12668285

NEWS REPORTING:
SCIENCE, MEDICINE,
AND HIGH TECHNOLOGY

News

SCIENCE, MEDICINE

Reporting:
AND HIGH TECHNOLOGY

BY **WARREN BURKETT**

THE UNIVERSITY OF TEXAS AT AUSTIN

THE IOWA STATE UNIVERSITY PRESS / AMES

*Dedicated to the lovely and loving Gay,
whose tender care and patience with an often-absent
husband made this book possible, and to my family,
Martha Burkett, Karl and Rebecca Burkett, and
Patricia and Tom Bishop and Chester V. Bishop.*

© *1986 Warren Burkett. All rights reserved
Composed by Texas Student Publications
Printed by The Iowa State University Press*

First edition 1986

Library of Congress Cataloging-in-Publication Data

Burkett, Warren, 1929-
   News reporting.

   1. Journalism, Scientific. I. Title.
PN4784.T3B84 1986   070.4'495   85-23102
ISBN 0-8138-1511-8

CONTENTS

ACKNOWLEDGMENTS

LITERALLY DOZENS OF PEOPLE CONTRIBUTED to the making of this book, just as they did twenty years ago when it first appeared under the title *Writing Science News for the Mass Media*. Members of the National Association of Science Writers are due special thanks for their candor in discussing the issues in often raucous debate. A debt is owed, also, to Professors Hillier Krieghbaum, Sharon Dunwoody, Sharon Friedman, Rae Goodell, James Tankard, Michael Ryan and others whose persistent research into the activities of science writers and readers over the past decade has added much depth and understanding to the process of how science writers go about their business. Dwight L. Teeter helped significantly through his encouragement, just as did his predecessors at The University of Texas at Austin, DeWitt C. Reddick and Norris Davis. Thanks also to Nancy Green and Art Rinn, who kept the computer up.

INTRODUCTION

THIS BOOK CHALLENGES YOU to enter the world of the science writer from whatever background you bring to the field. Earlier guides focused on the problems of translating technical terms into more general language for easier-to-understand stories. Another part of science writing lies in taking a broader look at the social and economic aspects of science, engineering, and technology. You, the writer, will meet a fascinating community of men and women engaged in purely individual endeavors that can have enormous impact upon the other communities in our society.

You are coming into a period of change and controversy as well as reexamination of the role of science in our society. Many important issues are under scrutiny. The traditional open research policies of scientists are being altered by the people who write the checks for science in the U.S. government. Those checks, however, are written on our taxes and represent public funds for the most part. Scientists themselves are divided on the issue of increasing secrecy in unclassified research that has doubtful bearing on our national security. Other issues include the question of whether or not science should intervene in matters of life and death among the handicapped and the aged and to what lengths this intervention should go. The questions of how much medical treatment you and I can afford and how much we should be given are under discussion. You are entering science writing at a time when new industries are being formed from basic scientific discoveries about the genetic material that is common to all living things. In choosing to write for popular rather than technical publications, you will play a role in engaging your fellow citizens in a debate of great importance in a democratic society.

This book encourages you to stretch your creativity to the utmost to find new as well as traditional forms of storytelling that will help your readers, listeners, and viewers understand the technical and social developments coming out of laboratories across our country and the world. Scientists themselves are showing more interest than than have shown in many years in achieving this understanding. In fact, as you will see, at one point the scientists were withdrawing deliberately from communication with the larger society.

This book cannot teach you science. It does point out some

common errors made by science writers and ways to avoid them. You are encouraged to develop your own special areas of knowledge about science, medicine, and engineering. Colleges and universities offer a variety of courses, and all science writers read a lot to improve their understanding. You may come to the task of writing with a background in one or more fields of science. As you will see, science journalism and science focus on what is new and significant. If you are trained in science, you are urged to seek out livelier, more interesting ways of explaining your subject than those used in the typical science journal. If this form of writing were an effective way of communicating technical information to the millions of nonscientists, then scientific journals would have much larger readerships than they have now, even among scientists. Howard Simons, former managing editor of *The Washington Post* and now head of the Nieman Fellowship program at Harvard University, advises science writers to become reporters first.

In the world of science writing for the mass media, a well-written and important essay directed toward a few select readers may be driven out of publication by stories of lesser importance that deal with the bizarre and the pseudoscientific or the mere human-interest subject. One of the challenges, then, is to communicate accurately and interestingly so that authentic knowledge will appeal to a wide audience. Accuracy need not mean dullness, although many in the scientific and the journalistic communities equate them.

It is important, also, to communicate with fairness and fidelity an understanding of the people who are scientists and their leaders. Misplaced awe and fear of the people who make science and public policy can handicap adoption of rational responses to the knowledge developed by the scientists. To the extent that a more complete and realistic understanding develops from your writing about the physical as well as the social sciences, you will perform an educational service for your readers and for society at large. It is fashionable to discount the effect any individual can have upon society. However the writer who respects the truth and the well-being of his or her audience will have impact that reaches far beyond words on paper and pictures on the tube.

Some parts of your trip may be rough and some ridiculous. For example officials of the United States government at mid-decade were questioning the patriotism of writers on *The New York Times* and *The Washington Post* for doing stories about classified satellite projects and nuclear weapons, although most of the material published either had been printed in other media with the blessing of Department of Defense officials or debated openly in parliaments around the world (Friendly 1985). At almost the same time, Defense and other government officials let *Times* science writer William J. Broad into the supersecret "Star Wars" world of a proposed American defense against ballistic missiles and nuclear warheads. So be prepared to meet irrationality from people who claim rationality as their strongest point. The journey as a science writer will not be dull, and if you question whether a few scientists can make a difference, use your research skills to explore the effect five scientists, known as the TTAPS Group, had on world thinking with their work on the "nuclear winter" concept (Smith 1984).

You will find a new type of science writing emerging. It is more aggressive, and science writers are willing to put scientists in some uncomfortable public positions to expose scientific practices that may affect public health and safety. At *The Wall Street Journal,* science writer Jerry Bishop explored the potential effects that a delay in publishing a major study about breast cancer surgery would have on women facing an immediate medical decision (Bishop 1984).

Have fun writing about science, but don't embark on a writing career because you think it will be easy. Writing is hard work, and you should enjoy both writing and the subject matter. There are pleasures in science writing for the journalist as well as for those who consider themselves scientists. Part of the appeal of science writing is dealing with an abundance of new knowledge. While many other stories begin to repeat themselves after a while, you will step into a flood of information that is always fresh and unfolding, revealing our ever-deeper understanding of the world about us and inside us. That is part of the enjoyment that scientists themselves find in research. This book will lead you into shallow waters where you can practice while developing your individual skills and styles of communicating to the larger community.

Quite likely you will meet some villains, quacks and charlatans as well as heroes on this journey. You will encounter promising stories about science and scientists only to find them going toward a dead end. As with any human endeavor, science does not always produce the unqualified success story, an image that earlier generations of science writers and scientists have instilled in the minds of media consumers. Movies and television programs have shaken this image with portrayals of scientists as dangerously obsessed, a situation that disturbs many scientists. The 1985 meeting of the American Association for the Advancement of Science devoted one of its programs to this problem of "image." But the general trend of scientific discovery has been to improve society simply because the more we understand about our world and ourselves, the better choices we can make for ourselves and our children. It is one thing to respect traditions that have served humankind well; it is something else to remain bound totally to old knowledge and outmoded practices that may lead to social disaster. Part of the science writer's task is to help people sort out these elements. Scientists may or may not be of material help in this task because of their closeness to the issues. Scientists do not necessarily have a unified viewpoint when dealing with political and social issues; they are often divided among themselves as sharply as any other group. You surely will meet interesting and even courageous individuals from the scientific community. They merit stories as persons worth your audience's acquaintance.

Another part of your challenge lies in piecing together the scattered enterprises of science into a coherent pattern. Scientific discovery emerges piecemeal, contradictory, and even with biases that may take years to weed out. A few scientists are asking for journalists to judge and evaluate science, as if they are unwilling or unable to depend on their own consensus alone. This calls on you to develop your own sense of the world and what it promises for those who depend on your reports. Writing about science and medicine carries responsibilities as well as pleasures.

NEWS REPORTING:
SCIENCE, MEDICINE,
AND HIGH TECHNOLOGY

Chapter 1
What is science writing?

SCIENCE WRITING IS ONE OF MANY NEW types of specialized communication evolving in the twentieth century. More than five thousand people in the United States alone consider themselves "science writers" because they spend all or most of their time writing about subjects in the bodies of highly organized knowledge known loosely as the sciences. This includes the obvious fields covered by the physical sciences, such as physics and chemistry, and the life sciences, biology and zoology, for example, and all their branches. Science writing also encompasses subjects in the application of science through engineering and technology and, especially, the art-sciences of medicine and health care. The social and behavioral sciences also fall into the province of the science writer.

Thousands of other writers sift this same body of knowledge without formally declaring themselves science writers. In the process of writing about this knowledge, these writers interact with many of the nearly three million men and women counted by the Scientific Manpower Commission as scientists. Science writers may or may not be trained formally in one or more of the sciences.

As a science writer you may write or broadcast the first story, for example, of new medicines, of the discovery of new stars or planets, or of the discovery of new life forms deep beneath the oceans—perhaps even on other planets. You could be one of the first writers aboard a spaceship; or you may be reporting stories dealing with the environment or energy issues of the world.

Generally speaking, science writers consider their careers to be built around explaining or translating scientific knowledge for people who may or may not be scientists. In 1847 James Prescott Joule could stand in a church in Manchester, England, and expound on his thesis that energy is transformed into the equivalent of heat, and he could expect most people at this public lecture would understand his ideas. The first published account of his reasoning and the experiments supporting his theory appeared in the Manchester weekly newspaper. A modern Joule would be expected to announce his discovery at a meeting of other members of his scientific specialty or publish it first in a scientific journal, and there are thousands of such journals. Joule would be expected, also, to explain his theory and experimentation in words so technical that many scientists in other fields could not grasp their meaning.

Thus science writing tends to be directed outward, toward audiences beyond the narrow scientific specialty where the information originates. The science writer becomes part of an education and communication system as complex as modern science and the larger society. At its furthest reaches, science writing helps bridge the gap between scientists and nonscientists. Such is the world of the two cultures seen by C.P. Snow (1961), a respected scientist before he turned to writing novels and to government service. Snow feared a situation void of communication and understanding between persons bound by scientific disciplines and those who would withdraw from science and attempt to follow only humanist disciplines. Science writing educates to varying degrees adults whose formal learning ends with high school or college. Science writing helps educate children about the natural world beyond their immediate environment, beyond their schoolrooms, beyond their limited experience.

As go-betweens, science writers must sort out for themselves, their editors, and their audiences some ideas and concepts that are less than clear even to many scientists. Take the concept of science itself. Dr. Dietrich Schroeer in *Physics and Its Fifth Dimension: Society* (1972) calls attention to paradoxical ideas about what science is:

Science is the control of nature. Although this concept has a tradition going back more than three hundred years to Francis Bacon and the beginning of what is accepted today as the "scientific method," it has faults. It covers product technology and manufacturing, which many who call themselves scientists disdain. If science means controlling nature, it cannot include cosmology, the study of the universe.

Science studies the material world. This excludes mathematical physics, which is mainly theoretical, intellectual, and speculative—such as Albert Einstein's conclusions about $E = MC^2$. It can be seen as excluding the social and behavioral sciences because they focus on social behavior, not the material world. This concept could shelter such new specialties as biophysics and biopsychology, grounded on assumptions that behavior is the result of people's physical or chemical state at a given time.

Science is public knowledge. While a beautiful concept for the science writer, this proposition hides several snags. The word "public" causes the problem. Does science include secret research, a practice opposed at many universities? Does engineering add to public scientific knowledge or merely to private technique? Are the notebooks of Leonardo da Vinci, for example, with their amazing insights, outside the realm of science because he wrote them in a mirror-code and kept them hidden? Scientists often tell science writers that a work is not science until it has been reviewed by other scientists, peers, and published in the scientific literature.

Science is the experimental method. With the experimental method as the standard, most anthropologists, naturalists, paleontologists, and social scientists could be excluded from science since their techniques are mainly observational. They can perform only limited experimentation with varying and controlled circumstances.

Another definition, "Science consists of logical inferences from many observations," is one Schroeer finds the least acceptable definition. Many of the best theories in science were based on skimpy, sometimes false, data. Insight and hunches may be as necessary to science as fact and logic. Seldom do published scientific reports indicate a certain messiness that accompanies scientific research. Science literature contains many papers where the data do not support the conclusions. Most of the published papers never have their hypotheses confirmed or even checked by other scientists.

Sir Richie Calder, scientist and popular science writer, called attention to other areas of science where science writers help illuminate the paths where scientists walk. One of these areas includes recognition of fads and cults in science. Scientists will flock to "hot" areas of research, especially if there are grant monies available, just as rapidly as youths flock to the latest fashions in music and clothes. Interferon, a natural body chemical playing a role in the human immune system, was a "hot" research area in the 1960s, cooled in the 1970s, and reheated in the 1980s. Virus as a cause of cancer, with or without environmental stimulation, has been in and out of favor countless times. Nuclear physics and solid-state physics, source of electronic marvels ranging from personal computers to video games, have had their eras. As predicted by Calder, now DNA in all its manifestations is getting top attention in many areas of scientific research and application (1963).

Calder also recognized the need for science writers to sort out for their readers the many types of scientists. "Pure" or academic scientists, it is assumed, seek knowledge for its own sake, exploring the paradoxes of the natural world, lighting the unknown, seeking grand theory. (Knowledge, Calder warns, is not necessarily wisdom.) "Fundamental," applied, or basic scientists explore problems whose study may reveal information that increases understanding of the problem—as in the mechanism of a disease, properties of a metal, or the operation of a living cell. "Applied" scientists work on a specific program, seeking specific answers; their research is often nongeneralized, applicable to a single area. Both fundamental and applied research often are called "directed" research. "Technologists," applied only with care to most engineers, meld fundamental knowledge into product know-how; they make scientific facts work for their living.

Technicians transform a product into industrial operations. One of the traps of science and medical writing has been to attach too much meaning too soon to a scientific discovery. In medicine, it produces false illusions of "cures" before there is a track record of disease remission. Stories of scientific "breakthroughs" often ignore the many steps between one or a hundred successful laboratory experiments and endlessly repeated production runs of a medicine or a new device. Laboratory accomplishments often cannot be duplicated profitably on the production line, almost never quickly. Typically it takes twenty to thirty years for a discovery to move through this chain to availability.

In Calder's world, basic-academic scientists are the "makers-possible." Applied scientists and technologists are the "makers-to-happen." Technicians are the "makers-to-work." Social scientists, operations researchers, market researchers, and commercial scientists are the "makers-to-pay."

As the science writers spread information outward from the core of the scientific disciplines, science loses some of its precision and much of its technical jargon. In the mass media—newspapers, radio, and television—science becomes popularized and even "sensationalized", and for good reason. Women, men, and children, often with limited time and often tired, have little incentive to wade through indigestible prose that offers little meaning to their daily lives. Science writers provide the meaning for their particular audiences. This is part of the translation process, often omitted from scientists' formal speeches and papers because their colleagues supposedly know enough about the field to grasp the meaning and would be insulted at having it spelled out to them. So the science writer must seek "meaning" for his or her particular audience.

Sometimes the writer's interpretation of this meaning may not coincide with the scientist's, whose intent was to inform his colleagues. This leads to accusations of misleading the public. Because much of the scientist's world is too small or dangerous to be sensed directly or so large that its size—as in the world of cosmologists—cannot be grasped, popular science writers attempt to explain science in terms of analogy and similie. These are by definition less exact than the precise terminology used by the practitioners of science or their highly compressed but precise language of mathematics. It is very possible that editors and writers underestimate the level of technical and scientific understanding their audiences hold in many advanced countries.

Science writers, especially those writing for the mass media, also tend to strip out many nuances of science. Those very subtleties delight the scientists and often demonstrate to other scientists the brilliance of their work. Thus popular science writing, in one way or another, can fall vulnerable to charges of oversimplification. As will be shown later, science writers are prone to follow the ideas of William of Ockham (1290-1347), the excommunicated Franciscan monk and philosopher of science, who helped lead early scientists into the empirical and experimental tradition. One of his principles, known as Ockham's Razor, held that the most simple explanation of a phenomenon probably was the correct explanation.

This does not mean advocacy of irresponsible simplification. Most science writers attempt to confirm the facts and interpretations in their stories with reputable and knowledgeable experts. These scientists include the original researcher and other scientists operating in a field. However, experienced science journalists know that scientists often make poor judges of the implications and possible applications of their discoveries.

Take the laser, for example. In the 1960s, shortly after the laser's demonstration, science writers were quick to ask about the laser's potential to become the "death ray" postulated by science fiction writers. Scientists almost universally tried to knock down the idea that lasers and their concentrated beams of energy could become useful tools on earth or in space by overcoming the handicaps of size, power supplies, and water, dust, or other particulate matter. However twenty-plus years later, the Department of Defense boasted of combat lasers powerful enough to blind enemy troops. The Air Force released photographs and declassified information about experiments using airplanes to test potential laser weapons. And President Ronald Reagan announced a national defense program to develop an orbiting system of laser and particle beam weapons to destroy missiles and satellites in space. Barring changes in the program, prototypes undoubtedly will fly aboard both the military and civilian versions of the American space shuttle.

The culture of science

There is another view of science writing. Dr. Joel Hildebrand, who taught chemistry and did research at the University of California-Berkeley almost until his death at age 101, offered this explanation of science: Science is what scientists do (1957). With all its ramifications, this definition offers much to the science writer. Jon D. Franklin, science writer for the evening *Baltimore Sun* and winner of two Pulitzer Prizes, has said that instead of writing about the esoterica of particle physics he would choose to write about the physicists (Lewis 1985).

Science, then, can be and should be understood as the very human activity it is. Yet this is nearly the opposite of how scientists usually reveal themselves in most of their own literature. Most profess to desire a complete denigration of personality in science. Reading their dry, dispassionate reports in the scientific journals, you might think each discovery comes from cool and rational thought, careful planning, and execution of experiments designed to trick nature into revealing its mysteries. You would never guess from the literature that most experiments are failures. Nor would it seem that science is an untidy arena of broken test tubes, power failures, dying mice, and competition. In one case, for example, pitched battle ensued between two Ivy League expeditions for possession of dinosaur bones. Only with the publication of *The Double Helix* by James Watson (1968) did much of the public realize how scientists may be driven by fierce competitiveness to claim a discovery such as the structure of deoxyribonucleic acid— DNA, the very stuff of life. Yet in the seventeenth century Newton and Leibniz scrapped as hard in public to take credit for inventing the calculus. Scientific life offers few rewards for second place, at least in the eyes of some scientists. Competitive pressures have been offered as excuses for scientists who violate the principles of research by falsifying their results, thus threatening the integrity of science.

In writing about science, science writers deal with a human culture of personalities that many scientists prefer go unpublicized. Science has its daring heroes, its victims of intellectual and political rape and pillage, its plodders, and its neglected. When Dr. Barbara McClintock received her 1983 Nobel Prize for research showing that genes were mobile and transportable in corn, she had virtually stopped publishing her research. Her early work had been virtually ignored until the idea of genetic manipulation became fashionable in science. She was rediscovered. And in J. Robert Oppenheimer, many scientists believe modern science has a political martyr to rank with Galileo. Physicist Oppenheimer led the Los Alamos National Laboratory team to develop the first atomic bombs. Playwrights have dramatized the story of Oppenheimers "leftish" political ties and how these were linked to his reservations about developing the more powerful hydrogen bomb. Less has been written of Edward Teller, advocate of the hydrogen bomb and one of Oppenheimer's opponents, and of Teller's years of near-ostracism by many in the community of scientists for his role in having the U.S. government remove Oppenheimer's security clearance.

As in any other human enterprise, the frailties of scientists occasionally show through: ambition, deceit, plagarism, theft, bullying, arrogance, fear, and conceit. Instances of physical and moral courage, work under impossible and frightening conditions, and cleverness lie behind the research reports. These also are material for the science writers, material that writers can dig out with work and imagination. Altogether they form a human side of science in the making that scientists prefer, in many cases, to keep hidden, much as their predecessors— priests and wizards—relied on mystery to dominate those multitudes outside the club.

Science writer Daniel Greenberg has identified some of the high priests and temples of science, its established power centers. These include Harvard University's laboratories and medical school, the Massachusetts Institute of Technology,

California Institute of Technology, Stanford University, select departments in other universities, and Bell Laboratories before the breakup of AT&T. The "establishment" of science includes, also, the National Academy of Sciences, the Smithsonian Institution, and the Cosmos Club of Washington, D.C. Among science's high priests are the heads of these institutions and those of certain independent institutes, such as the Sloan-Kettering Cancer Center and Carnegie Institute, and the winners of Nobel Prizes. Depending on personal influence, the high priesthood may also include the science adviser to the President of the United States. Science's "bankers," by supplying billions in grant money, include the National Institutes of Health, the National Science Foundation, parts of the Department of Defense and the Department of Energy, the National Aeronautics and Space Administration, and major charitable organizations, such as the American Cancer Society and the American Heart Association. A handful of companies enjoy establishment status because they devote significant percentages of their budgets to fundamental research rather than mere product development. These are found primarily in the chemical, electronics, and aerospace industries (Greenberg 1967).

In the culture of science and medicine, competition exists between the centers of power. For example, the recipients of the American Cancer Society awards carry almost as much prestige as the Nobel Prize winners. The ACS leaders are chagrined if they overlook outstanding scientists before they are recognized by the Nobel committee in Copenhagen. Competition exists between the established universities, hospitals and institutes for money and people, and between them and outsider institutions for these same resources.

Science also has its own established voices, primarily journals. Because these publications represent large segments of scientific opinion or the leadership, at least, these journals are sources of much information for science writers. *Science,* the weekly journal of the American Association for the Advancement of Science, circulates and influences far beyond the more than 100,000 members of this largest of the scientific organizations. Two U.S. medical publications carry heavy scientific and political clout: *The New England Journal of Medicine* and the *Journal of the American Medical Association.* Their editors speak not only of the technical matters of science but also of policy, politics, and conscience.

Science also has its public "voices." In part these public representatives of science are the creations of the science writers, especially those journalists writing for the national media. Dr. Rae Goodell, professor of science communication at MIT, has identified a group she christened "the visible scientists" (1977). These include Nobelists, heads of prestigious institutions, and administrators of science-oriented government agencies and federal laboratories. Science writers rely heavily upon this limited circle for expert information on controversial matters having a high scientific or medical content. This sometimes leads to problems. For example, in the controversy over the effects of marijuana usage, one study of published stories revealed that most of the journalists' information about the drug came from sources having no research experience with marijuana's effects. The science journalists did, to their credit, find and quote three of the five reports from researchers most often cited by other scientists involved in marijuana studies. But most of the printed and broadcast information came from highly visible scientists whose official or administrative positions kept them from direct contact with research in the field (Shepherd 1979).

Reliance on such distant sources of information is not wholly the fault of science journalists. Tribal customs within the scientific community can act as barriers to communicating science information through popularization and the mass media (Dunwoody and Scott 1982, 52). Writers entering the field of science writing will find these customs affecting how they deal with scientific news sources. Journalists tend to deal with senior scientists whose reputation within the scientific community is well established. They are more secure and willing to speak out. For younger researchers, peer criticism may jeopardize standing within the community for those seeking professional advancement, university tenure, or recognition for their work. However, Sharon Dunwoody and Michael Ryan (1983) established, for one group of scientists, that questions of ethics or jealousy may have less to do with granting interviews than with the fact that senior scientists give better interviews. Peer review, including publication of one own research in a reputable journal, remains the scientist's first priority. Increasing the public's understanding of science confers few material rewards on scientists.

Employer restraints may chill public communication also. Scientists in industry deal in proprietary information from which their companies expect to profit over competing businesses. Therefore they can be very closemouthed about their work. Research carried out in nonindustrial settings has not been guarded so closely in the past. That may be changing. It is too soon to tell if science writers will have difficulty talking to researchers now that Harvard University, for one example, expects to make money from genetic engineering research. Medical writers for popular media may face new competition from the universities and other research organizations. Both Harvard Medical School and the Mayo Clinic publish health care newsletters aimed at subscribers among the general public. Business also is increasing its use of academic researchers on ideas with potential commercial value; conditions of these research contracts may prevent scientists from talking about their work.

Politics can stifle open discussion. Some public university researchers told Dunwoody and Ryan they may be reluctant to discuss their work or opinions fully because they fear reaction from state legislators. Human origin and reproduction provoke strong politics. Research in the fertilization and growth of human embryos, for example, was caught up in the 1980s in an intense religious debate over exactly when "life" begins and if terminating an experiment could become murder. Scientists and engineers involved in classified military or space research may have terms in their grants and contracts specifying that approval of the funding agency must be given before any public discussion of the research is allowed. One open scientific meeting saw more than one hundred unclassified scientifc papers cancelled, after official approval, because of increased sensitivity in Washington to potential disclosure of information that might affect national security. To make the government's point, FBI agents once chose to arrest an accused spy at a scientific meeting rather than in some other setting.

One group of scientists often sought out by science writers seems less inhibited about press contacts. These are the social scientists. Dunwoody and Ryan, in work in progress, speculate that this results from the youth of the social sciences and their development in conjunction with the mass media. Publicity may help these scientists gain status and perhaps funding.

Another set of researchers show more willingness to popularize science activities. These are scientists who depend largely on public funds for their research. As they told Dunwoody and Ryan, public recognition helps overcome most disadvantages of public exposure. Publicity and public approval helps their supporting agencies look good at budget time.

Science writers learn the many sides of this remarkable community of highly educated and highly trained individuals. Its people and its institutions are the sources and the subjects for stories. Physicist John Ziman in his book *Public Knowledge* argues that science is less a body of formal, fixed knowledge than it is a public

consensus among scientists as to who does "good" work and whose work cannot be trusted, what information is accepted and what is ignored, and what is obsolete and what should be resurrected. It is part of the science writer's job, also, to find out when a maverick or nonconformist is worth listening to and where to go within this scientific community for evaluations of people and research.

Schroeer warns those who would understand science only as consensus: Consensus may place too much emphasis on science being public. It may give you the impression of a monolithic organization of selfless individuals rather than what Schroeer calls "a collection of egotistical prima donnas." Consensus may confuse science with religion, a faith in unverifiable data. The individual scientist may perform his or her own research for very different reasons from trying to achieve a consensus. Achieving tenure, getting a promotion, making a fortune or other personal ambitions drive scientists as they do the rest of us. Dr. Hans Mark, who rose to be deputy administrator of the U.S. space agency, said he stopped being a nuclear physicist and became a politician, an administrator. You will find many other administrators less candid.

In reporting on another of the cultural aspects of science and technology, Robert Reinhold of *The New York Times* found himself describing lunch hour at the Lion and Compass restaurant in Sunnyvale, California. Why? Because that is where the scientists and engineers of the "Silicon Valley" electronics industry go to eat and negotiate million-dollar deals for advanced computer technology. The owner of the restaurant, Nolan K. Bushnell, was the electrical engineer who invented video games and sold his company for twenty-eight million dollars. Wrote Reinhold: "The Lion and Compass is to the computer world what Sardi's is to New York's theater district" (Jan. 7, 1984, 7). The Cosmos Club in Washington holds similar status for those in academic science. Conveying a sense of the places that scientists frequent when they leave their labs can impart new understanding to the human side of science.

Science in government

Beyond interesting, often gripping stories of scientific discovery, and beyond the fascinating, often odd, personalities lies another realm of concern for the science writer—the financing of science. Science and its kin, technology, consume vast amounts of national resources. In the 1980s the federal research and development budget in the United States exceeded fifty billion tax dollars, the chief source of money for science. More billions poured into applied technology from private business, usually in terms of new products that can create problems for society and its governments. Companies get tax exemptions for research and development expenses, making private research and development indirectly financed by taxpayers. Solutions to those problems created by technology generally call for more technology to defend against enemies, to control new diseases, to produce more energy, to provide jobs, to establish colonies in space, to dispose of waste, and to perform dozens of other missions a complex civilization requires.

These social service functions are lumped by Philip Boffey into a beat he covers for *The New York Times,* designated as science and public policy. Daniel Greenberg produces a newsletter called *Science and Government Report.* Both report on the interaction of governmental decisions, political maneuvering, and public effects wrought by scientists and their technology. It is a world of power, money, influence, and often raw politics of the lowest, pork-barrel variety. For some Washington reporters, science is less an exalted enterprise than just another special interest trying to slide money from the public purse, as do road builders and others. The scientific community can unite, as it did in 1983, to oppose members of congress trying to get new buildings, laboratories, and other special favors

for their districts without first having the need for this allocation of scientific funds determined by science review panels in government agencies. These facilities are not small political plums. The Argonne National Laboratory outside Chicago, for example, commands an annual budget of $210 million, a staff of 4500 highly paid people. Battles for such facilities are well worth the fight because of their effect on local economies. While scientists may argue that they are using their influence to insure research money is spent in the places best equipped and staffed to spend it wisely, others may feel this exercise in power is merely a variation on pork-barrel politics.

Science writers covering public policy will look at a National Academy of Sciences report on how to diminish "acid rain" for signs of undue influence by power generating companies. Scientists employed by or consulting for an industry may serve on panels and commissions drafting recommendations to be effected by such regulatory agencies as the Environmental Protection Agency, the Consumer Product Safety Commission, and the Food and Drug Administration. In theory the scientists set aside personal prejudices and biases when they examine evidence; in practice it may be impossible. In public policy the science writer must deal regularly with the conflicting testimony of equally qualified scientists, engineers, or other experts who recommend diametrically opposite solutions to public issues. "For each and every Ph.D. there is an equal and opposite Ph.D.," runs one wisecrack. This puts the science writer in the position of consciously or unconsciously choosing which side of the testimony gets the most weight in a story.

Science writers also deal in the larger issues of public health and safety in times of crisis or breaking news. Expect to be accused of sensationalism. Science writers' stories may deal directly with the cause of the crisis, as when Mount St. Helens in Washington state erupted or when a series of mishaps at the Three

Mile Island nuclear power plant melted the fuel core, contaminating parts of the plant with radioactivity and possibly threatening nearby communities. These rare events put scientists and science writers in the middle of breaking news where their expertise in public communications directly affected audience members. In both cases, close residents monitored the news reports for indications they needed to flee for their lives. In looking at the element of sensationalism, it's clear both events were sensational by their very nature. In the case of the Three Mile Island nuclear accident, most stories from the journalists were far from sensational; where alarming statements outnumbered reassuring ones in stories, officials with the Nuclear Regulatory Commission were the source (Stephens and Edison 1982).

Science writers faced criticism in stories when traces of a powerful pesticide, ethylene dibromide (EDB) used to fumigate citrus fruit and grain, turned up nationwide in boxes of baking products. Because EDB was suspected as a very strong carcinogen, its pervasive distribution throughout the food system resulted in stories that alarmed readers and viewers. Was the alarm justified? Critics have claimed the U.S. government changed rules on EDB use simply because of the political uproar, not from fear of a genuine health risk. Part of the confusion over the danger from EDB lay in two concepts of the danger. Scientists and government officials could talk about the estimated risks that EDB in food and water could increase the risk of cancer by a few cases per 100,000 people. Journalists, as surrogates for individual readers, wanted the scientists to talk about the risk faced by a person buying a package of muffin mix. Science could not provide that answer.

On the other hand, the bias of a writer's sources on such public health issues can result in criticism of the writer. The issue of assessing risk offers many examples. Science writers have been accused of failure to understand and explain the "risk factors" when citing scientific studies that

claim increased death or disease may result from exposure to various chemical elements in the environment, in the workplace, in the home, or elsewhere. *Science in the Streets,* a report by the Twentieth Century Fund (1984), concludes that society's perception of technological dangers, including those from oil spills and air pollution, depends very much upon the presentation of that risk in the mass media. Some media users blame the media for creating unnecessary anxiety; so do some scientists. Often enough, those blaming the media have personal or financial interests in reducing the concern over various situations. In the Fund's report, however, sociologist Dorothy Nelkin notes that science journalists are vulnerable to the scientist or administrator who makes a clear-cut, easily quoted statement of danger (or lack of danger) on the basis of very little data. This shows up most noticeably in TV and radio where the "sound bite" of ten to fifteen seconds is standard for explaining any news situation.

Overall, the report concluded, science writers and journalists generally have not done badly. Chairman Harrison E. Schmitt, former astronaut and U.S. senator from New Mexico, disagreed with the rest of the committee, however. Learning to assess risk amid conflicting expert sources will be one of the science writer's continuing problems. Schmitt said that knowledge about potential risk sometimes should be withheld by journalists. Dr. Nelkin and the rest of the committee would have the journalist offer readers and viewers a reasoned, intelligent view of risks so that audiences can function as informed members of a democratic society.

Sometimes science writers use their special knowledge and news sources to provide secondary or background stories to help people understand a news event. When President Ronald Reagan and Pope John Paul II were shot by would-be assassins, science and medical writers delivered stories that detailed the nature and severity of the leaders' wounds and explained surgical steps taken to save their lives. Often the network of specialized news sources available to science writers can be used to other ends. When Soviet Premier Yuri Andropov disappeared from public life for several months, Victor Cohn of *The Washington Post* drew upon his contacts with doctors throughout the United States to find out what their colleagues in Europe and other areas knew about rumors of Andropov's illness. The result was a story sketching the seriousness of a kidney disease afflicting the Russian leader. Cohn's story was proved right after the death of Andropov a few weeks later.

Levels of science writing

Science writers operate at many levels and degrees of popularization, education and explanation. Their understanding of their readers or viewers guides both the selection of stories and the degree of popularization. Radio, television, and the community newspaper reach audiences that contain many age groups, many eduction levels, and diverse backgrounds. Writing about science for this audience calls for selection of topics with major impact or of great significance. Because of limited time or space, science subjects must compete with many other kinds of news and features.

Larger newspapers with more space, such as *The New York Times*, will view the audience differently. The *Times*, with a highly educated readership, will cater to an audience interested in reading about some advances in science or medicine that will be ignored by the editors of the *New York Daily News*. The choice of news depends almost entirely on the editors' views of the interests of their audiences, whether predominantly working class or professionally trained. Science writers for *The Wall Street Journal* cover science, medicine, the environment, and other subjects for the potential effects that new developments will have on their readers as humans and as business people. A new drug for heart disease, for in-stance, can interest a stressed executive reader as a person and as a stockholder in the drug manufacturing company.

Magazine science writers draw their image of their audiences even more narrowly: Space limitations and audience considerations force *Ladies Home Journal*, for example, to leave astronomy to other publications. *Time* magazine, by one study, uses significantly more scientific terms without translation than does *Newsweek*. Neither will carry as many science stories as *Science News*, whose subscribers buy the magazine for a large dose of weekly science information. But because *Science News* aims at an audience that contains young and old, the highly educated and students, and professionals with and without specific science literacy, its writers may actually do more translating of scientific terminology than the general news magazines. *Science,* the weekly magazine for members of the American Association for the Advancement of Science, makes no compromises with the technical language in its major articles written by scientists. However, it uses several journalists to follow the shifting political scene in its section "News and Comment." In addition, *Science* serves its highly educated audience with such departments as "This Week in Science" and "Research News." Both are written in more general language, often explaining technical articles elsewhere in the magazine, to help technically trained readers understand the jargon used in various disciplines.

Scientific American employs several editors to work with the scientists who write the magazine's articles. Nevertheless, the technical level remains very high for a publication aimed at a nontechnical audience. For a more popularized sense of what is happening in science, readers have *Science Digest* and *Science 85* (which changes numbers with the year), which is also published by the American Association for the Advancement of Science. For the science buff who wants science fiction literature mixed with thoughtful articles on science, there is *Omni* magazine. *Psychology Today* and *Society* magazines cater to those with a special interest in the behavioral and social sciences. *American Health* is one of many publications providing a broad range of popularized, reliable information for people concerned with all phases of their personal health, including the economics of health care.

Another class of publications employing science writers is known as business, industrial or trade publications. Magazines such as *Business Week*, or *Forbes* focus on the interests of managers and stockholders in major companies who require more popularization in technical areas than do readers of *Aviation Week and Space Technology* or *Chemical Engineering,* for example. However, the more narrowly focused the magazine is for its particular industry or segment of an industry, the more selective its interest in science.

Science writers also write for companies and institutions, producing reports for a wide range of purposes. There may be press releases promoting a company product, a brochure explaining a process in layman's language, or a magazine for stockholders or employees. Exxon, for example, uses science writers to explain its actions to protect the environment where it operates oil wells and refineries. The Exxon magazine goes to a broad general audience, including journalists, members of Congress, and others considered influential in the company's well-being. DuPont distributes a similar magazine that stresses the applications of new chemical products in business and industry.

Writers for newsletters will focus their science stories even more narrowly into a scientific or technical field. Some may cover only one subject or agency, such as the Food and Drug Administration or the National Science Foundation.

Often it is the degree of popularization that separates science writers from "technical writers." Technical writers aim for a very specialized audience of experts or give step-by-step instructions for operating, maintaining, or assembling something. Technical writers prepare manuals and scientific and engineering reports, often as part of a company's marketing or customer service effort. Many technical writers will also write popularized science or engineering material from their specialized knowledge, either as part of their job or as freelance articles. Some science and medical writers also moonlight as technical editors and writers, depending on their knowledge of a particular field.

International science writing

Explaining science, medicine, and engineering, and the men and women who make science, challenges writers around the world. Their methods reflect the nature and the media of their own societies and countries. United States science writers and Western science writers operate very much as individuals, even though each may be one of several science writers on as large a publication as *The New York Times.* Japanese science writers work within a system that is group oriented and hierarchical. A group of writers may work on various stages of any story. In Russia and China, where the media are integral to the government, training of science writers and selection of stories presented are of official concern that aims toward an understanding that advances the welfare of the state. European science writers tend to have a higher percentage of professional scientists in their midst. In the Third World or advancing nations, science writers have the desire but not necessarily the space or outlets for their work. Attempts to form associations of science writers in these areas, in the manner of the British Science Writers Association or the National Association of Science Writers in the U.S., have produced organizations that may or may not exist at any given time. These associations, formed to improve the skills of local journalists through educational seminars and communication with scientists, generally arise through sponsorship of one or more international organizations, such as the Pan American Union or the Organization of American States. The experience of the Asian Science Writers Association is typical.

The Asian Science Writers Association was first organized in 1970 following a seminar sponsored by the Press Foundation of Asia with the United States helping indirectly through the Asia Foundation. It lasted about five years and included members from Japan, the Philippines, Malaysia, Taiwan, and other nations outside mainland China. When grant money from the Asia Foundation was exhausted, the science writers association activities among the widely scattered countries declined amidst suspicions that the Asia Foundation was a front for the U.S. Central Intelligence Agency. An attempt was made to revive the organization at a 1977 conference in Manila attended by thirty-five members from countries around the Eastern Pacific Basin. The group agreed to seek money from sources other than their own governments or the United States. Neither the writers nor the newspapers involved seemed able to sustain their organization from their own resources, as do members of the National Association of Science Writers in the United States (Laing 1978).

Organizations of science writers in other countries have much the same goals as those in the United States. One scientist at the first Inter-American Seminar on Science Journalism more than twenty years ago declared:

Scientific research, and this is particularly true in Latin America, cannot develop without full government support. Therefore it is essential that statesmen become aware of the desirability and the need of helping science apply its results to the solution of many national problems. It is equally important to create a state of general opinion favoring scientific work. (Cardon 1962, 6)

Thus a heavier burden of national education may be carried by science writers in less-developed countries.

A report from the conference indicated that science reporting may be more politicized in times of tension and internal political or armed conflicts. Outside the United States, all journalism is much more politicized than Americans are accustomed to reading. Science in countries with a weak or nonexistent scientific tradition is easily driven out of the papers by news of political or economic conflict.

A later attempt was made to organize science journalists around their Spanish heritage through the Congress of Ibero-American Science Journalism held in Madrid in March of 1977. This resulted in an attempt to form the InterAmerican Science Writers Association since all Spanish and Portuguese speaking countries were represented with the exception of Cuba and Costa Rica. There was even talk of forming a World Union of Science Writers, although the meeting was highly partisan and marked by international rivalries (Cornell 1977).

Groups that existed for a while include European Science Writers Union and a Swiss Science Writing Association. The International Science Writers Association lives on. The ISWA counts about 200 members and has been held together mainly by Howard Lewis, retired information officer of the National Academy of Sciences. The largest and most stable of the science writers organizations, the U.S. National Association of Science Writers, has more than thirty foreign-based science writers among its members. The largest group is, not surprisingly, in Canada—eleven members. The rest are scattered through Australia (3), France (3), Germany (3) and England (2), with individual members living in Ireland, Israel, Japan, Mexico, Puerto Rico, Saudi Arabia, Sweden, and Switzerland. Although most of these are nationals of their country of residence, the number includes a few Americans who live overseas and write for American media.

Western European countries offer science journalists less assistance in gathering information than the United States. When Lois Wingerson, former science editor of the Bergen County, New Jersey, *Record* worked in England, she found little encouragement to go beyond reporting from science articles as they appeared in *The Lancet*, the British medical journal and other technical publications. She also concluded that government information officers existed mainly to glorify their bosses and did not return phone calls. This was especially true at the National Health Service. Scientists, including those of the Royal College of Physicians, seemed as puzzled in Britain as in the United States with journalists' concern for getting fresher information than that in the journals. However Wingerson's persistence in seeking direct contact with the scientists produced interviews and tours of laboratories (Wingerson 1979).

Scientific meetings on the Continent generally offer media few special accommodations, reported John F. Henahan, NASW member and freelancer (1981). He used Dublin as a base for covering meetings in England and Europe. Language frequently proved to be a barrier, although meetings generally included one or more scientists who delivered their papers in English. The few meetings that provided multiple-language translations worked well in the early stages, but translations became sketchier as the translators tired. Most science press conferences are held in the national language, and public announcements may not be made at all. Being the only American science writer in a country can produce exclusive stories, but the writer spends more time arranging interviews than in the United States.

In China, popular science writing seemed more in the hands of scientists than journalists, says David Perlman, science editor of the *San Francisco Chronicle*, who made two visits there. This probably occurs under the social responsibility theory of the Marxist countries that makes everyone responsible for educating the masses in the "proper" way. However the Chinese editors have the same problem as U.S. science editors: dealing with scientists who write incomprehensible articles

for laymen. Perlman found the Chinese journalists surprised at the ability of U.S. science writers to make personal contact with scientists without going through the hierarchy of ministries and laboratory directors to obtain interviews. The Chinese science writers consider it important to focus on the practical applications of science rather than explain the abstract and fundamental. The Chinese were concerned also with how to develop materials to introduce children to science (Perlman 1984).

For more than thirty years, at least, foreign science journalists in the United States have plowed fairly easily through the same routines of news coverage as American journalists. This may change in the climate of intense political and commercial competition that is developing. In 1983 the Reagan administration refused a work permit to a Canadian journalist, writing for Canadian publications, who wrote stories contradicting administration policies on technical aspects of arms control and air-water pollution. The British science journal *Nature* and the *Economist*, a newsmagazine, maintain staffers in the United States and regularly seek access to scientific and technical material that is increasingly being restricted by policy to Americans only.

This may provoke retaliation overseas in the form of denying access to both American scientists and science writers at conferences dealing with industrially important subjects such as computers and biotechnology. American science writers abroad may find they have to arrange access through science officers at the American embassies. For the present, however, conventional and direct contact with scientific organizations and institutions works.

Looking ahead to the next chapter, you may wonder: why publish news and features about science, engineering and technology at all? A socially significant answer would include the importance of science economically and politically in a democracy. There is no doubt that what happens in science and technology affects us all. However, many science writers will tell you they cover the science beat because there are good stories to be written there. Besides, it is a lot of fun. As Victor Cohn of *The Washington Post* has said, "Scientists are to science writers what rats are to scientists" (Goodfield 1981, 94).

Experiments

1. Read a major national or metropolitan newspaper's Sunday edition. Count the number of stories you consider science related. Are the sources scientists or some other sources? Count the number of stories in the paper. What percentage is science related?

2. Read a popular science magazine. In which category of science do you think each story fits best: pure, basic, applied, technological, cultural, or science-policy?

3. Find the business and industrial magazines in your library; read one issue of a magazine and report on science related stories. How many are there? What kind of a scientist is their source?

4. Get an issue of *Science, Journal of the American Medical Association,* or the *New England Journal of Medicine.* Submit a list of technical articles that you think would be worth popularizing and give your reasons why.

5. Draw up a list of potential science stories for discussion in class. How would you and your classmates classify these stories by the criteria in this chapter?

Chapter 2
Evolution of science writing

SCIENCE WRITING, AS IT IS TODAY, stems from a centuries-old communication system. It began in the sixteenth century when early scientists faced censorship by church and state for their activities. They met quietly in various cities to inform each other of their discoveries in the new natural philosphy. From meetings of these elite groups of nobles, scholars, artists, and merchants sprang the tradition of open, oral communication in scientific matters.

The Accademia Secretorum Naturae began in Naples, Italy, in 1560 as the first of many scientific societies flourishing in cities where the new "scientists" could gather easily. Rome had its Accademia dei Lincei, which lasted from 1603 to 1630. In Florence the Accademia del Cimento was founded under the protection of the Grand Duke Ferdinand de Medici and his brother Leopold in 1657. It lasted ten years, ending soon after Leopold received his cardinal's hat. Historians speculate that the price of the red mitre was Leopold's help in dissolving the Accademia, a group troublesome to the church. Members of the group had come under scrutiny by the Inquisition, and one member of the Florence society killed himself to avoid torture (Jeans 1958, 148)

In England the Royal Society for the Improvement of Natural Knowledge was proposed by Francis Bacon in 1620 and approved in 1662 by Charles II. Many of its members had been meeting for years in Gresham College, London, and in Oxford under the name of the Invisible College. Louis XIV established the Académie des Sciences in Paris in 1666. Elector Frederick of Prussia followed suit with the Berlin Academy in 1700. The United States chartered its National Academy of Sciences in 1863.

Exchanges of letters, monographs, and books in Latin laid down the pattern of communication between individuals, between societies in the cities, and between the national societies. Scientists favored letters (often printed so that copies could be sent to several scientists) because government officials were less likely to pry into what looked like ordinary mail. Their fears had some substance. In 1667 Henry Oldenburg, secretary of the Royal Society, was imprisoned in the Tower of London when the British secretary of state thought some remarks in a scientific communication criticized England's conduct of war with the Dutch for the East Indies trade.

It was Oldenburg who invented scientific journalism. Oldenburg began publication of *Philosophical Transactions*, the Royal Society Journal, in March 1665 as a personal effort. Through his command of several languages, Oldenburg was able to translate letters from many sources for publication in English and Latin. Had he not, the world might not have known about the strange things that a Dutch-speaking garment maker in Delft saw when he examined drops of water with the same magnifying lenses he used to study cloth. Oldenburg coaxed nearly two hundred letters from the garment maker, Antoni van Leeuwenhoeck, father of microscopy (Boorstein 1983, 330, 390-417). It was many years before the Royal Society assumed responsibility for the scientific journal. Oldenburg established precedents for scientists acting as editors of the scientific society journals and for publication in the vernacular. These concepts strengthened scientific research in Europe.

Much of what was published could be understood by any of the relatively few literate persons of the times. As literacy increased, early versions of newspapers and magazines emerged in Britain and in Europe, and their publisher-editor-printers rewrote and reprinted such articles from the science journals as they thought might interest their readers. They also arranged for members of the societies to write for the general readers of the new papers.

In the British colonies of North America, this pattern of science communication repeated the European experience, with accounts of fever, ague, and smallpox appearing in Boston's *Publick Occurrences* in 1690. Benjamin Franklin, one of the founders of American science, printed an account of his kite and lightning adventures in the October 19, 1752, issue of the *Pennsylvania Gazette*, which he published. However, during a century of great scientific innovation, successful demonstrations of the steamboat (1807), the steam rail car (1830), the telegraph (1844), and the telephone (1876) received relatively bare mentions in the newspapers. The chief interest of the editors then lay in party politics. In the era of personal journalism, Horace Greeley wrote about his interest in farming and other aspects of science. This evolved into a weekly column, "Science for the people," which first appeared by that title on March 3, 1877, after Greeley's death. This was a period of writing in a scientific vein about discovery through exploration. As the nineteenth century faded, so did writing about exploration as "science." Adventure it might be, but not "science."

Separation and Sensation

In the 1880s, the paths of science and popularization were diverging. Science moved toward the extreme professionalization evident now. Science and scientific research were becoming full-time occupations outside the province of hobbyists, merchants, and clerics. Afficionados of science and its wonders still flocked to public lectures by scientists. In 1883, the editor of *Science* felt comfortable inviting amateurs to collect specimens of rocks, plants and insects that the local scientific societies could discuss and analyze.

A common interest in new knowledge still existed between scientists and nonscientists, but it was unraveling. "Pure" scientists who denigrated the state of American science led the separation. There were about five hundred serious, publishing researchers in the country then, and they emphasized advancement of their disciplines over service to local public and industrial interests. They wanted the amateurs out. The scientists were mainly in university or government employ, and some historians say their motives may have included enlarging their share of prestige and financial assistance (Kevles et al. 1980). In truth, American science of the time was neither as primitive nor as simple as leaders in the professionalization movement, often physicists, claimed.

Specialization, however, was in the air. Scientific researchers left the local societies, founded their own professional groups, and took control of "national" organizations, such as the American Chemical Society. In the name of better science, control of the American Association for the Advancement of Science (AAAS) passed to the research scientists. Public education through lectures, exhibits, and museums remained with local societies as an artifact often managed by the social and financial elites.

In its peculiar way, popular journalism of the time helped this movement along. Although some newspapers and magazines accurately reported science news, others used pseudoscience and sensationalized science to wage newspaper war. Excesses of the William Randolph Hearst and Joseph Pulitzer papers, to name two, left behind the name "Gee Whiz Science." Says Dr. Hillier Krieghbaum "The trauma of having their activities misrepresented was so intense that even decades later and despite the rise of professional, full-time science journalists, older scientists told newcomers of the 'horrors' of having work reported in the mass media" (Krieghbaum 1978, 6). These horrors, of course, were magnified by journalism's critics and served those raising the barricades between scientists and the unknowledgeable.

Americans had no national scientific journals in the strict new sense of "science." *Nature* started in Britain in 1869 and attracted notable scientists as authors. Americans had *American Journal of Science*, started in 1818 to report on local scientific societies. *Scientific American*, started in 1845, emphasized patents, invention, and technology. (New life and meaning were given the magazine when the name and content were rejuvenated after World War II.) *American Naturalist* began in the 1860s when a group of Harvard students set up their own science center in Salem and spun off *Science News* magazine in 1878, under the editorship of William C. Wyckoff, who had been covering science meetings for *The New York Herald Tribune. Science News*, as a title, was also rejuvenated in the twentieth century. In part this was a response to the apparent success of *Popular Science Monthly*, started in 1872 to print news and analyses of national science issues and reports from scientific institutions. A covey of other magazines rose and fell in this period, often lasting less than a year. Even as the scientists specialized and fragmented their own publications into highly technical journals, they complained that the news of science was fragmented and did not inform across the hard-drawn disciplinary lines.

It was in the late 1800s that Thomas A. Edison, whose technology and publicity were abhorrent to many pure scientists, founded a magazine with staying power. John Michels, amateur microscopist, was a freelance writer who reported scientific society meetings for *The New York Times*. He convinced Edison to back the magazine *Science*, which first appeared July 3, 1880. The magazine carried major stories about Edison's work among its other accounts. One of *Science*'s early "scoops" was Alexander Graham Bell's report on his "photophone." But in the time of professionalization of science, Michels's amateur status and Edison's tight hand on the purse kept away distinguished contributors. They liked pay. Eighteen months later, Edison transferred ownership to Michels and paid off the magazine's debts. Michels, back covering scientific societies for New York newspapers, eventually interested Bell in the magazine, but in doing so lost his publication. Bell conferred with many scientists in the AAAS and convinced himself that *Science* had potential. Subsequently he helped buy Michels's interest. As editor he installed Samuel H. Scudder, a Harvard scientist and librarian with good academic and political connections. Daniel Coit Gilman, president of Johns Hopkins University, headed the board of editors. To underscore *Science*'s academic and professional orientation, Gilman wrote: "*Science* will never be easy reading and will never entertain the seeker of curiosities" (Kohlstedt 1980, 33-41).

Bell and his father-in-law Gardiner Hubbard invested in *Science* from 1883 until March of 1894 when then editor N.D.C. Hodges folded the magazine for lack of sufficient funds. Ironically, even though Bell bemoaned the money lost, Hubbard lent Hodges money toward the end. He could afford to for he also had started a new publication called *National Geographic Magazine*. It was popular and successful to an extreme.

Leaders of the AAAS, having lost a journal made to their liking, proposed subsidizing a reborn *Science* that would publish papers from the society's meetings. In a way not even the AAAS understands, psychologist James McKeen Cattell became editor. Before the AAAS agreed to adopt *Science*, Cattell had persuaded Bell and Hubbard to give him ownership. Cattell had a solid research background and connections in New York through his Columbia University professorship. Family money left Cattell no financial worries. Cattell edited the magazine for fifty years, becoming a wealthy publisher instead of a professor. Ultimately the AAAS would pay his widow more than $250,000 for ownership of the magazine in 1945 (Sokal 1980).

It was the best buy the AAAS ever made. As with many other scientific and medical society magazines, its advertising boomed as billions of dollars in federal money poured into research and development after World War II. Advertising from makers of scientific equipment, government contractors, and universities hiring scientists turned the magazines into the main source of income for many scientific, medical, and technical societies. By 1980 *Science*'s budget had passed $7 million. Circulation, down from a 1971 peak of 163,000, was still more than 152,000 and rising in 1983 (Wolfle 1980, 57-62). Only in acknowledging its one hundredth birthday in 1980 does *Science* remember the two false starts by technologists Edison and Bell. It numbers its issues from Cattell.

Unlike those in scientific societies in Europe, notably in France, American scientists remained aloof from political issues. Neutrality in politics for themselves and their work became the official position. American journalism also followed a neutral path termed "objectivity." The AAAS also proscribed concern with the American education system; it ceased publication of *Science Monthly*, which had been organized through the AAAS to explore issues in the education community. The AAAS would pick up interest in education again when war-born federal education subsidies provided warm bodies to work as graduate students in science, expand the ranks of Ph.D.'s, staff laboratories for new scientist-administrators, and churn out research papers enhancing the reputations of the labs, the universities, and the administrators. Scientists declared themselves and their work to be above politics. Some held out even when Adolph Hitler's policies caused Jewish scientists, such as Albert Einstein, to flee the German universities.

Wild and popular science

Although scientists withdrew from professional contact with the larger audiences and practical concerns of general society, laymen were not bereft of scientific and technical information. Popular press editors wrote about what they and their readers could understand, but in the interest of excitement they often embellished their stories with the bizarre and the imaginative. Both science and sensation were served by Wilhelm C. Roentgen in 1895. Journalists described his X-ray photographs of the human skeleton and other hidden objects. They fed and increased their readers' curiosity by printing hosts of related but fanciful ideas including the possible need for radiation-proof female underwear. Medical science performed badly also. In the ignorance that follows any new discovery, *Lancet*, the venerable British medical journal, proposed that men run a small cathode ray tube over their faces each morning instead of shaving off their whiskers. With this authoritative support, physicians and quacks (often indistinguishable) tragically applied large doses of X-rays to their patients for depilatory purposes.

Serious magazines, such as *Harper's* and *Atlantic*, explored events and issues in science. A new breed of magazine flourished in the form of trade and industrial journals aimed at businesses aligned with the new technologies that produced chemical, mechanical, and electrical wonders. Farmers were the targets of magazines about scientific agriculture. These publications were in private hands and free to discuss topics the science journals preferred to ignore, including political and personal battles within the specialized societies.

Newspapers, which were rapidly growing into mass media, gave laymen an impression of science focused on the bizarre. Stories of the odd, outlandish, and impossible filled the popular press after the turn of the century. Yet the papers also caught the portent of Albert Einstein's theories of relativity and the revolution in physics flowing from it. Expanding use of the newswire services carried stories of two-headed calves and claims of Darwinian missing links across the continent. Such worldwide links as underseas cables and wireless increased the speed and range of communications and the embarrassment of scientists whose work was misreported. To others the times offered publicity opportunities. Archeologists opening up buried cities and pharaonic tombs carried journalists with their camps. So much seemed possible that little seemed impossible, no matter how improbable, to editors.

Then as now, editors were sympathetic to anything that fit their definition of "a good story." Some scientists, with their increasing dignity and authoritarian manners, offered irreverent journalists targets for humor. Samuel Pierpont Langley, head of the Smithsonian Institution, attracted their barbed reporting with his unsuccessful attempts to coax a powered aircraft model into flight by launching it off a barge in the Potomac River. Yet many newspapers ignored the Wright brothers' story from Kitty Hawk, North Carolina, which followed Langley's last splash by a few days.

Albert Einstein unleashed his theories of relativity in 1905. Science, in the press, still included much about daring physical exploration. While some adventurers risked everything in balloons and zeppelins, handwired airplanes, or bangy automotive speedsters, others reached for the ends of the earth: Robert E. Peary for the North Pole in April of 1909 and Roald Amundsen of Norway for the South Pole in December of 1911. Science also was moving toward war, with the rest of the world, and the discovery of how much the United States depended on Germany for chemicals and chemical expertise. World War I was characterized as the chemists' war as scientists (and engineers) found new ways to produce the materiel of war. As the scientists reported, in their conventions, the journalists relayed and glamourized the discoveries of chemistry—for better living, all agreed. The visible role industrial chemistry played during and after World War I helped journalists and their bosses recognize that the scientists deserved more serious attention. War II became the physicists' war for their contribution in splitting the atom to derive fission bombs and nuclear power. This time not even the scientists agreed that better living resulted.

Between the wars a new type of science journalist emerged. These journalists were better educated than many of their predecessors. This gave them a better grasp of many of the new ideas and the larger themes of science. Earl J. Johnson, who rose from reporter to vice president of United Press International, was one of the old school. Reporters were expected to cover a bloody railroad strike one day, he told a William Allen White Memorial Lecture audience, and shift to reporting on a meeting of scientists the next. "No doubt I was a versatile fellow, but it was a superficial versatility neither wire service would tolerate now" (Johnson 1965, 1).

One of those effecting the changes in popular science writing was journalist David Dietz. Dietz wrote his first science story in 1915 for the *Cleveland Press* while he was a freshman and campus correspondent at then Western Reserve University. His science classes gave him the vocabulary and the knowledge of the science of that time to exchange ideas easily with the scientists. His was a significant contribution to the specialization in science reporting by serious, educated journalists. In 1919 Britain's Sir Oliver Lodge granted Dietz an interview, producing what Dietz considered to be the first newspaper story on the release of atomic energy. Dietz, who wrote science and medicine stories for more than sixty years, considered Nobel scientists Arthur Compton, Robert A. Millikan, and Wendell Stanley his friends. He and astronomer Edwin P. Hubble played cards in the Mount Wilson observatory while waiting for the right time to turn the telescope to the Orion Nebulae. Dietz recalled telling Millikan he would have to miss the scientist's lecture. Millikan's answer: "Go ahead and write your story. You don't need my notes. You know as much about the subject as I do" (Dietz 1977, 25, 26). Dietz's knowledge of his subject and acceptance by scientists were unparalleled in his time and remain so today.

While Dietz moved about the country reporting on little else than science and medicine, he became one of a handful of regulars on the science trail. Among his companions were Alva Johnston of *The New York Times*. As *Times* owner Adolph Ochs remade the newspaper, he replaced freelancers with regular staff members who specialized in reporting science news. Assigned to cover the 1922 annual meeting of the AAAS, Johnston convinced *Times* editors to give most of a page each day to his stories from Cambridge, Massachusetts. These stories won Johnston a Pulitzer Prize in 1923, the first of several given journalists for science news coverage.

For the first time, in 1921, a news service dedicated to science reporting appeared. Dietz's publisher, E. W. Scripps of Scripps-Howard Newspapers and United Press wire service, launched Science Service to disseminate responsible science news and features. He put Dr. Edwin Slosson in charge, aided by another Scripps-Howard journalist, Watson Davis. Science Service evolved to the present-day *Science News*, the only popular weekly news magazine of science.

In this period between wars, other newspapers put full-time journalists onto the science and medicine beats. Waldemar Kaempffert was named science editor at *The New York Times*, but William L. Laurence wrote some of the *Times*'s most memorable stories. Howard Blakeslee moved into science writing for the Associated Press. New York's *Herald Tribune* matched the *Times* with John J. O'Neill. Even William Randolph Hearst joined the move to restrain the wilder aspects of science news reporting, making Dr. Gobind Behari Lal, then an Indian graduate student in social sciences in San Francisco, the chain's science editor.

Although these specialized reporters covered a lot of scientific gatherings, all was not well in their dealings with the scientists. In typical American fashion, the reporters organized to increase their bargaining power for press privileges with the scientists' organizations. The National Association of Science Writers (NASW) began in 1934 with twelve members and Dietz as president. Other members included Kaempffert, Laurence, Davis, Blakeslee, O'Neill, Lal, Slosson, Robert Potter of the Medical Society of the County of New York and Science Service, Delos Smith of United Press, and Allen Schoenfield of *The Detroit News*. Another member, Robert Dwyer of the *New York Daily News* and its City Press Association, concentrated on the medical researchers at Bellevue and other New York hospitals (Hohenberg 1961). Over the years the NASW won a set of operating amenities at scientific meetings that included official press liaison, pressrooms, phones, typewriters, copies of papers for study, news conferences, reference books, and other accommodations to make reporting easier, thorough, and more accurate.

O'Neill, Laurence, Blakeslee, Lal, and Dietz, five founders of NASW shared the 1937 Pulitzer Prize for their reporting of Harvard University's tercentennial and its emphasis on efforts to understand humans and their world. In the middle of World War II, *The New York Times*'s Laurence disappeared from sight and print; only after the atomic bombs were dropped on Hiroshima and Nagasaki was the reason revealed. The U.S. government had taken the *Times*'s science writer into the secret world of nuclear energy and the latter stages of weapons development and testing. Laurence witnessed the atomic bomb's first test at Trinity Site, New Mexico, on July 16, 1945. He would write the first stories of the atomic bomb's use at Hiroshima and Nagasaki and the cracking of the storehouse of nuclear energy. This brought Laurence the 1946 Pulitzer Prize, his second.

In 1984, John Noble Wilford of *The Wall Street Journal* won the Pulitzer for the bulk of his work, primarily his writing about the U.S. space exploration programs. The most honored, although not the best known of NASW members, however, is Jon Franklin, science writer for the evening *Baltimore Sun*. Franklin won unshared Pulitzers twice, in 1979 and 1985, for stories about the mind and brain. Through the years, many journalists have won the Pulitzer and other major journalistic prizes for articles on scientific and medical subjects, although they have not necessarily identified themselves as full-time science writers.

Pressures of world war, and their removal, helped bring the scientists and the science writers closer together on many issues. There were shared desires to understand whole fields of science and technology, such as radar and electronics, that had advanced tremendously behind the walls of military secrecy. Disturbed physicists, among others, shared with journalists a desire to keep open and unclassified as much as possible of the nuclear energy information. Wartime development of penicillin, coupled with new biological research and production techniques, promised that life sciences could make medicine a true science. Jet propulsion, taken from the defeated Germany's military laboratories, promised a new type of air transportation, the breaking of the sound barrier, and flying speeds and distances unimaginable before. Out of the war came millions of men and women eager to be educated into these new sciences. So useful had science been in winning World War II, scientists worldwide sensed a transformation in the ways nations regarded and financed scientific research. Big science had arrived, consuming large amounts of public funds and entering the political debate on public policy and financing, the natural field of journalism.

The competition of science news for space in newspapers and on the expanding commercial and educational television broadcasts led science writers and editors to examine the readership and audience for science information. The ability of publications to attract and hold readership is crucial in the commercial media to financial stability. In television and radio, maintaining audience size against competing networks and stations is the heart of the game.

Why read science stories?

Writers and editors often assume people want to see—should see—what they want to broadcast, write, and publish. Hundreds of dead or dying newspapers, magazines, and radio-TV shows memorialize this attitude. A few scientific journals, *Science* among them, prosper because they go to a large dedicated audience of scientists whose interests are perfectly aligned with the journal's content. Most of the thousands of scientific journals cannot support themselves out of membership dues but are subsidized in some way, and scientists pay to have their research published in most journals. Often the money is part of their research grant. Editors and writers for unsubsidized periodicals seldom have this financial option. On most commercial publications, paying to have an article published would mean having it labeled as paid advertisement.

Mass media editors and writers have no guarantee of reader interest and so attempt to gauge what readers want. Over the past forty years, readership surveys have consistently given high marks to reader interest in science information. Although all the surveys are not directly comparable, this interest appears to be on the increase.

One of the earliest readership studies covered 130 newspapers published from 1939 to 1950. News about science, invention, health, and safety ranked above accidents, national government, local government, recreation, sports, art, music, and literature. Outranking science-based news were war, defense, fire and disaster coverage, the comics, human interest stories, and the weather (Swanson 1955).

The National Association of Science Writers commissioned two later surveys by the Survey Research Center at the University of Michigan. "Science, the News and the Public" was conducted in 1957. The second NASW study, "Satellites, Science and the Public" (McLeod and Swinehart 1959), came after Russia put up the first Sputnik. The researchers found the general categories of science, medicine, and health retained about the same rankings, and that 90 percent of the readers were then aware of Sputnik. Two points stood out: awareness of a scientific event is stimulated by printing news of that event, and a sizeable group of individuals are curious about anything in science.

Dr. Hillier Krieghbaum, one of the leaders in teaching and research in science popularization, concluded from these surveys that the typical "science reader" is a high school graduate or beyond, older than most readers, affluent enough to live in the metropolitan suburbs, and a heavy user of media—newspapers, radio, television, and magazines (1959, 1092-95). This picture continues to hold up. Wilbur Schramm further concluded that knowledge of science is widely but not deeply distributed in the United States. There are areas of ignorance and misinformation. Level of education and mass media use are the two most important predictors of interest in scientific information for an individual, the basis for aiming new science

publications and programs at a highly educated audience. Readers selectively choose science information on the basis of their perceived "needs." Women, for example, read medical news more than men do.

This audience wants more science news. Readership increases where science writers put their information in a narrative or "story" form, make it apply to the audience's needs, personalize, and even sensationalize it. And, Schramm concluded, most learning about science information comes from the media after people leave school (1962, 1-20).

Fifteen years later, in 1971, the Newspaper Advertising Bureau surveys of media usage placed news of science and invention in eleventh place. However, public health and welfare, science and medicine related, ranked fifth. Environmental news, also heavily dependent on scientific research, ranked ninth. By 1976, in the middle of concerns over energy supplies, energy ranked first, accidents-disasters-natural phenomena second, public health and welfare third, weather (a science field) fourth, environment fifth, and science-invention eighth. In spite of these indications of rising interest, space devoted to such science-related categories of news and features has remained around 5 percent for newspapers since 1942 (Krieghbaum 1978).

What are these readers and viewers looking for in science? Psychologists and sociologists have derived several levels of "needs" that people seek to gratify through media and other means. On one level, media help meet survival needs. For any organism these are basic: securing food, shelter, and sex. Where scientific research bears upon these areas, particularly if the information threatens personal security in meeting these needs, interest should be high, as with interest in the disease AIDS.

Most people who are heavy media users have solved their basic survival needs. They seldom face the question of where their next meal will come from.

However there are many needs beyond survival. Maintaining or enhancing the quality of their survival ranks high among these needs. Ways to get better food, better housing, better health, and better sex, as reported by scientific researchers, offer immediate applicability or gratification in people's lives. In modern terms, ways to earn the money necessary to secure a higher level of survival for oneself or family may be revealed through promising new industries or more enjoyable occupations that are inherent in science and its potential applications. Often this relation to recognizable human interests accounts for publication and broadcast of stories derived from science but of nonscientific import. *Money* magazine holds a membership in the NASW, and stock analysts attend scientific news conferences for advance information that could affect the price of shares in publicly held companies, such as those making and selling drugs or advanced technologies, as well as for science information of interest to its readers as consumers.

Reader interest determines subject matter, but another factor enters in before a story goes into print. Science writers must first get their stories past the "gatekeepers," editors who make the final decisions on publishing a story or book or putting a broadcast on the air. One science writer complained that he could get any story about hemorrhoids into print because every editor has them. When an editor is familiar with a subject, he or she will handle it differently than an unfamiliar subject. Familiarity helps, even with less personal subjects. Earl Ubell, a science writer for print and broadcast media, once told of a science writer whose first story on a new subject landed deep in the newspaper. "And, finally, by the third time around it almost hit the front page because by that time the editor had begun to understand that perhaps it was news and he ought to do something about it" (Communication 1964, 35). Some publications use the science writers as gatekeepers; editors ask their opinions on whether or not a science wire story or press release story is important enough to print.

Science news helps satisfy another human need. This is the need for diversion, variety—entertainment. New knowledge fits this need. Charles Darwin's evolution theory, Roentgen's X-ray photographs, and Albert Einstein's views of the universe captured imaginations, provided conversation, and stimulated thought, no matter how misconceived, because they offered fresh ideas. New discoveries about the natural world in general, if they are significant enough, satisfy a need for knowledge in mankind. However, educating the public is not necessarily high in scientists' priorities. Some think it is not their responsibility. Eric Ashby, master of Cambridge University's Clare College, once asked: "Ultimately there is the question of why scientists should compete with crooners" (1960, 1166). Cosmologist Carl Sagan, after producing a widely heralded astronomy show for public television, was criticized by scientists for having abandoned science. Editors generally do not consider themselves in the business of education either.

Scientific projects sometimes wind up as the focus of ridicule because of the media's need for variety. Scientists seldom take their work lightly; to them, media humor at their expense stings for a long time. But some projects are natural targets, no matter how significant or insignificant or how valid or questionable their scientific result. Such was the case with Dr. Erwin O. Strassman who set out to research any correlation between the size of women's bustlines and their intelligence (1964b).

When the story appeared in the journal of the doctor's specialty, the job of reporting on the doctor's study went to a reporter known for his colorful writing. The product was a witty story evoking images of brainless beauties and bustless Phi Beta Kappas. The somewhat banal conclusion that three-fourths of the women studied were mixtures of the two was ignored. Complained the doctor:

You took a small observation from the last pages out of context and made it the leading issue of the entire report with a sensational headline. This gives the impression as if there are only two kinds of women, the ones with flat chests and brains and the ones with large breasts and low I.Q.'s . . . in order to dramatize the "busts-or-brains" slogan you added pictures and interviews with bosomy movie stars to your articles. The comments of these ladies, based on distorted information, made my investigation a joke (Strassman 1964a).

There is another side of the readership question. Popularization carried to an extreme may alienate readers two ways. First, because science news has a steady, reliable corps of readers, bringing the specialized language of science, its jargon, down to too low a level may offend the readers who understand science best and cost a medium the respect it wants with knowledgeable readers. This may restrain popularization where a general audience publication, such as The New York Times, has a large bloc of scientists, engineers, and doctors among its readership. The other danger is that the writer or publication alienates future news sources. Because the science writer is very dependent on the goodwill and respect of those inside the various scientific disciplines, the danger of a loss of communication may inhibit writers. This possibility often leads publications to assign critical stories to generalists to protect the specialized reporters from offending their sources and to avoid having a reporter write a weak story for fear of losing contacts. This tactic has been used frequently on the sports and police beats where reporters may become too close to their sources. Some news organizations shift reporters to new territories regularly to avoid such occurrences.

Science writers: who and where

Who are the people writing about science, medicine, and technology? In the broadest sense, they include anyone building their stories with bricks from the heap of knowledge developed by the scientific, engineering, and medical disciplines. This could cover every writer doing reasonably thorough research for a story since the most recent information on any subject probably lies with some research scientist. In a more restricted sense, science writers are those spending most of their time writing about science or related subjects for an audience that is primarily outside the scientific disciplines. There are also a number of scientists and doctors who write an occasional popularized account of science, as does Dr. Lewis Thomas, chancellor of the Memorial Sloan-Kettering Cancer Center in New York, but writing is not their primary occupation. Thomas's collection of essays, The Lives of a Cell, won the National Book Award in 1974.

In the opinion of Dr. Miroslav Holub, author of thirteen books of poetry and an immunology researcher at the Institute of Clinical and Experimental Medicine in Prague, Czechoslovakia, Thomas's work is exemplary. "The best form of writing about science is in my view the scientific essay, by Lewis Thomas, say, the essay which presents selected problems and the scientific way of thinking about them in a refined literary form" (1982-83, 21). In addition to writing poetry, Holub edits a popularized science magazine but operates under a considerably different press system than do science writers outside the authoritarian-bloc countries. Education in the "right" form of thinking in communist regions takes precedence over immediacy, subject matter, and competition. Philosophically, newsiness is not of high priority.

Because such polished essay forms take time to achieve, they seldom fit readership and writership needs for the mass media. Science journalists who have a regular column—and time to smooth the writing—can approach them, as can very good, facile writers.

Controversy exists among science journalists over those eighteen to twenty newspapers that publish weekly science and health supplements. One group favors the supplements for promoting a regular readership and showcasing their stories. The other side holds that such sections may deprive readers of daily science stories by restricting science coverage to one day a week. These science writers claim such a concentration may, in fact, reduce the science news content of a publication as well as withold news from readers.

Some writers, scientists among them, use provocative approaches to science writing, even though this risks criticism for being flippant. Sarah Blaffer Hrdy, an anthropologist who writes for many popular and semipopular magazines as well as journals, is one of the best. In her article, "Heat Loss," for *Science 83* (1983) she catches you off guard with this lighthearted lead-in to a serious subject, why human females do not experience "heat" cycles.

> "Women are really dreadfully complicated," muses a lovesick veterinarian in Alan Ayckbourn's trilogy *The Norman Conquests.* "With other animals, well, the majority of them, they're either off heat or on heat. I probably should have been born a horse or something" (p. 73).

Some scientists write entirely for a popular market. Dr. Isaac Asimov, a biochemist, is a virtual writing machine. He has written more than three hundred books of popular science and science fiction; he has lost count of the number of magazine and newspaper articles in his collection. However, science-trained writers make up a small but growing minority of the science writers. At one time Earl Ubell, with a bachelor's degree in physics, working for *The New York Herald-Tribune,* could boast that he had the only scientific degree among newspaper staff science writers. This is no longer true. Lawrence K. Altman of *The New York Times* holds the M.D. degree. Asimov and nearly three dozen other members of the National Association of Science Writers hold Ph.D. degrees. Research chemist Irving Bengels-

dorf was science editor of the *Los Angeles Times* before going to the Jet Propulsion Laboratory as a specialist technical writer; he continued to write a science column for the *Los Angeles Herald.*

Regardless of training, most science writers do not work as journalists or on the staffs of newspapers and popular magazines. Only about 250 to 300 members of the 1000-plus members of the National Association of Science Writers are staff writers; only about 10 percent of the 1700 daily newspapers employ science writers (NASW 1983). Moreover, most newspaper science and medical writers work on the larger metropolitan and regional dailies. For many years, the Rochester, Minnesota, *Post-Bulletin* has been the smallest newspaper employing a full-time medical writer; it is, of course, published where the Mayo Clinic is a major employer and source of news. Most small newspapers get their science news through general assignment reporters, wire services, or public information writers employed by local medical and science centers. Many science journalists got their start covering local medical and science news and developed this interest into a specialty.

Although full-time science and medical writers work for such magazines as *Time* and *Newsweek,* most magazine staffers work for specialized science and, in the main, medical publications. The newswire services—Associated Press, Reuters, and United Press International—each deploy a handful of science writers around the world. Another small group of science writers is affiliated with the radio and television networks, including the Public Broadcasting System.

The majority of full-time science writers work in institutions such as universities, hospitals, science and health organizations, government and business, and public relations agencies. They may work for an organization turning out press releases, newsletters, newspapers, magazines, television scripts, or other popularized science and medical information for distribution to the media, hospital patients, association members, employees and stockholders, contributors or other publics that may offer a commercial or institutional benefit from public contact. The same pattern of employment holds for the nearly 3000 members of the American Medical Writers Association, whose membership overlaps considerably with the NASW, and for the smaller Aviation and Space Writers Association, the environmental and energy writers organizations, and several agricultural writers associations.

Membership in these writing groups expands and contracts with economic conditions and with communication crises that demand writers with specialized knowledge and contacts. Science writers shift into these newer specialties as the market demands. The environmental associations were born out of the enactment of legislation to reduce air and water pollution. Energy writing became an organized specialty in the 1970s with the oil shortages produced when foreign countries reduced their petroleum exports to the United States. Likewise with the reduction of the U.S. space exploration program in the 1970s, membership declined in the space writers association. Fearing the appearance of undue commercial influence, most science-technical news organizations vest control in the group of "active" members writing directly for readers or viewers. Educators, government information officers in science-oriented agencies, and public relations people usually hold "associate" status. This bars them from voting control of the organization and preserves the journalists' independence from dominance by those science writers in nonnews organizations. Such restrictions are galling and frequently produce conflict inside the organizations.

Science writers number a large proportion of freelancers among their members. Because of the higher than average fees available for their specialized knowledge and the large number of medical publica-

tions operated on the basis of drug company advertising, science and medical writers thrive as freelancers where many other writers barely scrape by. Some freelancers work mainly for public relations and information offices. Many staff science writers for media also freelance books and magazine articles about science and technology.

Science writers appear to be an exceptionally mobile group. The roster of the NASW, for example, warns that about 20 percent of its members change jobs or addresses every three months (NASW 1983).

Geographically science writers tend to be an eastern and urban group. New York City, Boston, and their suburbs contain large numbers because of the major publishing and scientific-educational institutions in these metropolitan areas. Washington, D.C., draws another cluster to write about science politics and research at the National Institutes of Health (NIH) and other government facilities in the area. The American Medical Writers Association has its headquarters in nearby Bethesda, Maryland. Many Washington science writers work for government institutions and scientific-medical associations. The *Journal of the American Medical Association*, for example, has one writer specializing in politics and hard sciences and another covering NIH. Other science writers are assigned to Washington bureaus of major news organizations, including *The New York Times*, Associated Press, and United Press International, *Time, Newsweek*, and *Business Week*—McGraw-Hill World News.

California, principally around Los Angeles and San Francisco, also harbors a large number of science writers who write for the area's larger newspapers, government institutions, university and other medical centers, the aerospace industry, and a growing number of aerospace and other specialized magazines. Chicago as a center of trade publishing, government and private research, health-medical research and drug production, and universities provides a base for many other science writers. Concentrations of science writers are very dilute elsewhere; Texas with the third largest state population had only a dozen science writers listed with NASW in 1985.

How did they get there?

As has been the case throughout their history, science writers come from all directions and educational backgrounds. There exists no recognized training program or licensing requirements. Interpretations of the Constitution's First Amendment "free press" clause hold journalists cannot be controlled through licensure. In authoritarian countries, membership in one or more recognized writers' "unions" is required before you can work. Some countries may require official credentials, such as graduation from an approved school. Some American professional writers' associations require a year or more experience for new members.

If a science writing requirement exists (or success can be assured), it probably lies with education. The most generally recognized division between science writers rests in educational background or training. Scientific fields rely heavily upon credentials for admission; advanced degrees carry status. Status for journalists can come from the news gathering organization, and news sources generally deal with someone of equal status more openly than with someone they perceive as having lesser status. Network TV and *The New York Times*, for example, command attention from all but the most haughty.

Training in science, knowledge, and credentials convey authority. Syndicated medical advice columns by doctors have been a staple of American journalism for many decades. Donna Buys, a registered nurse and freelance writer, is successful in writing under her own name or under a byline shared with other health professionals, including doctors. One must have credentials and training to write semi-technical articles for many specialized magazines.

Although some writers originally trained as scientists, most science writers come from liberal arts and journalism backgrounds. Three waves of science writers have occupied the field over the past sixty years. After World War I general reporters prevailed, often without college training. They simply covered what came their way. A few people were assigned primarily to science coverage. Numbers of science writers increased in the period after World War II through the mechanism of managing editors simply assigning someone with promise or an interest in science or medicine to make contacts with people in the scientific community. Editors perceived that their jobs would be easier with someone who knew publishing and writing. The editors despaired of teaching science and medical people how to replace technical jargon with words or ideas appealing to the editors' perception of some "common man." Most of these science writers learned their business on the job and relied on their few college courses in science and outside reading. They also received help from seminars and briefings offered by scientific and medical associations. Many journalists consider such sessions as badly disguised ploys to gain publicity.

Education in science may help a writer specialize but may place him or her in an awkward position as a working journalist. Editors reluctantly create specialists in their publications, especially on newspapers. Becoming a full-time science writer may require apprenticeship to general reporting or desk work for a year or more on a smaller publication before going to a publication with science specialists. Budget controls at smaller newspapers force editors to use a few people to cover the dozens of different types of stories happening in even the smallest communities. Editors are also wary of specialists being captured or "co-opted" to become advocates of the people or the viewpoints they cover regularly. Editors have decades of precedence for this on such established beats as sports and police. Thus developing science writing experience depends heavily on how well a writer generates stories about science or medicine while covering other assignments. The coin of broadcast, newspaper and magazine journalism is how well a story comes out, how often a writer gets printed or on the air. Credentials are worth something but they are not everything. Editors still want good stories.

The success of the Soviet Union with Sputnik brought a turning point in science journalism. Columbia University persuaded the Sloan and Rockefeller foundations to finance midcareer science training programs for journalists with basic science reporting experience. The program was modeled on Harvard's Nieman Fellow program, which encouraged study in the sciences. Other universities in the 1960s began specialized science, environment, and energy reporting courses or programs emphasizing formal technical, economic, social, and historical aspects of science. MIT offers midcareer training to a selected group of would-be science writers. So science writers today include a large number of people with more formal science training in their background, including more ability to evaluate critically the statistical proofs and other evidence scientists offer for their discoveries.

However familiarity sometimes affects objectivity. Some editors, journalism researchers, and sociologists of science worry that the mental conditioning needed for science expertise makes the media science writer less able—or willing—to see flaws in the scientific community's activities. Experience long ago demonstrated tendencies of specialties to adopt the attitudes, dress, standards, and speech of the people they cover. Sports writers slide into jockspeak, police reporters act like cops, and State Department and business writers adopt the protective coloration of their surroundings.

Science journalists have been so admiring of scientists that Dr. Dorothy Nelkin, professor in the Departments of Science, Technology and Society and Sociology at Cornell University, wonders about the reports of conflict between scientists and journalists. Idealization of science and scientists is endemic in the journalists' writing. Newspapers, she points out, hire critics of politics, the arts, and other fields, but not in science. She writes,

> While political writers criticize and analyze, science writers elucidate and explain. . . . All of which leaves me with two questions: Why is science writing so uncritical of science? And why are scientists so critical of the press, so convinced of its antiscience intent? (1984b, 4)

A recent survey of science writers by Conrad J. Storad indicates a number of science journalists inclining toward a more critical and analytical stance. While Storad's overall demographics show science writers tend to be of early middle age, highly educated and very experienced in reporting, those willing to assess the social and economic effect of science tend to be younger and more tuned to in-depth reporting. Often they are the product of university science and science writing courses.

Science writing proves no handicap to career advancement. It is not a backwater of journalism. Editors Michael O'Neill of the *New York Daily News*, John Troan of the *Pittsburgh Press*, and Marvin Stone of *U.S. News and World Report* came out of science news experience. So did Howard Simons, head of the Nieman program and former managing editor of *The Washington Post*, and Abigail Trafford Brett, an assistant managing editor of *U.S. News and World Report*. David Hendin moved from science editor and columnist to vice president of United Features Syndicate and Newspaper Enterprise Association. Gerard Piel, publisher of *Scientific American* left his job as science editor of *Life* magazine to build *Scientific American*. In 1985, the American Association for the Advancement of Science installed Piel as its president, the first science journalist to head this largest of the scientific organizations. But career paths to the executive suites, such as they are on newspapers and magazines, depend more on how you relate to larger issues of society and to publications management—and luck—than on your specialty. Just as many superb editors and reporters enjoy small town or community journalism, many science writers are content to spend their lives covering the people and the subjects that interest them. In the pursuit of their interests they parallel many scientists who prefer research to administration.

Experiments

1. In your library find newspapers and magazines, particularly in New York, Chicago, or San Francisco, from around the turn of the century. Find a science or medical story of the time and compare it with a science story of today.

2. Find a science article for every five years from 1890 to 1950. Did you recognize the names of the scientists of the late nineteenth century? How about the scientists and adventurers from 1900 to 1950? Look them up in histories or encyclopedias of science and report on what they accomplished.

3. Look through the *Readers' Guide to Periodical Literature* or the early volumes of *The New York Times Index*. What subjects were covered as science of the times?

4. Interview one of your former science teachers or a graduate student in science about his or her attitude toward popularized science. What does he or she think about newspaper science writing? Does he or she need or want to know about other fields of science? What is the attitude toward public understanding of science? Can your scientist suggest ways of improving public knowledge of science?

Chapter 3
Choosing science news

THE ABUNDANT INFORMATION ABOUT science, medicine, engineering, and technology can be overwhelming. All of it potentially interests someone, somewhere. Choosing from the outpourings of hundreds of thousands of scientists is one of the hardest tasks for the science editor and writer. Writers for such publications as *The New York Times* and *The Washington Post* get a foot-tall stack of scientific journals, reports, and releases from universities and other institutions every day.

In addition, federal, state, and local government agencies almost daily propose, effect, or alter regulations and public policy affecting health and safety. Woven through all this are personality clashes, conflicting plans, requests for financing at public expense, and issues of priority. Science-based industries feed this stream of information with claims of new products and processes. Nature also plays a hand, offering new diseases, unexpected floods, volcanic eruptions, earthquakes, and other phenomena of spectacular scale. Choosing what small part of this outpouring merits communication is a major aspect of being a science editor, writer, broadcaster, or information specialist. Scientists are very critical of how well journalists do this.

This aspect of journalism also puzzles scientists. Studies indicate that scientists who have many contacts with journalists from the mass media cannot predict what the journalists will make of their research any better than can scientists who have little contact with the media (Ryan 1982). But scientists likely would derive little comfort from knowing that deciding what is news puzzles journalists and publicists almost as much as their sources.

Good news judgment enters into the decision-making process of the successful journalist. Understanding some of the criteria that determine newsworthiness will help develop news judgment. The game is played by the rules of the media. As one medical writer said of a doctor acquaintance: "We reached an agreement. He'll decide when his patients are sick. I'll decide when they are news."

Traditional news criteria

In part, the choice of what gets published is made by a consensus of writers and editors. There are no binding rules, although there is general agreement on factors considered in the decision. Some factors are based on tradition and others are of more recent origin. Caprice also plays a part: an editor or a writer simply enjoys writing or reading about a subject and assumes others will also. Sometimes good writing can outweigh other detracting factors. In general, timeliness, timing, impact, significance, uniqueness, and human interest are important. Variety and conflict are also considerations.

TIMELINESS. With some exceptions, media people do not consciously dispense stale information. If they know something has been previously bruited about and new developments have not occurred, they will seek out another story. However timeliness in science reporting means more than just immediacy. An event may happen today that requires a look at yesterday's news. For example, a scientist may be interviewed about an old topic simply because a researcher gives a paper today at a meeting of specialists. Today's event gives a "newspeg" on which to hang the story.

Also what appears to be yesterday's news may not be. Because of delays in science publication, the information may be several months or even years old, but it merits a story when a reputable science journal appears today containing the research report. In fact, you can pick up Sunday or Monday newspapers and find at least one story digested from the latest issues of the *Journal of the American Medical Association, The New England Journal of Medicine,* or *Science* magazine. The release of the publication is the newsbreak. Because weekends are notoriously slow news days, the editors of these magazines provide advance copies to wire services, newspapers, and other media. Science journalists sometimes question whether or not every issue of these and other journals contains a worthwhile story, but they do offer stories that meet standards for both reliability and timeliness. Since the date of publication of a given scientific paper usually is known to the author, public relations officers at universities will attempt to alert the media through a phone call or a press release about the coming publication.

TIMING.   Closely related to timeliness is timing. A subject may be worthwhile, in the judgment of writers and editors, if it is tied to some event extraneous to science. Thus a writer can publish at Christmas a story based on new psychological research into Christmas melancholy. Every winter also sees science writers delving into the status of research on weather patterns, influenza, and the so-called common cold. Such material would have less meaning to readers on the Fourth of July.

IMPACT.   Impact is another factor in deciding what to publish. Many editors say the best story is the one that affects the most readers. A trivial science story can get worldwide publication when writers and editors perceive that it will affect a large segment of their readers. Research into sex and many other human relationships comes with a built-in audience. Medical research gets attention because people universally recognize disease as a threat. Given a choice of medical stories, most writers and editors will choose those dealing with cancer and heart disease or other major killers over less-deadly afflictions. A deadly or debilitating malady can become an orphan for both science and media when too few people are afflicted by it to catch the attention of journalists or those who award research grants.

SIGNIFICANCE.   Significance, as seen by writers and editors, contributes also to the decision to popularize a science topic. Many science writers lose their stories because they cannot show their editors that the subject has meaning to the audience. Jerry Bishop of *The Wall Street Journal* writes about basic research, particularly in medical fields, and gets printed because he establishes a personal health or economic angle within the story for his readers. Often this is one of the more difficult tasks for a science writer when researchers are wary about speculating on the potential applications of their research.

For example, most newspapers ignored early attempts to transplant genetic material from cells of other living species into bacteria cells. Because scientists said little about the implications of the work, writers were unable to establish what many call a "significance paragraph" in their gene transplant stories. The phrase "genetic engineering" entered the common vocabulary, however, when scientists and industrialists began talking more freely about the risks and benefits of using this technique to manufacture human insulin and other chemicals with bacteria containing the transplanted genes or plasmids. The technique also made possible the production of interferon, a naturally occurring chemical with potential as a disease fighter. For the first time since the substance was discovered nearly thirty years earlier, scientists could obtain enough of the chemical to test its potential uses. Transplants of human tissue cells containing fragments of hormone-producing nucleic acids promised potential remedies for some genetic diseases. Once scientists acknowledged these possibilities, writers could establish a meaning for general audiences of what appeared, at first, merely a neat laboratory trick of significance only to scientists.

Significance to science rather than to readers can get a story published. Discovery of a new phenomenon, such as a "black hole," or the confirmation of some event or phenomenon predicted by one of the great theories, such as gravity waves, are examples. These stir our imaginations although they do not affect our lives directly, provided the science writer recognizes the story or coaxes the researcher to explain.

FIRST EVENT.   First event and uniqueness comprise a news factor that scientists sometimes curse. Being first with a discovery or a theory is what research is about. Firsts are news. Sometimes the competition among scientists to claim first credit approaches the unethical, as shown by James D. Watson in *The Double Helix* (1968), an account of how Watson and Francis Crick found the structure of the DNA molecule. On the other hand, being first may not draw universal acclaim. When MIT scientists held a press conference to announce their assembly of the first artificial gene, other scientists criticized the media for giving them so much publicity. In the view of these critics, the credit should have gone to those who first discovered the biochemical techniques that made possible the construction of the gene. That was the real trick.

Uniqueness, as a news criterion, often carries a built-in trap when writing about science. Science as a method rests upon the ability of an experimenter to duplicate the results of another. Failure to get similar results has exposed hoaxes in several cases. Failure of other observers to obtain predicted results may indicate faulty research techniques, a botched experiment, or merely a one-time event—an aberration that cannot be expected to occur or be observed generally. Such things as twin-headed snakes or bizarre mutations in plants exposed to heavy radiation are oddities beloved of some journalists, but they smack of sensation in the world of science. They are not the predictable results of testing against a reliable theory. Some scientists frown upon publicizing a "first" discovery; they prefer that duplication by another scientist occur before stories are written. But for journalists, that would conflict with the criteria of timeliness, since some experiments take years and others are never duplicated or duplication is never attempted. The journalists' solution is to write the story.

HUMAN INTEREST.   Human interest, another news criteria, is found in stories that appeal to the emotions. But taking this feelings approach is potentially at conflict with scientists' attempts to present an objective, dispassionate view of their work. An example of this approach would involve probing a scientist for quotations reflecting the elation, fatigue, or other visceral aspects of research. A writer may choose to tell a story through the person when dealing with very abstract material. The natural interest of people in other people leads some writers to approach all stories this way.

Human interest is often used in efforts to raise money. Public relations people and journalists focus sympathetic stories upon an ailing, crippled, or handicapped child. It is a technique commonly used by private organizations and in hearings before congressional committees when federal research budgets are under discussion. Describing one suffering victim who represents the thousands or millions similarly afflicted evokes a stronger response than statistics. One scientist, hard-pressed for research funds, proposed a "telethon" to raise contributions for basic research.

Then there are animal stories. Monkeys sent up to test the first space ships made what writers call "good copy." Baby harp seals, eagles, snail darters, wolves, wild horses, and others win media attention. The issue of experimental animals is particularly touchy among animal rights proponents. They have been known to break into laboratories and free the animal subjects. Scientists working with dogs, monkeys, and other animals are wary of stories that may reflect real or imagined abuses of the animals.

Related to the human interest story is the personality profile. People like to read about other people. When a scientist's work has significance and impact or yields recognition or fame, such as the Nobel Prize, science writers may find it easier to describe the science by focusing on how the person works at science. Human quirks, hobbies, or other non-scientific interests may help the writer show the scientist as a warm, searching, often fallible human being with whom the readers and viewers can identify. An audience may not understand the science but will appreciate the person. Dr Paul de Kruif discovered nearly fifty years ago how effectively the stories of Pasteur and other pioneers could be told through the human drama of their lives in their quest for scientific truths. His stories formed one of the most successful series ever published by the *Reader's Digest*.

Indeed, the world of scientific research contains possibly more than its share of colorful, strong, distinctive, even egotistical personalities. Yet the way scientists present their research emphasizes sterile methodology while minimizing the human factors involved, including error, accident, and luck. Scientific reports detail little of the history of discovery, almost nothing of the missteps that distinguish dead-end paths from those leading to new insights. The impersonal style required of formal scientific reporting comes through dry and dull, contributing to the view of scientists as cold and uncaring. Yet for a scientist, particularly a young one, to reveal too much in print or appear too irreverent of process and methodology invites criticism from his or her elders for debasing science. In the undocumented folklore of science there are many stories of scientists whose professional advancement was hindered by publicity about their work. In the medical world professional jealousy can bring censureship, charges of unethical advertising, and even loss of license.

Yet there are marvelous stories to be found in exploring the human side of science. Dr. Gustave Ekstein, the great neurosurgeon and teacher at the University of Cincinnati, was a world-class authority on budgerigars and let hundreds of the birds fly free in his house. Others go to great lengths to hide all aspects of their lives beyond their professional activity. Colleagues probably can help you develop such personal information.

Luck plays a part in successful science. As W.B. Gratzer of the Cell Biophysics Unit of Britain's Medical Research Council pointed out, "After all, more valuable discoveries than one would dare mention have been the outcome of accidental observations from misconceived experiments conducted by incompetents" (1984, 17). Perhaps more scientists would be received better if they were understood as having the quickness to recognize the importance of the unexpected.

CELEBRITY SCIENTISTS.   A relative of the personality profile is the celebrity or authority interview. Few scientists equal the name or face recognition of actors and other well-known people we usually think of as celebrities. Einstein was perhaps an exception. On the other hand, there are a large number of scientists whose offices and/or accomplishments project status and power. The secretary of the Smithsonian Institution, the president of the National Academy of Sciences, winners of the Nobel or other major prizes, the executive officers of the American Association for the Advancement of Science, American Chemical Society, American Institute of Physics, National Institutes of Health, and others may attract mass media attention as "visible scientists" whom the media ask to speak for the scientific community. They lend a cause respectability and extra consideration because of who they are. Nobel chemist Linus Pauling, for example, espoused, with some success, massive doses of vitamin C as curatives, a stance viewed skeptically by many of his colleagues. Such people merit attention for their views and for the understanding of power figures.

PROXIMITY.   Proximity is another of the traditional news values. The closer readers and viewers are to the location of an event, the more likely they and the editors consider the event newsworthy. Thus, thousands of people dying during a flood in China get less space than a hometown flood that kills no one. This has several aspects that the science writer must be aware of. They help make relations between scientists and journalists very sensitive. First, the significance of proximity may outweigh significance to science. Media in sprawling countries such as the United States and Canada are very distance-limited. FM radio and TV signals reach out only a limited distance from the city, no matter how much power stations install or how high they raise their towers to expand their line-of-sight horizon. Most newspapers can distribute copies of each issue profitably only within a limited area. This limit is often defined by where they encounter another strong newspaper, available transportation facilities, terrain, and trading patterns. Usually this maximum extends a few hundred miles, at most, from the city of publication. Individually, the media must develop enough loyal readers and listeners to provide a market to local advertisers or they will go bankrupt. Studies of these readers and listeners indicate the media must carry information about local or regional events to hold the audience in their territories.

The desire for attention from network and cable TV, radio, national magazines, and a few national newspapers, such as *The Wall Street Journal* and *USA Today*, obscures many implications of the fact that most media are local. One consequence is that a local university scientist who delivers a paper at a meeting in town or out of town may receive news coverage even if the subject and the increase in scientific knowledge is minor. Likely the university's public relations office will inform the local print and electronic media of the event, perhaps even providing a summary of the paper or journal article. Both the university and the news media have a stake in maintaining coverage of the local people and their activities. This stake may outweigh the scientific importance of the research.

Second, the occurrence of a special event can test and hone a writer's abilities. When a local, state, or national science or medical organization meets in a city, local media will report on the meeting. This brings journalists of varied backgrounds, experience, and expertise into contact with specialized scientists. Even in the cities of 500,000 people or more, a general reporter or one with a nonscientific specialization may draw the story assignment. The smaller the city, the more generalized the assignments of the reporters. Some very large cities may have a medical reporter but not a science reporter. Except on the largest papers or those of national scope, science and medical reporters may deal in nonscience aspects of news coverage. In Cincinnati, for example, the science-medical reporter may cover fund-raising drives by the heart association, Red Cross, and so forth. This is not necessarily a disadvantage; it acquaints reporters with the realities of science-medical politics and with economic competition between various health and research organizations.

Yet another consequence of the geographics of media distribution is that the smaller the city, the more proximity plays a role. Small city media will have fewer sources of science information available to the writer and less experienced science writers, if any. There are exceptions, such as in Rochester, Minnesota, home of the famed Mayo Clinic. In addition, the smaller the staff, the more work is expected, and the less time allowed to research and write. Survivors of this career system generally move to a larger city, to a wire service or to a magazine where more resources—including time—are available. Reporters develop their specializations in this period on media of small to medium size and make most of their mistakes. Thus the science writers and public relations people that scientists encounter on the national and international scene have most of their errors behind them, have more time and research support, and have more science contacts. The larger the media, the less news value accrues to proximity.

A third consequence of localization is that journalists and public relations people will call upon local scientists to explain other scientists' work and to comment on issues involving science and technology. The same readership research that tells newspaper managers they neglect local people and subjects at the peril of losing circulation also tells them readers want to hear local experts' opinions and explanations about larger events. This is another area of science news coverage that offers the beginning science writer or publicist an opportunity to develop. Overweighted, proximity turns into comic parochialism. Most writers and editors try for balance.

VARIETY AND BALANCE. Variety and balance are strong factors governing the content of newspapers, magazines, and news broadcasts. They permeate all media, including scientific journals, because every medium is limited either by time or space or both. Broadcasters program for a selection of the "best" mix of stories for an audience on any given day. Science material may be squeezed out by politics. An astronomy story will be balanced with a medical story rather than another story about one of the physical sciences. Popular science magazines want a mixture of physical, biological, and social science stories.

CONFLICT. Conflict, for better or worse, is a component of news selection. Often the conflict may be personal or hidden. It may involve two famous heart surgeons who can no longer share credit or facilities because their personal conflict is too intense. Conflict may emerge over research aims and testing, as it did between doctors, biomedical engineers, and hospital managers during the implant of the first artificial heart. Theories may conflict. Conflict also may involve the science writer in larger issues of ethics and public policy. A sensitive medical or science writer will record the dispute and its causes.

The adversarial approach to resolving conflict is a tradition in the United States. Win, loss, or compromise results from pitting one or more viewpoints in more or less open combat. In a more simple era of science, each laboratory development was assumed to be progressive, beneficial, and rewarding. Scientists as well as science writers and the public in general subscribed to this view, judging from the uncrtitical acceptance accorded announcements of scientific discovery prior to World War II and for many years afterward. Many science writers, one suspects, enjoyed their careers because reporting these advances seemed noncontroversial. A fact established by the scientific method seemed more fixed, almost certain.

The political combat between scientists who developed the atomic bomb and other nuclear fission and fusion products shook some of the complacency out of journalists and their audiences. World War II's intense research and development climate produced both penicillin and DDT, an effective pesticide in tropical combat zones that helped spawn environmental concerns because of its lethal effect on birds. More than twenty years after a U.S. surgeon general's report condemned cigarette smoking, after most doctors themselves stopped smoking, the tobacco industry could find credentialed scientists willing to represent that links between smoking and lung cancer or heart disease were not established firmly enough.

Now science writers talk about reporting as the journalism of uncertainty. Much of the uncertainty stems from the fact that scientists in a given field may agree on numbers but not on what those number mean to people in terms of physical, social, economic, and political effects. Often even the numbers do not agree. Another factor in this uncertainty conflict lies in the nature of science. It is statistical and random. Readers of science news are seeking personal, individual answers that apply to them from this information. Scientific information may supply general information that can only guide prudent decisions by individuals.

Science writers are deeply involved in reporting what some call "trans-science," society-wide effects of science and technology. Medical issues no longer revolve around whether or not a disease can or will be cured. The new focus, how long to prolong life itself and whose life shall be prolonged, involves a package of monetary, ethical, professional, social, and political considerations. Energy writers face similar knotty problems in reporting. They are asked to report on battalions of scientifically trained experts arguing the best way of converting raw materials into usable energy, and its costs. Agricultural use of pesticides and herbicides, the dangers in hormones given food animals, and use of food preservatives are similar battlegrounds. So is the field of human and animal nutrition where concern exists over the potential for animal bacteria to develop immunity to veterinary antibiotics. Such immunity could lead to human infections that cannot be treated successfully because the human versions of the antibiotics also have been rendered ineffective. At stake for readers are pocketbook issues, health and safety issues, and political infighting whose outcome will have potentially serious consequences.

These and other issues generate intense emotional pressures. Sometimes these boil over into physical conflict, imposing on science writers the need for extra care in news coverage. People on various sides of such issues as nuclear power plant construction, nuclear weapons, abortion, and saving the whales have disrupted scientific and medical meetings with demonstrations, some of which ended in violent exchanges. Such conflict tempts journalists to focus their stories entirely upon this event, often with the enthusiastic cooperation of their editors. To avoid losing all other news from a scientific gathering, the consensus among responsible science writers has been to relegate such diversions to a separate story, known as a "sidebar." Other writers consciously weigh the importance of such a fray to the overall assembly and give it space in their stories accordingly.

Environmental writers face similar complexity. Their selection of news and emphasis in selection is complicated by the probability that environmental dangers show up first in small ways, develop slowly, and take a long time to reverse. Solutions may offer many combinations of technique and costs. Power shortages and failures offer demonstrable emergencies. Environmental and health dangers from nuclear power stations are not only arguable by experts but so laden with emotion that calm discussion is difficult. In addition, firm data may take years to develop.

Some critics of both science and science writing would have the journalists, traditionally neutral in reporting conflict, take a role in sorting out which sides in these conflicts offer the most credible evidence (Goodfield 1981). If the media are merely agents of power in the societies where they operate, as some communications researchers contend, this is indeed a heavy-duty role for a group that only twenty or so years ago considered it sufficient to report what was said by a scientist and translate jargon into easy-to-understand words. Practically, journalists as neutral observers in conflict situations attempt to report fairly on all aspects of conflict situations as they unfold.

Other news values in science

Conflict, proximity, human interest, personality, and such are not the only news values operating in the media. Psychologist Abraham Maslow expanded the proposition that people act to fulfill certain "needs and gratifications." The idea that some of this fulfillment can come through print and electronic media steers large portions of the science news selection process. One newspaper prints an abundance of stories about female sex organs and their disorders. The staff calls them "uterus stories." The editors assume every woman has one and worries about it; male interest is thought to be automatic. These stories fit into Maslow's "needs" as survival information. Readership and intensity of readership presumably increases with application of these psychological guidelines.

SURVIVAL NEEDS.   High reader and viewer interest attends those stories or subjects dealing with such survival fundamentals as food and shelter, basic mobility, personal health and safety, sex and procreation, and some level of affection and social contact. Also postuated by Maslow as survival needs are meaningful time use, basic work skills, and some minimum of free time to use as one pleases. Threats to gratification of these needs evoke deep and powerful responses.

Environmental preservation laws may owe their birth to such responses. The surprising speed with which the environmental laws passed in the 1970s reflected strong public support. The regulations passed with relatively short public debate either in Congress or in the media, a rarity for laws mandating such great changes in a society. Regulation of fluorocarbon, which a few scientists pegged as a threat to the upper atmosphere ozone layer that protects earth from heavy ultraviolet radi-

ation, moved rapidly through research, study, and toward enactment. Another seemingly pervasive threat to health surfaced in 1984 and evoked public pressure on state health officials and the Environmental Protection Agency. Health officials were concerned over amounts of the carcinogenic pesticide ethylene dibromide (EDB) discovered in underground water. When traces of EDB showed up in cornmeal and flour mixes and citrus fruit, the pesticide's use was banned and other control measures ordered. Similar powerful responses have been elicited by fears of public exposure to nuclear wastes and dioxin, a chemical by-product linked to cancer and birth defects. The EPA bought an entire Missouri town that was contaminated by dioxin contained in the waste oils sprayed to hold down dust on the town's roads.

Reporting of such activities can bring accusations that "the media" are frightening people unnecessarily. Missouri doctors, for example, managed to get a convention of the American Medical Association to pass a resolution chiding the media and the public for overreacting to the threat of dioxin. The resolution was cancelled the next day by the delegates.

A field of science known as risk analysis has come out of such occurrences; they have caused social scientists to look at such questions as whether survival risks are more acceptable if people can choose their risks, such as smoking or driving, and less acceptable if a risk is thrust upon them by others. Such are the disturbing effects accompanying the reporting of survival issues.

CULTURAL NEEDS.   "Lifestyle" or cultural needs may dominate reader interests, after survival needs are met. Subjects in this area include how to make better food and nutritional choices, how to improve working conditions or make career choices. Sex and sexuality likewise may be examined for quality. How others use their time and money is of great interest, perhaps to guide readers in improving their choices of housing, transportation, recreation, and clothing.

At this level, where most media users live, people have the need and opportunity for increasing their self-knowledge and for self-improvement. Thus, research projects, especially in the social sciences, may hold wide interest even though scientists may consider them limited in applicability to only the small groups involved in the tests. Reporters, editors, and readers can empathize with the people involved in the experiment and draw meaning from it that may not have been immediately apparent. Journalists may feel more comfortable dealing with the social sciences because they have had similar courses in college or the material seems more closely related to human experience than the physical sciences.

KNOWLEDGE NEEDS. Beyond the necessities emerge "knowledge needs," satisfaction of the curiosity in the human organism. These needs may be linked in science and technology to possibilities for growth in personal and economic areas or to developments offering new career possibilities. Only marginally can they be regarded as entertainment although the human organism appreciates variety. Receptivity to new information out of science, medicine, and the social sciences increases, although the knowledge contributes little or nothing to daily life except knowing something new. Readers and viewers of the mass media also, at this level, can be interested in seeing how people very unlike themselves work and live. This probably is reflected in the success of celebrity publications and in the continuing interest in such figures as Albert Einstein. It possibly accounts for the willingness of many readers to follow very complex subjects when the writer tells the story through the personal life of the researcher.

Stories developed to supply answers to survival, culture, and knowledge needs tend to be called "service features." They provide a service to the readers seeking guidance in daily affairs. The science writer may be called on to supply such service features as "How to find a doctor" or "Nine ways to a healthy life."

DEMOGRAPHICS. Magazines are especially sensitive in their news judgment to the composition of their audience, the demographics. Defining science news means defining it as "News for whom?" Examples of two extremes are science written for the children's magazine *Highlights* versus writing for the adult subscribers of *Science Digest*. Birth control research will have a different meaning for readers of *Seventeen* than for readers of the publications of the American Association of Retired Persons or for certain church-sponsored magazines. *Science* and *Science 85* magazines come from the same organization, with different expectations from the audience of each about the content of the publication. Even within *Science* you will find different degrees of popularization; editors of the "Research News," for example, may find it necessary to explain a specialized technical report so that the broader audience of scientists understands its importance. Considerations of an audience's education levels, types of education, occupation, income, age, female-male distribution, any special interests, and other identifying characteristics play large roles in determining which stories will be printed or broadcast.

The influence of demographic considerations extends to metropolitan newspapers. If you are a science writer or editor, you may select and write stories on the basis of whether or not the newspaper's philosophy holds that every story should interest all readers. Different story choices apply if the material is considered to be written for a select, educated, perhaps technically trained segment of the readership. Somewhat different criteria will guide judgment if you are a science-technology writer assigned to the business section of the publication. Specialists in business news encounter this sort of conflict over whether to approach a topic as a "consumer" story or as one aimed at the business community.

Social disorder news

Sociologist Herbert J. Gans (1980) identifies another news value in *Deciding What's News*, a report of his time spent in the offices of CBS, NBC, *Time,* and *Newsweek*. This value assumes that certain behavior standards, myths, or beliefs guide a community. These may be promulgated by its leaders, given as paradigms or models for apprentices, and touted as virtues to those outside the communtiy. In the scientific community these include honesty in recording observations, accuracy of data, completeness of reporting, impartiality of peer review, publication judged on merit alone, credit for first discovery, and so forth. Gans concluded that violations of such norms offer examples of social and moral disorder that news media find irresistible. In the latter part of the twentieth century—and reaching back to the early days of science—enough examples of violations of the norms of scientific research have surfaced to merit a congressional investigation and a spate of stories.

Depending on whom you talk to, these examples are rare or they are only a small part of what actually goes on in scientific research laboratories. Two *New York Times* science writers, both former staffers on *Science* magazine, analyzed these occurrences in *Betrayers of the Truth* (1983), which should be supplemental reading for any would-be science reporter. Broad and Wade maintain that instances of discovered violations represent only the tip of an iceberg of fraud, theft, cover-up, favoritism, and failure of self-policing in the scientific community. Scientists testifying before the Subcommittee on Investigations and Oversight of the Committee on Science and Technology, United States House of Representatives, from March 31 to April 1, 1981, (U.S., Congress, 1-350), held that the researchers identified with the violations were those of a few individ-uals who broke under the mental and physical intensity of their work.

Such stories fall also into the science writer's domain. He or she is likely to hear of them first through covering what scientists do as members of the community. These occurrences take on meaning for the larger audiences where considerable sums of public money support the research, where research must be publicly repudiated because of its errors, and where danger to the public health and safety are involved. Frequently prescription drugs (often referred to as "ethical" drugs) must be removed from the market because deceptive or incomplete data mask deaths, birth defects, and less severe side effects. In the case of Great Britain's Sir Cyril Burt, a pioneer in developing public policy from extensions of his social studies, his research won him a place in the British education system so that government school policies, based on his alleged research, affected children for decades. After Burt's death in 1971, reexaminations of his data and scientific papers led other researchers to question the validity of both (Kamin 1974).

In terms of traditional news values, the science writer in American journalism operates as a watchdog of the scientific research community. How well journalists can do this is certainly open for debate. In politics and public affairs, more examples of malfeasance are uncovered by police, district attorneys, and the like than by journalists. Given the technical nature of scientific and medical research, other scientists or regulatory officials in such agencies as the Food and Drug Administration are more likely than journalists to see the signs of inconsistent or overly consistent data than will journalists. Journalists likely will hear of questionable situations first through official announcements from governmental or institutional officers unless the journalists have very good sources in the gossip mills of science.

Ambiguity in science news

In these media news values lie the

sources of much ambiguity and conflict between science writers and their sources. Tensions that exist may be exaggerated, but scientists have lodged some serious complaints against science as presented in the mass media. Both scientists and science writers agree that the worst distortions of scientific material come in the headlines placed on daily newspaper stories. Virtually every science writer can recall at least one instance in which a headline was misleading if not erroneous. In part this results from the system of newspaper editing in which the story editor's need to stress color and impact leads the editor beyond what is in the story itself. Headline writers use different yardsticks than scientists and science writers, who place first importance on accuracy and significance. Editors place color and excitement as primary standards for rating the science story (Johnson 1963).

Part of the conflict arises because science writers fail to draw the points of their story plainly and clearly enough for their first reader, the editor. Some scientists suggest that the science writer also write the headline, but such a practice would conflict with many internal operations of newspapers. Many newspapers ask science writers to counsel editors on selection of local and wire stories. It may be possible for the writer to suggest headline words or themes that fit the stories. A few writers have experimented with putting "test" headlines on their stories before sending them to the copy desk.

Greater conflict in attitudes lies in the question of whether science should be covered as "news" at all. Scientists argue that deadlines and space limitations work against getting accurate and adequate science news coverage. Instead of covering science news as "event," some scientists and journalists would report scientific developments as "process," using the longer, more thoroughly researched feature or series format to show how scientific developments build up gradually from a series of discoveries by several researchers. However, this conflicts with the demands of competitive news coverage by the daily print and electronic reporters and the expectations of daily stories by editorial department managers.

One response to the critics' complaints has been a consensus system operated by members of an "inner circle" of science reporters for major news media. By consulting with each other, and with attending scientists, in the pressrooms at such events as scientific meetings, they reach a generalized agreement on the best stories of the day. They become more collaborators than competitors in their attempts to clear up subtle points and assure accuracy. This allows them to concentrate on accuracy while relieving them of complaints from their editors about failing to cover a story that may seem better to their editors because the competition has it (Dunwoody 1978). This inner circle of writers supplies much of what the public reads as news of science because it includes staff members of such large publications as the *Los Angeles Times, The Wall Street Journal, The Boston GLobe, New York Daily News, Newsweek, Chicago Tribune, The Washington Post, San Francisco Chronicle, Philadelphia Inquirer,* and *The New York Times.* Other members represent the Associated Press, United Press International, Scripps-Howard Newspapers, and Hearst Newspapers— *Baltimore American.* Thus, much of science reporting often represents an editorial consensus.

Herein lies a paradox all science writers must live with. These science writers produce most of the popularized science news printed in U.S. newspapers. But the scientists who criticize the science writers as a group regularly award them, as individuals, prizes for excellence in science writing. As with many paradoxes in science, causes await further research.

In looking at the puzzle, Professor Sharon Dunwoody, who teaches science writing at the University of Wisconsin, has found these science writers get much of their material from press conferences. Since the press conferences are arranged by scientists and scientific associations, whose staffers are qualified to judge significance or obtain advice, she concluded that *scientists seem to exercise a great deal of influence over what the media print and broadcast.* On the other hand, many science writers have said that Dunwoody's observations misperceive the situation, that it is the science writers who request press conferences on specified topics at scientific meetings. Since journalism prizes frequently are established to encourage improvement, the sponsors may be rewarding the pick of the litter.

Some of the scientists' criticism of popularized science writing and presentation may be posturing. It would conflict with nearly a hundred years of tradition in the scientific culture for a scientist or a group of scientists to begin praising the journalists too freely. Scientists are far from shunning the media. Dunwoody surveyed one group of scientists and found that 75 percent of them would welcome talking with a journalist again. Fifteen percent of the scientists had initiated the first press contact, and 30 percent or more had written at least one story for popular print. While the scientists said the worst science coverage was done by radio and television reporters, they were most interested in appearing on television (Dunwoody and Scott 1982). So the science writer should keep in mind that the seeming reluctance to be interviewed may or may not be genuine. Science writers may have to endure the same sort of hazing given other specialty journalists until they prove to their sources that they are accurate, knowledgeable, and skillful. Writers need to distinguish between a source determined to avoid an interview and one who can be coaxed. Thus writers should work at improving their human relations skills.

A test of the writer's human relations skills will come when he or she encounters some of the prejudices underlying scientists' views of the press. As noted by Dunwoody and Scott, this perception includes the idea that journalists are of lower status than scientists. This image may be offset by the power or prestige some publications confer upon their writers or the strength of the writer's personal reputation. One's medium may make a difference too. If you represent a magazine, the scientist likely will be more accepting. Scientists prefer print over electronic media for conveying a public message and rate magazines higher than newspapers. Perhaps this reflects their recognition that more research and writing care go into magazine articles, thereby decreasing chances for inaccuracy. This preference may simply mean that magazines more closely resemble the scientists' familiar journals.

Newspapers, on the other hand, are alien creatures in some aspects. First there are those problems with headlines. Then there is the company that science stories keep in the daily papers—murders, political battles, crime, faddish diet advice, "black boxes" that turn water into gasoline, and horoscopes. In the sensational publications this company also includes miracle cures and visitations by extraterrestrial beings.

Human relations skills may never conquer strong biases. Sometimes the reluctance of the scientist to talk cannot be overcome for an interview. If the situation is too difficult, find another source. As will be shown in the next chapter, seldom are you without alternate routes to scientific information.

One subject that most scientists, particularly those at politically-sensitive state universities, are reluctant to touch is the debate over origin of life: creationism versus evolutionism, the Bible versus Darwin. On the other hand, there are scientists who enjoy scrapping with creationists. Many scientists are religious, and they hold two great faiths. One is the existence of a God. The other, the faith of science, tells them that there is order in the universe, that humans can discern that order, and that it is good for them to do so. Others hold only their faith in science.

Technological risk

Scientists as well as science writers are divided over the reporting of risks in the high-tech environment of our complex world. Since much experimentation with humans is greatly proscribed, risks must be estimated statistically and through experimentation with nonhumans. Beyond that generalization, using animal data to estimate the risk of carcinogenicity or other pathologic condition runs into problems. One problem is acceptance of animal results as valid for humans. Different test animals yield different results. Another reporting problem lies in putting a scientist's interpretation of the data into perspective—is the finding conservative or liberal? Another problem with "risk" numbers is that different types of tests often yield different numbers. Some of these problems of estimating the validity of animal tests have been outlined in a report by the Interdisciplinary Panel on Chemical Carcinogenicity (1984). Extrapolation of animal results to predict human incidence must consider the following four factors:

1. Where response (cancer) occurs at rates of 10 percent to 100 percent, the so-called mathematical dose-response models yield similar results.

2. Where response rates are lower, and perhaps unobservable, the several mathematical models of predicted human incidence give widely varying results.

3. Reactions to low doses of a potential carcinogen also vary; this keeps alive the theory that a tolerable "threshold" for exposure exists; not all researchers accept the threshold concept.

4. Lines of experimental animals and cell cultures used in testing have a nearly homogeneous ancestry and environment, yet their response to toxic exposures vary—not all get cancer; human ancestry—and possibly response—is diverse.

Because the panel was convened at the request of the American Industrial Health Council, supported by chemical manufacturers with a stake in the outcome of the panel's deliberations, not all researchers agree with its reservations about the use-

fulness of predicting cause-and-effect for individuals in large human populations. Statistically, few people are affected in relation to total population, but individual members of the mass media audience have difficulty in assessing the meaning of such risks.

Reporting of risk on a different scale confronted journalists of all kinds, including science specialists, on December 3, 1984. The leak of a poisonous chemical gas from the Union Carbide Corporation pesticide plant in Bhopal, India, resulted in estimates of 2000 dead and possibly 200,000 injured. This most serious industrial accident on record represents a risk of low probable occurence—but with a high probability of death or injury to anyone involved. One result of the Bhopal accident was a public demand that companies make public the type and nature of all chemicals on their premises. Reporting on the risk such chemicals pose in a very controversial, emotional, survival issue will fall on science writers.

Experiments

1. Scan a week's newspapers or several magazines for stories containing science or medical information. From the writer's theme or approach to the subject, can you categorize them as event or process stories?

2. Can you characterize these stories by traditional news values as being used for reasons of proximity, personality, impact, or other traditional values? Do you see survival, cultural, and knowledge values at work?

3. Make an appointment with a scientist or ask your instructor to arrange a class visit by a scientist to discuss his or her view of the news judgment used in the mass media. Can the scientist name some writers who do good work?

4. Scan a week's newspapers. With a ruler, measure the length of each story and headline containing science, social science, and medical information. Which category gets the most space?

5. Invite a publicist from the university or the local medical society's staff or the chairman of the medical society's public relations committee to visit your class. Discuss how he or she goes about deciding which stories to recommend to the local media.

Chapter 4
How to gather science news

TWO STORIES ILLUSTRATE KEY ASPECTS of gathering news of science, engineering, medicine, and technology. Reporters once asked a famous criminal why he robbed banks. "Because that's where the money is," he replied, amazed that anyone should ask. Making a career in science writing means locating the vaults of scientific knowledge, penetrating them where they meet the public interest, and coping with a series of protective measures.

The other story may be apocryphal, but a scientist reportedly growled to the late William L. Laurence, Pulitzer-winning science writer for *The New York Times*, "You science writers live off the crumbs from our table." Said Laurence, "Unfortunately, sir, it is a hard life because the crumbs are so often stale."

Laurence reflected the impatience of many science journalists with some of the tribal customs of scientists. With the exception of the first mechanical heart installations in humans, piloted American space flights, the dropping of the atomic bomb, and certain natural disasters, science writers rarely are present at the making of scientific news. Science surfaces as news most often at conventions of scientists, doctors and engineers or with the distribution of their professional journals. Weeks, months, and even years may lapse between a scientific or medical discovery and its appearance in the scientific literature. A journalist with good sources inside the scientific community may learn of an event and be unable to write about it because the work has not been reviewed, blessed and published. Overcoming such obstacles to a fresh science story is part of the game.

The typical science story

The typical science story is a "how-to" article, familiar to anyone who has taken a feature-writing course or read any of the numerous books or articles on expository writing. The writer's task is to understand the "how" or "why" of some scientific or medical process, and its significance, and transmit this to the reader or viewer as accurately as possible. Even if the form of your writing is the standard 5-W news story, much of your research will be directed toward obtaining an understanding of the process of science, its step-by-step procedures, and the often subtle logic of scientific reasoning. Key points of the logic, process, and procedures will make up the background material your audience will need to understand for either news or feature stories.

Securing the necessary cooperation and information comes easier when the journalists show scientists they are working toward some of the goals they share with the scientists. The success of experienced science writers in dealing with scientists comes, in part, from the mutual trust established over years in the integrity and good intentions of both parties.

Seekers of reality

As many people point out, the journalist and the scientist have several basic points of agreement. Both seek to know reality and, possibly, truth. Journalists usually deal with specific, timely information about events they judge important and interesting. Scientists use these details to build generalities about the natural world, predictabilities, even universalities. Scientist and journalist share an interest in objectivity (Tankard 1976, 42; Mehlberg 1958, 14). Both scientist and science writer believe in open, public knowledge of this reality. Secret science is not science. Both believe in reporting this reality accurately and honestly. Scientist and science writer espouse timeliness in reporting, although their time scales differ greatly.

Some of their differences come from the rubbing together of two faiths. Immense news in a field of science may escape the journalists if they cannot understand it, cannot see a relationship to their readers and audiences, cannot convince an editor of its significance, or cannot put its complexities into words they think will interest readers, viewers, and editors. Lack of pictures or other "visuals" may stymie a television science reporter. Journalists' faith in the necessity of these elements is as strong as the scientists' faith in the scientific method. Both disciplines' faiths have withstood severe tests.

Faith in the need for timeliness often brings conflict, especially when medical and safety concerns are a factor. Journalists thrive on the immediacy of events. Scientists fear prematurity in disclosure of their knowledge until their data, procedures, and conclusions have been studied by their peers and published in an approved way. As practical humanists, journalists feel uncomfortable when a potentially lifesaving discovery may take a year or more to get into general circulation because of the scientific publishing process. Medical researchers, on the other hand, know many promising therapies go nowhere or turn sour even after acceptance by doctors.

Scientists and science writers often disagree, too, over degrees of accuracy and

thoroughness in reporting. Reality to the science writer includes rounding or deleting some numbers because readers quit reading if their newspaper or telecast sounds too much like a classroom exercise in mathematics. Translation of technical terms into analogies or pictorial terms inherently threatens the scientists' love of precision. And with research scientists, knowledge is a very personal thing. Wide popular dissemination, even with full credit, lessens—however slightly—the satisfaction of knowing more than anyone else about an aspect of the world about us.

As discussed in the preceding chapter, journalisms's practitioners have faith in a very different set of news values from most scientists. The journalists' faith is reinforced by their peers, just as the faith of scientists is reinforced. Of such faith J. Herbert Altschull, former professor of journalism at Indiana University, warns, "Articles of faith are by definition irrational, that is to say, they are not arrived at by reason. They are often held with the passion of true believers. An article of faith is not subject to critical analysis. One believes or one does not believe. One is of faith or one is an outsider, and infidel" (1983, 287)

As with any faith, there are members who, in religious parlance, have "fallen away" in varying degrees. Perhaps all have, if you insist on the ideal in a less than ideal world. Scientist and science writer often focus on each other's failings and sometimes these are news. This chapter aims at increasing your knowledge of the congruencies of the science writer and the scientist in selecting news about what the scientists are doing. But as Altschull observes, "The difficulty of accommodating opposing articles of faith ought never to be minimized." Your choice of science news will not always satisfy all scientists all of the time.

Where to find science news

Like the bank robber, science writers go to the sources—the people, the meetings, and the journals—to gather science news. Choosing among the potential stories can appear overwhelming, immobilizing some writers. This multitude of potential sources includes any of the three million scientists, any of thousands of scientific journals printed worldwide, or any article within those journals.

In the river of publications the difficulty of choosing the best science story from this Amazonian flow is increased because well over half of these articles make little impression on the scientific community. In fact the numbers of journals themselves are something of an embarrassment; some have the reputation of being started as places for science and medical researchers to publish papers rejected by more prestigious journals. Scientists try to publish in the journal or journals read by most of their colleagues. Commonly this is the journal of their scientific society or specialty. Finding out which journals are important to a field of science is a first step to locating articles of significance. The editors of one of the premier medical publications, the *New England Journal of Medicine*, found that more than 80 percent of the papers they rejected subsequently appeared elsewhere. So significant research is not necessarily found only in the best-known journals.

Part of the significance of a scientist's contribution to understanding is how often other scientists use that work in their own research, build new experiments upon it, or cite it in their own journal articles. Relatively few journal articles are cited more than once by other researchers, indicating how little scientists rely on or test others' research. One way to gauge "good science" is to check in the literature or with other scientists on how often a report or a scientist is cited in the research of others.

Although much second-rate research fills obscure publications, journals are a place to start. Scanning a publication's table of contents may alert you to a potentially newsworthy article. Rather than read all of an interesting sounding journal article, many writers go first to the "conclusion" or "summary" section of an article to begin judging whether or not the subject or the results may interest a larger readership outside the specialty. The common style for writing the scientific paper is the opposite of the popular article. Scientists generally put the research problems, theories, and research methods toward the front of the article. Then they present data, and last of all they give their conclusion. It is very logical for the scientist's purpose, but not for the journalist. Sometimes abstracts give a quick guide to the importance or the potential news interest, but too often they offer only a dry or almost ethereal account of what actually took place. Besides, in the conclusion the scientist must present his or her most forceful and quotable words.

Complicating the choice of a suitable story from journals is something known part humorously as the "LPU," which stands for "least publishable unit." An LPU paper deals in only a part of the results of a series of experiments or a research project. Scientists, particularly in the universities, gain pay raises, prestige, promotions, and tenure in part as a result of the works they publish. Because most scientific experiments are hard work involving several people, heavy expenses for labs and/or research animals, and long periods of time, some researchers wring as many publications as possible out of their data. They split the results into many facets to give each team member credit and maybe some credit to the department or institute administrator as well. Several published papers from the same basic data help demonstrate productivity when the team asks for more money from government or from private foundations. When a science writer finds an intriguing journal article, he or she would do well to ask the scientists if it is part of larger research project and where it fits in that project. Such questions can lead to a more significant story.

Probably you will pick out a potential science story on the basis of its journalistic news values—significance to science, impact, or the needs of your readers or viewers. Giving some perspective and background to the story is important. Because scientists write for other scientists, they often do not explain what the results mean to larger questions of scientific knowledge or ignorance. The science writer needs to get comment on what the newly reported results mean, whether they are new or not, and whether they are significant. But even if you think you know, it is worthwhile to confirm your judgment with a second opinion.

Science writing, like all journalism, is built upon five factors: documentation, verification, interrogation, observation, and participation. Journal publication provides acceptable documentation. Science writers are less likely to make mistakes in transcribing data or quoting from the article. The work also carries verification of a sort because other scientists, supposedly as knowledgeable as the researcher, read the paper and checked assumptions and data for plausibility. Stories derived from a scientific journal carry the most acceptability for scientists, generally speaking. Published articles are credible because of the assumption of scientific honesty in making and reporting the experiments.

Journal articles have journalistic handicaps, however. The events described in them will have taken place months or years before. The style is dry, detached. Many scientists doing related research will have known about the report for a long time. Although publication alone is sufficient as a newsbreak, prudent science writers will contact the researchers and others in the field before doing a story. New facts may add color and timeliness to the story, updating it. In extreme cases, fresh evidence or other influences may force the scientists to modify, even retract, the article.

Interrogation of other scientists should yield their evaluation of the work and the researchers. These evaluations can be extremely critical, requiring you to seek a balancing reply from the original researchers. Names of people to call may be obtained several ways. Many articles list coauthors. Footnotes to published articles contain references to the work from which the new research stems, and a directory of scientists or a *Who's Who* will give you their hometown or university locations. When you talk to the researchers, ask them for names and locations of others working on similar research problems. Often the information officer at a local college or university will help you locate someone on its campus who knows the subject or knows someone who does. Librarians can steer you to other published works, including popular articles, that will help put this development in perspective. An increasing number of libraries and news organizations subscribe to computerized information services that can speed up your literature research. *Reader's guide to Periodical Literature* and other indexes are good places to start. These techniques take time and effort many science writers say they cannot spare close to deadline. Frequently the story is written solely from the journal, with credit to this source. Most writers could find the time to read an encyclopedia article on the subject. After you have been writing science information for some time, you will develop your own list of contacts, built with mutual trust, for evaluation and information.

The best stories, and hardest to interpret, frequently come from journals associated with a narrow scientific specialty or society, such as the subsections of the American Institute of Physics. Because scientists like to publish their best work where there is prestige and their colleagues know their field, the science writer will find less background and broad perspective in these journals. The most frequently cited journals used by journalists include the *New England Journal of Medicine* (NEJM), the *Journal of the American Medical Association* (JAMA), and the British publications *Lancet* (for medicine) and *Nature* for general science. Contributors scramble worldwide for inclusion in these publications. Their editors set strict guidelines on peer review and originality of research. The most frequently quoted U.S. journal is *Science* published by the American Association for the Advancement of Science. Part of the reason journalists rely on *Science* is its weekly frequency and its "News and Comment" section, a guide to conflicts over science policy and public affairs, government funding, and other topics. While the broad science articles in the front of the magazine may be dated, from a news standpoint, they afford popular science writers good background material for "event" stories and broader interpretative features. Signed articles from government officials also offer insights into how federal science policy develops. Its "Research News," section, written and edited by Ph.D's, helps science writers spot significant new developments because the section is written to be understood across disciplinary lines. Reporters for "Research News" have won several writing awards. In the back of *Science* is "Reports," a section sometimes read by science writers for the first notice of scientific discovery or research with human interest. Because *Science'*s editors can offer a relatively speedy six-week, or less, time period to publication, the National Aeronautics and Space Administration and other agencies used *Science* for publishing the first scientific analyses from moon and planetary explortion data and other major events. Some of the first research on the identification of the AIDS virus appeared here. Letters to the editor occasionally reveal disputes over scientific and policy issues.

Science News, a thin weekly magazine published by Science Service in Washington, D.C., is another part of the "alerting" system for science writers. The *Science News* journalists read many more journals than most journalists have time to scan. Their highly popularized but accurate news and features stories provide starting points for other journalists to research

their own stories for their particular audiences. Sometimes newspapers and magazines will reprint these stories intact, with permission and credit.

Advance notice of journal publication is common. Many of the important scientific society journals send advance copies or proofs of articles to science writers at the major newspapers, wire services, and magazines. Some have public relations staffs who call selected reporters in the print and electronic media. Many universities will alert local science writers when one of their scientists has an article printed. Some will send a press release when an article is accepted for publication, although a few journals insist on secrecy until actual publication. A long time may pass before actual publication, although the science writer may get a manuscript copy of the article or a digest. If the new discovery is significant enough, local publicists or even the national society will set up a formal interview or press conference upon publication. The science writer should get on the contact list of institutions dealing with science, medicine, and technology.

Scientists—face to face

Interrogation, or gathering science news by a direct interview with the men and women responsible for new scientific information, is one of the most pleasant of the science writer's tasks. Your attitude and approach are important. Prepare for the interview by reading as much about the scientist's topic as time permits. If you waltz or boogie into the researcher's lab expecting to joke about his or her life's work and your total ignorance, the atmosphere can drop to Absolute Zero unless the circumstances are very, very special. Blair Justice, who financed his Ph.D. in psychology by writing science news, says the real test of a science writer's acceptance comes when he or she calls up a researcher directly and says, "I'd like to talk to you about your work." This means stripping away frills such as press conferences, public relations people's arrangements, and hometown connections. You are depending on your own reputation, your approach, and your persuasion to get an interview.

Doing your homework is essential. Learn something about the scientist and the subject. Before an interview, sometimes before seeking one, you should at least go to a national or regional *Who's Who* for biographical material. Librarians can steer you to other references. A newspaper's "morgue" or library may contain more information. This will give you much personal background, saving interview time. If the person works at a university or technology-oriented business, chances are good that the public relations department or the scientist's departmental secretary can provide a biography and maybe even some copies of articles other writers have published about the scientist or papers she or he has published.

Until you establish your own reputation with scientists, you may have to depend on public relations people for a lot of assistance. Most public relations offices maintain biography and clipping files on their people. Sometimes the PR department will get copies of scientific articles a researcher has published.

You usually have a reason for singling out a particular scientist, but getting some background files on his or her field never hurts. Reading an encyclopedia article is better than no preparation. Some previous science course work and a genuine interest in the topic are assumed, as is reading in news and science magazines. No one knows everything, however, and everyone gets caught short on prepartion now and then. A visiting scientist can arrive in town unexpectedly, for example. Scientists so fear the legendary ignorance of journalists that even a little preparation and knowledge can evoke a disproportionate amount of good will from a source. Scientists expect to have to explain their work to outsiders, but it's too much to ask him or her to educate a writer from scratch.

A useful and little-known reference for science writers is *Encyclopedia of Ignorance* by Ronald Duncan and Miranda Weston-Smith (1978). The editors persuaded nearly sixty scientists to write essays on what is known and unknown in their fields. It can serve also as a source of story ideas.

The scientist should know in advance what you want to talk about. I once asked a major figure in science politics for a get-acquainted interview, nothing more. His public relations man somehow lost this in the information transfer. We both lost— the scientist because he wondered why I was there and I because I could not fathom his irritation about getting to the point of the appointment. So make it clear in advance what you want to talk about. This helps your interviewee get ready for your questions, some of which you should prepare before the interview. Avoid posing "closed-end" questions, ones that can be answered yes or no. Open-ended questions cannot be shut off with a one-word answer. They will bring out more information and offer both of you more pleasure from the encounter. Closed-end questions are best for getting and checking specific facts: numbers, times, places, and dates.

Sometimes, even when you have prepared, your interviewee will remain taciturn, uncommunicative, and unhelpful. For the science writer this is the equivalent of an attorney's "hostile witness." It may be prejudice against science journalists, it may be fear, it may be a bad lunch, it may be bad faith in accepting the appointment. For whatever reason, the writer will do better seeking other sources, of which there are many for almost every subject. As noted earlier, mature and experienced scientists are more willing to talk. And most scientists who have had contact with media representatives welcome other contacts. Exit with what you get. The other side of this coin is that more often than not, your preparation will enable you to convince your subject that your are educable. The interviewee will open up to you and sometimes suggest new aspects of the story. You should go into the interview prepared to drop some questions and follow new leads if you get the chance.

Probably you will have to encourage the scientist to drop the jargon of his or her technical field and use plainer English, analogies, and explanations. "You wouldn't talk that way to your mother," one scientist chided his colleagues for using highly technical language when explaining their work to nonscientists. Of course, you're in trouble if mother has a Ph.D. in physics.

Occasionally you may encounter someone who wants questions submitted in advance. Newspapers generally frown on doing this in political matters. You may have to make your own judgment call in science if your publication has no firm rules. Writers have found that a set of provocative questions can intrigue a person who is tired of the same old questions or is known as hard to contact. Some businesses provide their executives, scientists and public relations people with sets of standard answers prepared in advance of anticipated questions. A few companies and individuals use the written question routine as a way to discourage journalists.

A good interviewer tries to take no more of a subject's time than necessary. You can always come back, with your reputation probably enhanced. Be sure you have both office and home phone numbers of the scientist so you can call back to check facts, quotations, and perspective—and to fill holes in your story left by questions you forgot to ask or answers you did not fully understand. Offering to do so can head off the difficult request to "read the story for accuracy when you are through." Few organizations let a subject read finished stories and scripts or preview a tape or film story. However, showing your own concern for accuracy often reassures the subject and helps you brush aside requests for "showing your copy." On the other hand, public relations science writers working for a

scientific or medical organization can expect to have all their stories reviewed by one or more people in the organization, including the subjects of the stories. Some magazines follow this practice too. Newspaper and wire service reporters avoid showing stories because the high speed editing processes to meet deadlines may result in changes to copy.

Because of sensitivities about disclosing research before peer review and publication, some scientists may be reticent about research in progress. If the chance of premature disclosure is a threat to getting published, the scientist may close off talk about certain areas. However, the writer should not fall into the trap of self-censorship before inquiring. Be straightforward. If scientists are concerned, they will tell you and appreciate your recognition of the problem.

It may be possible to elicit a promise for notification when the time is right. Dr. Barbara Gastel, a physician and a writer for both popular and medical publications, advises researchers who fear premature publication to offer to call journalists back when they are ready to discuss their work (1983). However, following up remains the writer's responsibility. Scientists have notoriously bad memories for science writers except for those from the major newspapers or TV networks. The same holds true for many PR people.

Gastel also points out two problems that often confuse scientist-journalist interviews. First, there exists a group of scientists who think journalists should get all their material from journal publications. These scientists take the position that interviews waste time when all the necessary information is available in the publications. She warns scientists that when they try to write outside their own specialty, they may be just as lost and mistake prone as any journalist. Dr. Gastel admonishes scientist-writers that they too would need to obtain fresh information on the research and confirm the validity of work done long before it was published. She tells scientist-writers they they, too, would need what the nonscientist journalist needs: quotations, human interest details, impressions, color, and descriptions. These add flesh and blood to the bare bones of scientific life described in the literature.

Gastel deals with another problem, getting the details accurately while missing the larger focus of a story. Make sure you grasp the central concept or the general picture and can state it clearly to your readers or viewers before you start talking details. Give yourself and your readers perspective and orientation; show them the forest before you lead them into the trees. This information is part of the "signficance paragraph" or background.

Reading Gastel will provide you a good review of science practices from the scientist's view as well as ways of opening new lines of communication to a source who remains skeptical about popularization. Besides, you like many other writers and editors may want to approach a scientist or doctor to write an article for your publication. If the expert better understands some of the problems and techniques, you will be serving your audience in a new way. A copy of Dr. Gastel's book could make a useful present for your sources.

The reticent scientist has an opposite, for science also has its publicity seekers, as do most professions. Some are very good scientists who break stereotypes about shy, retiring laboratory inhabitants. A few understand too well how to manipulate journalists into giving airtime and ink to subjects that have little value but may help decorate a grant application or the university's public relations scrapbook. These scientists acquired the sobriquet of "operators" decades back. A second opinion may be helpful if you suspect you are being used excessively.

Observing science close up

Direct observation by journalists of science-in-the-making is rare. Most of the significant events cannot be seen at all in many sciences. Discovery comes out of manipulating data, either in scientists' heads or in long computer analyses.

Applications and technology offer better chances for the writer to see and report what happens. For example, science writers have ridden airplanes into hurricanes with weather researchers. Ritchie Ward, author of books and magazine articles, was invited on a flight to South America where he spent a week with ocean scientists aboard a research ship simply because the scientists liked one of his books that had found its way into the ship's reading material (1978, 19).

Archeological digs, field trips, laboratory tours, and other opportunities, may open up to the science writer who asks. Scientists, particularly administrators, enjoy showing off their facilities. Even if you do not watch an actual "discovery," descriptions of the places and conditions under which science is performed make interesting reading for those who may wonder but never have the chance to step behind the curtain. Until you see some of the equipment used by physicists or energy researchers, you lack any feel for their scale of operations. A laboratory tour is not quite the same as roaring down an Everglades channel with an aquatic biologist, but any personal experience will help you put subjects into better perspective.

Participation even more rare

Scientists wish there were more science writers with research experience. You may not appreciate the problem without understanding the location, the conditions, or the physical experience. Some writers strive to experience what they are discussing. Oceanographer Bill Cromie, science writer and head of the Council for the Advancement of Science Writing (CASW), has helped scientists with the backbreaking effort of capturing and tagging giant turtles. He once had to be rescued from a melting ice island. David Perlman of the *San Francisco Chronicle* also participated in scientific field expeditions as a working member of the team. Both report their understanding of science and their science writing is better because of the experiences. Because of their contribution to the work of the expeditions, both experienced more personal acceptance of their reporting efforts and friendships with members of the expeditions. A number of universities, private laboratories, hospitals, and government facilities, such as the National Institutes of Health, will take science writers inside their daily routines for a few weeks or months. By performing useful work, ranging from writing press releases to taking observations and even washing glassware, the writer gets direct experience with how science is made.

Sometimes formal internships are available for upper division or graduate students and working journalists. Often there is a stipend. MIT offers two types of research-study experiences for those who can take time away from their work as science writers. One lasts a few weeks, the other covers an expense-paid academic year. Harvard's Nieman Fellows program pays journalists for an academic year, which can include taking science courses. Science writers training at Columbia University cut up cadavers in anatomy classes a part of their educational experience. The American Association for the Advancement of Science for several years has offered a few young scientists an internship program with newspapers, TV, and magazines to show them how the media operate.

These experiences add authenticity and drama to stories of scientific research. Even those whose training includes science courses and labs should take advantage of any opportunity they can wrangle, even if it is only a few hours spent with researchers working through the night on a cranky experiment. Even tedium has meaning. Your experience will add detail and insight that otherwise elude you unless you are an imaginative interviewer.

Special reports

Another source of scientific stories can be found in special reports. It is common for government officials and agencies to hand especially difficult topics over to an expert panel, such as a "blue-ribbon commission." Often this is a method of stalling a decision or justifying an unpopular political decision. Such special investigative panels were used to look into the causes of the Three Mile Island nuclear power plant accident and whether fluorocarbons, widely used in air conditioners and refrigerators, should be controlled because of their potential for damaging earth's protective atmosphere. The science writer can base stories on the reports' conclusions. In the competitive world of journalists there are rewards for having contacts who will give you an advance copy of a report or its findings before official release. You should also learn who makes and who wins appointments to such commissions. It is not unusual to find a panel filled with members whose personal or business backgrounds make impartial consideration of the issues difficult. When found, this potential for distortion in the report should be reported.

Reports can be found in progress throughout most federal and many state government agencies. The National Academy of Sciences and the National Academy of Engineering manage an investigative organization known as the National Research Council (NRC). It is the academies' major source of income. The council's main business is evaluating scientific data on specific problems and compiling reports that recommend technical actions by the government agency requesting the study. The National Research Council does no research directly, although it may contract with private or government laboratories to make specific tests. With the exception of some studies dealing with weapons and other national security problems, the NRC work is public record. Usually the report will be released by the sponsoring agency to journalists. The NRC reports carry handicaps similiar to those of blue-ribbon commissions. Panelists who evaluate the data and make the recommendations may be drawn, because of their expertise, from businesses and institutions with an economic interest in how the problems will be resolved. Members of the panels need not be members of the academies; they may serve as volunteers because of the prestige, or other rewards, of association with the academies. The academies try to make appointments that avoid conflicting interests.

Many government agencies conduct much of their own research. The National Bureau of Standards and the Consumer Product Safety Commission, for example, turn out test information of interest to trade journal writers and to consumer oriented publications. Often the first warning of safety hazards in the United States comes from the injury reporting network operated by the product safety commission. Depending on the political or commercial biases of federal officials at any given time, the policies of an agency in gathering and releasing this information may vary. Alert science writers may be the first to detect such shifts in policy that merit stories. William J. Broad of *The New York Times* was the first to find out when the Department of Energy stopped reporting underground nuclear bomb tests.

The Department of Defense, the three armed services, and the National Aeronautics and Space Administration (NASA) support giant research budgets for their own laboratories and for research contracts given to universities, nonprofit institutions, and business firms. Their projects range from basic and fundamental research to developmental and final engineering work for large projects. Much of the defense work is unclassified or easily declassified by someone wanting a little publicity. When a project is in political trouble, writers find it easier to gain access if military managers think a little public understanding will help. Contractors also can get a journalist visits and interviews on militarily sensitive stories. Any of these organizations can provide the science writer with a starting point for researching a story. The National Insti-

tutes of Health and the Centers for Disease Control often compile situation reports on medical problems and the research they finance. You can use these as beginning references sources for your stories, just as you use journal articles. Write these agencies for such material and get on their mailing lists.

Scientific meetings

One of the most ambiguous sources of science stories is the scientific meeting. Usually held annually, these meetings bring members of a society together to talk about professional business and to hear reports from scientists on their research and, frequently, policy, ethics, and financing. Doctors have them, virologists have them, and so do nurses and experimental biologists. These meetings honor the scientific tradition of open discussion and criticism of research reported at the meeting. Various societies also hold local, county, state, and regional meetings as well as national ones.

Several reasons make these meetings attractive to news gatherers. Of themselves, the scientific meetings are a local news event. Very large societies, such as the American Medical Association, American Geophysical Union, or the American Association for the Advancement of Science (AAAS), draw thousands of attendees from all over the world. Famous personalities are in town, available for interviews if you catch them. The programs, available in advance, list presentations of scientific papers, a dozen or so for a small society, hundreds for giants like the AAAS, American Institute of Physics, or the American Institute of Aeronautics and Astronautics. Selection of science stories from agglomerations like these pose hard choices for the science writer.

In addition, there's competition. Meetings of the AAAS can attract hundreds of journalists to the pressrooms. Such major conventions bring the wire services and writers from the national newspapers and large regional dailies. News magazines and trade journals will staff the meeting.

In addition freelance writers from across the country flock to these meetings to pursue stories, pick up new ideas, and contact scientists who may be useful sources of information. Local and network TV staffers come looking for stories. Among the journalists will be public relations people and government information officers promoting their institutions' speakers and renewing contacts with media representatives. A restrained carnival atmosphere exists. Some of the formality that rules contacts even with hometown scientists is lifted.

In the pressrooms of the larger associations, copies of most of the papers to be presented lie in stacks to be picked up. Release of stories written from these papers usually is pegged to the day and time each paper is scheduled for delivery. At other meetings, the staff may reproduce a file copy of a paper on request. Many science journalists write their stories from these papers and avoid sitting through the talks. However, this proves embarrassing if the speaker fails to show up or makes major changes. Science reporters using such material in advance of actual delivery usually include a phrase such as, "in a paper scheduled for delivery . . ." And they check back to see that the paper was delivered as scheduled.

On the occasions papers are withdrawn from the program, the reasons for this may be worth writing about. In 1983, for example, the Reagan administration ordered scientists to withdraw about one hundred unclassified papers from a meeting of the Society of Photo-Optical Engineers. It was the first indication of how strongly the administration felt about enforcing a new policy of keeping American science and technology from other countries. Interestingly, few of the scientists—most of whom were supported by government grants and contracts—protested this censorship of scientific research. The story became known only because a *Science News* reporter attended the meeting.

If the pressroom does not have a copy of a paper, speakers often bring extra copies for distribution to anyone who asks for it. At medical research meetings, obtaining copies may be complicated by the fact that some journals will refuse to publish research if other publications have used detailed stories and data pulled from a paper given at a public meeting.

PRESS ORGANIZATION.   If the occasion is important enough to draw science writers from the national media, as mentioned earlier, a small group of about a dozen writers from the largest newspapers and the wire services will reach a consensus about which story to write about for that day. They also will consult with the pressroom staff and society public relations directors about which groups of scientists should be asked for news conferences. This group of senior science writers exerts enormous influence for several reasons. They represent powerful mediums with large circulations. Generally they know more about contemporary science issues that other reporters because they attend most of the major association meetings regularly. They also know personally many of the leading scientists and officers of the societies.

Science writing analyst Sharon Dunwoody has concluded that the press conference arrangement allows manipulation of the media by the scientific association staffs (1979a). The news that comes from the meeting is controlled by the press conference schedule because it makes certain topics easier to cover. Usually the consensus of the writers on which story they will emphasize concerns a story from one the press conferences where the writers have a chance to get further details directly from the authors of the papers chosen for that day. The convenience and efficiency of the press conferences lead other science writers, who may have less understanding of the subject, to follow the leaders. Science writers protested that the press conferences evolved from the requests of the science journalists (Bishop 1980).

Dunwoody also concluded that science

writers with more education in science and science writers unencumbered by deadlines, such as magazine writers, did more stories that were different from those written by the pack, and they picked different subjects. Freelancers and magazine staff writers will use meetings to background themselves and get interviews for longer-range features more than will the journalists facing one or more daily deadlines. Often these writers will be satisfied with collecting the papers for their background files (a useful tactic for other writers also). The meetings are a good place to arrange future visits and interviews. A writer also may pick up minor papers that provide material for stories later or in other departments of the newspaper or magazine. Psychology research may initiate a story for the lifestyle section, for example, or a physicist may report on the flight of baseballs or golf balls, a feature for the sports pages. Biologists can be found reporting on the habits of game fish, birds, and other wildlife.

The larger the organization, the more sophisticated will be the press arrangements. Small organizations may not maintain a pressroom, leaving you to hunt down individual speakers and officers. Larger ones will offer typewriters and telephones, copies of papers, and some scientific reference materials. The larger meetings also set up separate interviewing areas for radio and television, providing power outlets and phone connections as needed.

RELYING ON CONFERENCES.   In spite of the advantages of meetings as a source of stories for journalists and the respected tradition of scientific meetings, many scientists dislike seeing stories written from the oral presentations. The research presented, they claim, is often tentative and the data insubstantial. Subjects may be trivial and grab headlines while more solid work goes unreported. The papers are not reviewed as strictly as those presented for journals, and research presented at a meeting may never appear in a refereed publication. News conferences, the scientists say, offer slick operators a chance to grab publicity, indicating some possibility that jealousy as well as concern for "science" is at play. Another mark against meeting stories, according to some of the scientists, is that serious researchers yield space to graduate students and that papers often go on a program just to fill time.

This is a curious position. Journalists have no say in what the scientists include on their programs. If there is an abundance of second-rate science, this is a quality control problem for those who plan the meeting, not the journalists who report it. If this research is as untrustworthy as some scientists indicate, why do scientists waste time arranging or attending these meetings? Perhaps they attend for the same reasons as the press— it's an event and you always get something out of it. Researchers claim they get more from chatting with others in their fields than from the formal sessions. Professional jealousy may also play a part in the carping. On the other hand, attendance by scientists and the press corps decreased significantly at the 1985 annual meeting of the AAAS, raising questions about the continuing appeal of gatherings aimed at the general body of scientific concerns.

Despite what scientists say about stories from meetings, journalists are as unlikely to ignore a large meeting in town as they are likely to ignore a big fire or explosion. Covering what's happening in town is one of journalism's traditions. And meetings have surfaced new trends in science. Some of the initial speculations about viruses as a cause of cancer were first made public at scientific meetings. So, sweeping statements about the unimportance of the material seem unfounded. The fact that the professional societies invite coverage indicates that the leaders of the organizations feel some benefits exist in news coverage. The spotty character of the papers, if it exists, merely increases the pressure on the science writer to select a worthwhile story for his or her audience. Meetings give writers a chance to catch scientists out in the open, unguarded by secretaries, grad students, and laboratory doors.

Instead of relying on individual papers, you might substitute interviews with the visiting scientists. Make sure you do your homework in advance to help insure a fruitful session. Sometimes you will see an original story by spotting a common theme running through several papers. And part of the news coverage of meetings deals with the routine business of the society itself, such as election of new officers. Getting away from the pack of other writers can yield exclusive stories for the writer who prepares for the meeting.

Covering scientific meetings will remain on the science writer's agenda for a long time. Meetings offer too many advantages to risk ignoring them. The supposedly shoddy quality of papers offers a challenge to see or sniff out a better story from the sources available. As a writer with some background in science, you can find original stories here. If the field is alien to your background, seek guidance from the local program chairmen as to the best topics of the meeting. Usually these people can be contacted through the society or a university public relations office in advance of the meeting.

A list of meetings or conventions scheduled for your area usually can be picked up at local chambers of commerce or convention centers. *Science* magazine publishes a comprehensive listing of scientific meeting dates and places. Members of the National Association of Science Writers routinely get notices of coming meetings from public relations offices of the various societies. Writers are advised to check about press access well in advance of the meeting date. Some of the smaller, more specialized societies have discouraged press coverage in general, and others admit freelancers only if they produce evidence, such as a letter from an editor, that the freelancer is there working on a specific assignment.

Public relations sources

More science writers work for businesses and institutions than work in the media. These public relations writers offer another useful source of science information. Some newspapers and radio stations will print and broadcast science press releases as given to them, although larger and better staffed media will report and edit to suit their audiences. However, some of the best science writing is done by public relations people. Some press releases make better science stories than their rewritten media versions. Most do not. The quality of writing plays little role in the media's decision to prepare their own version.

Media science writers keep in mind that stories prepared by business firms, universities, hospitals, and other institutions are aimed at promoting the welfare of the organizations, not at satisfying the needs of readers or viewers. This means that you should ask a lot of questions about story ideas gleaned from press releases, brochures, and institutional magazines. These sources may need supplementation because they seldom mention related studies at other institutions, for example. A hospital may trumpet its purchase of a new piece of medical equipment but neglect to say there are others in town just like it. A hospital or clinic may announce the availability of a new medical procedure without giving background or perspective, such as the risks involved or alternative treatments. Drug companies' publicists are notorious for promoting slight variations on existing drugs ("me too drugs") without mentioning competitors' products. Side effects, those reactions that accompany any drug's intended effects, seldom get mentioned in press releases. It is the science writer's business to stay alert to these omissions and give the needed perspective and balance.

On the other hand, public relations people can offer media science writers assistance in spotting stories and arranging interviews. This, in theory, is their purpose for being, although any prudent observer will recognize that their first goal is promotion and protection of the organizations that pay their salaries. In many organizations, public relations is considered part of marketing and sales. Early in the development of public relations offices, evenhanded treatment of the local media was one of the stated principles of operation. Within the last few years this has changed. Under the rationale of marketing for the highest return, the needs of local media science writers may be sacrificed for the assumed benefits of planting an exclusive story in one of the national publications or on network television. Sometimes local journalists negotiate with an institution for an even newsbreak with national media, but getting the story first remains the goal.

Thus the science writer risks getting beaten in his or her own territory by an outsider. This argues for keeping on decent terms with the public relations office but developing as many of your own personal sources in the scientific community as possible. This placement of the best stories for maximum national media effect is an outgrowth of the number of press releases being sent to media science writers. Because of their numbers, the releases often are opened and sorted by a news clerk, not the science writer. Many organizations are reducing the number of press releases in favor of more personal and specialized placement of individual stories.

The public relations science writer often chooses which stories of a major institution to publicize. At smaller institutions, the PR department must work very hard to locate fresh information and get a release approved by upper echelon administrators. The PR job includes working up background information for distribution and staging press conferences. Too often PR science writers are criticized because a scientist or administrator wants to publicize material that is trivial or incomplete. Media writers may simply ignore such a story or, at worst, poke fun at the publicity attempt. In 1981, Harvard University found itself ridiculed for publicizing some research as "new" when it was an extension of work done a decade earlier at UCLA. Although the earlier work was cited in the footnotes, its relation to the newer research was not made clear in the materials given reporters. Paul Jacobs of the *Los Angeles Times* stumbled across the originator of the technique, dealing with stimulating bone growth, while seeking other scientists' evaluation of the news announced by Harvard (Silberner 1981).

Stories promoting new drugs give science journalists many bad moments. Too often the drugs prove disappointing or unexpectedly dangerous after stories have been written from data provided by drug manufacturers and government agencies. Press releases have been known to play down dangers or omit mentioning them, says Jim Sibbison, a former Associated Press and Food and Drug Administration writer. Drug makers may also avoid questions on the dangers, if they can, at press conferences. Thus reporters who rely only on the press releases can miss significant information. Relying on government handouts does not offer sure protection. Sibbison found much coordination and consultation between the FDA and drug companies on publicity materials. Sometimes warnings about serious risks in new drugs are edited from reporters' stories, so the lack of warning does not lie entirely with writers and public relations people. Good reporting on new medicines should include asking for copies of the "label" or "package insert," that law requires to be placed inside the box containing a prescription drug. Reporters also can get copies of the formal letters that manufacturers must send all doctors when danger signs emerge. The FDA's free quarterly *Drug Bulletin* can also tip science writers to the discovery of fatalities and other medicine related problems. (Sibbison 1985).

Media staffers, however, can get help in setting up interviews through the public relations office. Good science PR people should know the specialties and significance of work in their institutions. Often they suggest stories for science writers. Their counsel to company executives on what stories will attract media attention, the necessary packaging, and backgrounding can help improve the usefulness of a press conference. Public relations officers also can make available to a media writer university and company library privileges or facilities for computerized literature search on major stories. At the rare event of a "breaking" science or medical news event, such as the first artificial heart implants, a public relations officer who understands what the media need to adequately report a story can provide a welcome order to newsgathering in what can become an unruly competitive situation.

Experiments

1. Implied in the chapter are several questions you should ask as a science writer selecting a story subject. Write down as many of these questions as you can.

2. Locate several science journals in your library and scan them for story ideas. Bring a list to class and tell why you think these are good story possibilities.

3. Look through *Science* magazine and another journal for the list of science meetings. Are there any meetings scheduled near your city? Prepare a local science meetings list. Ask the class to vote on which ones sound most promising for popular science stories.

4. From your chamber of commerce or convention bureau obtain a list of science meetings, if there are any. Can the class attend? Contact the sponsors listed by the convention office.

5. Some university libraries are repositories for government documents; if yours is one, get a list of recent acquisitions and see if any offer the possibility of a science story.

Chapter 5
Distortion and how to avoid it

SELDOM, IN PRACTICE, WILL CHOOSING A science story and its sources be as complicated as it appears in the process described earlier. Balancing significance, audience interests, and news values becomes habitual as you mature in writing science news. Indeed, writers and editors risk falling too easily into routines for deciding story selection. Only a constant alertness to the need for fresh material and fresh approaches to old subjects can keep the writer out of dullness.

Less manageable is the risk of distorting science news in this search for something new for readers and viewers. Somewhere between the topic selection process and the writing process, scientist and writer diverge. This accounts for some of the criticisms about popularization giving a false impression of what is good science and good science reporting. A series of critical questions will help the science writer narrow the range of potential error. There will remain differences of opinion that the disciplines of journalism and science (or journalists and scientists) may never resolve. To scientists who respect only scientific journal publication, popularized science and medical writing represents the ultimate entropy. If you miss the point, look up the second law of thermodynamics in a physics book.

Scientific hypotheses

One source of distortion in science writing comes through different views of the scientific hypothesis. With many notable exceptions, experimental science moves in small steps, each preceded by a hypothesis that proposes an explanation of a natural phenomenon or part of one. Baruch S. Blumberg, M.D., Ph.D., and 1976 Nobel Prize winner for his work leading to identification of the Hepatitis B. virus as a factor in cancer of the liver and to a vaccine against Hepatitis B., puts the case this way in a 1983 commencement address.

Either science or myth will explain satisfactorily the phenomena observed in nature; myth is established for acceptance as the only explanation. No other possibilities are permitted. One example was the church-supported theory of the planet earth (and mankind) as the center of the universe.

Scientific hypotheses (explanations) are established to be tested; the hypothesis will be a strong "unequivocal" statement, and the experiment designed to produce data that will reject the hypothesis if it is false. If, after enough tests, the data show that the hypothesis has not been rejected, it may be accepted—tentatively and provisionally. However, later data and related hypotheses, may weaken, modify, or disprove the hypothesis, because each testing can generate ideas for new hypotheses. Thus the original hypothesis may never be "proven" in the commonly understood way, even if it survives many tests. The hypothesis remains only "unrejected," always available to be proven wrong and supplanted by a more complete hypothesis, or theory, that explains reality in a better way. Researchers can act as if the hypothesis or theory is proven (true) until it breaks down or is replaced. Sometimes you can find two theories in use at the same time. Newtonian universe, for example, is sufficient for planetary space travel and much other astronomy; however only the Einsteinian view of the universe will suffice for explaining other phenomena. Says Dr. Blumberg, "It is an interesting paradox that science often is viewed as a series of established facts, whereas it may be more correctly understood as an integrated collection of non-related hypotheses" (1983,12).

Journalism, however, prefers established facts; a story with too many qualifications and hedgings appears weak and unreliable. If the scientists claim in their speeches, papers, or publications that the data support the hypothesis, the journalist accepts that, absent any protest from other scientific quarters. The scientist, not the consensus of the community, is expected to accept responsibility for the work. The modest, often overmodest, hedgings get ignored or the story gets killed. However, more science writers are posting warnings in their stories through qualifying phrases such as, "if the report holds up" or "until confirmed or rejected by more research." Science reporters may seek out and quote scientists who disagree, risking enmity from the researcher whose work is called into doubt.

It is doubtful that editors will ever allow such prominent warnings in science stories as journalists use to mark political stories from governments that censor stories, flagging readers that the content may be official but not necessarily accurate. If the gatekeepers of science, those who review scientific papers or screen speakers at a meeting, were to insist that scientists use prominent disclaimers, there might be little point in writing about what scientists are saying. Scientists themselves might balk at having their results so proscribed by their peers and for their peers.

Where scientists offer information outside the setting of a meeting or a journal, the writer can supply warning signs. Such warnings need not be obtrusive. These include noting that "the work has not been published" or that the scientist "plans to present the results" at a specified meeting. Another unobtrusive hedge, "in a formal report to be published soon in," can be used where a journal has accepted the research for publication at a future date. When two scientists released their research report to the National Science Foundation on the possibility that trees might "communicate" by warning other trees when insects or disease attacks them—by releasing airborne chemicals similar to pheromones—an Associated Press story carried this phrase: "If confirmed, the findings from the University of Washington would mark the first time that plants have been shown to emit chemicals that convey information to others." (Leary 1983, A-2). Thus writers can devise wording to convey the sense of scientific discovery and its tentativeness without weakening their stories.

Fragmentation

Another source of distortion lies in the nature of event reporting or handling science as spot news. Without at least some background for the story, science stories can leave readers without a perspective on the relative importance of what is being reported. Such perspective may involve defining a term and the way doctors use it. An "epidemic," for example, means to health scientists an incidence of disease that is above the normal occurrence. It does not necessarily mean a widespread geographic occurrence or large numbers of people. It can mean these things, but determining that requires other questions to ferret out the locations and numbers of victims.

Charges of distortion may involve the writer's approach to a story. That was the conclusion of National Cancer Institute people who analyzed 2138 stories published about cancer in one three-month period. The study indicated that small coverage was given to information that would help people prevent cancer or deal with its effect. And newspaper coverage tended to reinforce what the NCI information director called "negative" (dying) aspects more than "positive" (coping with cancer) strategies. Stories about cancer-causing effects of chemicals seldom gave information about relative dangers from the substances or how individuals could deal with the hazard (Van Nevel 1979). Journalists need not accept this charge since almost every group with which they deal will have its own idea of the appropriate style of presenting its message. However a common mistake of the beginning science writer is failure to distinguish between the many different types of cancers and the varying estimates for survival of their victims. When President Ronald Reagan underwent surgery for colon cancer in 1985, cancer and surgical specialists gave estimates for his survival for five years without further cancer at 40 percent to 80 percent.

Such charges do, however, suggest that science writers and editors should insist on providing some background in stories to put new information in perspective, should address individual risk where disease is a factor, and should report ways to minimize the survival risks. (This may require more space than some editors are prepared to give.) The Cancer Institute analysis concedes, however, that where perspective is missing journalists need not bear all the fault. Sometimes cancer specialists and their information assistants do not know how strong one carcinogen is in comparison with another, have no recommendations on avoiding exposure or, in cases of a new disease, the causes. In this study, 92 percent of the stories were hard news reporting, with only 7 percent features and 1 percent in-depth reports or backgrounders. Ironically, while only 7 percent contained scientists' recommen-

dations for individual action, 46 percent contained recommendations on what government agencies could do to minimize exposure of individuals.

Journalists must bear some responsibility for distortion. The National News Council censured The New York Times in 1983 for misusing facts in its story about the health dangers from herbicides used in Arkansas rice fields. The council said that a biochemist's statement was used out of context to support a lead that "doctors and scientists" supported claims to danger. The report said the Times reporter omitted facts showing that some rice areas had low cancer rates while reporting death rates from a one-year report instead of using a lower, average figure over several years or even higher death-rate figures from an area that did not grow rice. The newspaper story also mentioned a study correlating the incidence of cleft palate and use of herbicides, without mentioning the study's conclusion that the increase in cleft palate was the result of better medical reporting, not the use of herbicides. Perspective and background must include full reporting on scientific studies. Selective reporting that ignores contradictory facts harms the credibility of scientists and journalists (National News Council 1984).

Reporting scientific uncertainty

Ask scientists a clear question: does their data support a decision regulating or suppressing a chemical, a product, or an activity? This is the advice of Barbara Culliton, an editor at Science magazine and former NASW president. This type of questioning is crucial where public policy is concerned, particularly in trans-science debates about toxic waste disposal, acid rain, and other environmental issues. In 1981 the U.S. surgeon general recommended that pregnant women avoid alcohol to minimize the risk of their babies having fetal alcohol syndrome. Science writers pointed out that the data were old; the surgeon general's new interpretation was conservative. Culliton observed, "In light of the obvious psychological stress the surgeon general's stance could create, it is reasonable to think that a story reporting his decision should include information about the uncertainties in the scientific information" (1981,19).

Often the scientific data alone will not support a decision and it should not be expected to. Data and scientific opinion may guide a decision, but intuition, judgment, and politics also play roles in the decision. Toxic chemical wastes seeping from abandoned dumps, for example, obviously are unhealthy and ruin homes or other surrounding property. Can all the data ever come in? Often decades may elapse before a pathological condition is fully established. But should policy decisions be postponed until every scientific indicator has been reported? Unless mercy drops out of political and governmental decisions, it will remain a powerful factor influencing public policy and one the media can and will influence. On the other hand, Robert C. Cowen, natural science editor for the *Christian Science Monitor* and another former NASW president, warns that simplistic treatment of emotion-laden issues that are technically complex verges on embarrassment to science writers (1984). Yet should science writers or any other journalists be restrained to reporting only the hard data, sufficient or insufficient? Should decisions always be rational? Should only scientifically established facts support decisions?

Unorthodox science

Into every science journalist's life will come someone with new, startling, "Gee Whiz" claims for discovery. It could be an inventor with a machine that allegedly produces more energy than it consumes, another "perpetual motion" gadget. Or it could be a journal article proposing a completely new way of looking at a scientific issue. Orthodox scientists will urge you not to publish the story. But competition between yourself and other journalists or between media may demand some sort of action. Your editor expects expla-

nations. The unorthodox claim for new insight into nature may be valid. Virus as a possible cause for some cancers was hooted at when first proposed. Soon after, almost all cancer researchers were swept into the virus hunt. How do you sift, for your readers, the real from the false? The answer is not easily and sometimes never.

Physicist Jeremy Bernstein, who writes popularized science for *The New York Times* and *The New Yorker*, among others, doubts that nonscientists can tell unconventional but good science from what he calls "crank" science. Nor does he believe scientists themselves can make the distinction in fields distant from their own specialties. Bernstein asks three questions when he picks up an unconventional proposal:

1. Does it explain anything? (And, tell us plainly, what does it explain?)

2. Does it predict anything? (Prediction is the heart of scientific hypothesis and theory; results must be susceptible to independent testing. Ask what predictions are implied—not what use is a discovery.)

3. Is it connected to anything? (Claims must be suspect where they do not connect with other great theories that have so far survived the test of many researchers in many different situations.) Einstein's 1905 paper that set physics onto a new course connected with the physics of Newton and others and predicted effects that could be tested experimentally against the theory (Bernstein 1982, 21A).

Three other questions, amenable to even nonscience writers, offer some utility that is based upon credentials. These go beyond Bernstein.

1. Where does the scientist work? Connections with a reputable university, institute, or research company can witness to competence to perform the claimed work; implied acceptance from well-trained colleagues in research may reassure you and your editor. Lack of such a connection can raise suspicions about the researcher

and may deserve a place in any resulting story, along with the scientist's reply. If you have doubts, call a researcher's colleagues or the information officer of the institution for specific facts.

2. What is the educational background of the researcher? Can you trace his or her training? The pride most researchers take in their lists of degrees and other credentials usually makes them willing to supply this information. You may not feel you can ask the questions directly, under some circumstances. Biographies of most doctors of philosophy are in *Who's Who* or other specialized directories. Such biographies are prepared by the person, however, and may not be totally reliable. Entries have been faked. Again, a call to the institutions may reveal discrepancies between the person's claims and the record. Until a series of hoaxes plagued universities and medical centers in the 1980s, credentials and references were seldom checked. Universities and hospitals still find themselves tricked now and then by clever masqueraders. You may find, also, that the person is working in a scientific area outside his or her field of training. Nothing says that a scientist trained in digging out information cannot learn a new field, but experts outside their expertise are at risk.

3. Has the scientist published recently in reputable journals? As with the other questions, that one offers no sure litmus test in and of itself. However, acceptance through peer review is one more "plus" toward credibility in science. The lack of recent publications may indicate a long absence from research or entry into a new area. Unless the researcher is fresh from the university, absence of any publications record merits further inquiry. If the work appears in an obscure journal, you should find it worthwhile to check out the reputation of the journal with other scientists in the field. Does the journal have any standing with the scientific community? Is it a journal at all? Some scientific "giveaway" magazines use submissions to fill around the advertising from drug

and equipment companies with little questioning. Others maintain high standards for accuracy, significance, and timeliness. Forged, faked, and stolen research papers have shown up in the secondary journals and in carelessly edited publications designed more for profit than for information.

Other new research

Even with reports of orthodox research, science writers can improve their reporting with questions that may head off possible distortion in the final story. These questions include:

1. Can your scientist give you names of others working in the field? If not, why not? Because much of science is built upon the work of others, a competent researcher likely will have in mind other scientists who have expertise in the same or closely related problems. Footnotes in research reports often contain leads to other researchers if the materials truly apply to the work under discussion. In addition, if the work is genuine, you may turn up other contributors who deserve mention. One criticism of popular science writing involves charges that writers ignore those who deserve equal, and perhaps more, credit for this latest step. University press releases may imply, through omission, that their schools are the only ones with scientists doing a particular type of research. This is nonsense. Insist that the press office or the scientist supply names and places where related work is underway.

A few PR officers may resist naming others, claiming they have no business publicizing work outside their own institutions. This spurious reasoning indicates a willingness on the part of the scientists and the PR people to allow distortion for their personal gain. A few science writers claim that research is so competitive that this line of questioning risks offending a scientist. If feelings are this tense, the situation argues openly for getting another opinion. You owe no favors. This is just the type of press agent or scientist who will expose you to criticisms about your accuracy and lack of thoroughness if you let them dissuade you from finding an alternate source of information.

2. Where does the research money come from? The cost of research makes self-financing or on-the-cheap experimentation unlikely, except in those rare cases that will make good stories because of their rarity. Federal government grants, which can be checked with the supporting agency if answers raise your suspicions, are the most common form of support. These grants are identified by agency and by a grant number, which some agencies require to be used on any printed matter, including press releases. In the case of some drug and health products and other applied research, identification of the sponsors may indicate potential bias toward favorable results for the sponsoring company. Vagueness about sponsorship by either the scientist or the public relations officer may indicate the need for specifics. A university scientist used as a "neutral" spokesman at the press conference introducing a new drug was later discovered to be a hired consultant for the manufacturer.

3. Is the grant up for renewal? Science writers suspect that publicity around the time a grant expires may help win renewals. This seems unlikely to many scientists, who expect peer review of grant applications and results to guide renewals. But if an occasional scientist thinks publicity helps, you may have some hastily crafted discoveries handed to you. This is a possibility for institutional public relations officers also, and the resulting criticism may embarrass the school or company as well as the scientists involved.

4. What other companies make this product? Media science writers hold a wary view of drug and other product-oriented companies, with some reason. Each company, including its scientists, is in business for its own advantage. Therefore a lot of press releases arrive daily from the many companies announcing new drugs,

hip joints, pacemakers, artificial limbs, and other appliances. Viewed out of context, each can appear to be a significant advance. The track record of science writing, however, leads writers to believe they have too often been used for free and misleading advertising. The writers relied too heavily on the ethics of their sources. Many new drugs and devices are "me too" products made to compete with those sold by other companies. Products may be worth a story by journalistic standards, but to avoid misleading readers, editors, and yourself, ask if they are truly new or even any improvement over existing products. Ask also about limitations on their use and, with drugs, about side effects that can make them unsafe for some potential consumers. Check out drug safety claims against the drug's "label" or "package insert" listing contraindications for use of the drug.

Distortion by omission

Leaving crucial information out of a story, because of space and time limitations or laziness, or ignorance, tempts serious consequences. A classic instance occurred when the Rand Corporation, a research firm, released a report indicating that a few alcoholics might be able to resume drinking after treatment. Although the major newspapers and wire services that received the story in a briefing did carry information about the uncertainties of this conclusion, many of the qualifiers disappeared in the editing by lesser newspapers and broadcasting stations carrying the story. As a result, Rand was castigated by people in all sectors of alcohol abuse treatment for—supposedly—saying flatly that alcoholics could drink again, which, in fact, it did not say. As mentioned earlier, Sibbison (1985) found press releases that omitted warnings in the labels, science writers who did not look beyond the press release, and consumer warnings that were edited out of reporters' stories.

In another example, few science stories questioned the dangers of x-ray exposure when mammography was proposed as a general health measure for breast cancer detection. When the risk of this proposal became apparent later, stories appeared urging women to avoid breast x-rays. In turn, the implications of avoiding x-rays when doctors recommend them were later surveyed (Shaw 1977). A third example comes from the 1980s. At that time companies began marketing health boots that allowed people to hang by their heels from a bar, theoretically relieving pressure on spine and back muscles. Few stories carried by newspapers and broadcasters noted that this activity should be done with someone to help you down before you blacked out, or that the rush of blood toward the head could burst weak blood vessels. In fact, few stories even checked out the alleged benefits with medical sources. These examples show that science writers should ask about adverse effects of new technology, mark stories of new medical techniques as experimental, and query doctors and scientists about potential effects of new discoveries if they are intended to be applied generally.

Perspectives on distortion

Few guaranteed prescription remedies for avoiding distortion exist. Much depends on the writer's sense of integrity and responsibility. As with all journalists, science writers bear the responsibility for fully understanding and reporting any story they touch. If you fall short of the ideal, it should not be for lack of trying. That is the first protection against distortion.

Another protection lies in an open, tolerant attitude toward critics. In spite of often vigorous criticism, the scientists and science writers are closer together on most points than either group often admits. Exceptions may be those in both science and journalism who fall into the intolerance of believing too much of their own rhetoric. Perhaps illustrative of how splintered science has become is the fact that scientists are much more critical of stories done about them personally than about scientists in similar or different fields. This is a common story for journal-

ists; they hear it also from county sheriffs, judges, criminals, and other segments of society, except when the subjects are portrayed heroically. Such criticism does not necessarily reflect significant distortion (Tichenor et al. 1970).

One product of distorted science and medical news, scientists have charged, is that people are led into erroneous decisions. Fortunately people seldom rely on only one source of information when making decisions about their lives. They check media information with friends, personal experiences, and authorities. Scientists and doctors are mistaken when loading all the blame on the media when they are inconvenienced by calls about new treatment or mistaken assumptions. This does not excuse the science writer for inaccuracies and misleading impressions, but he or she seldom bears the sole responsibility.

Some distortion is self-induced and likely unavoidable. Any medical writer can tell you of carefully warning readers that a new treatment or drug is experimental, has been tested only on animals, and likely stands years away from general use. People will still call their physicians to ask for the treatment. However, science writers should review their stories for phrasing that would encourage such false hope. Another source of false hope is that scientists tend to exaggerate their accomplishments, just as do mayors, governors, and presidents. Sometimes this leads to press conferences on minor discoveries or, for example, the overoptimistic curative powers attributed to X-rays early in this century. Scientists also are known to claim misquotation and misrepresentation when their hyperbole gets into print, as do politicians.

In the case of distortion, much of the scientist and writer disagreement comes from the differences in the two faiths. While professor Michael Ryan has found scientists and journalists in agreement on more points of science reporting than they are in disagreement, he points out that journalists do not agree with the scientists' desire to read their stories before publication or with having reporters write the headlines on science stories. Seldom will a scientist agree with reporters that science news is rarely sensationalized; one's sensation is the other's color and human interest. There is no agreement with the idea of having only the scientist evaluate the contribution of his or her research. Nor will the science writer accept the contention that the science writer should not interpret the scientists' conclusions. Scientists think too much significant information is omitted; most science writers think not. The two disagree totally on writing about science as news only after it has been published in a journal (Ryan 1979, 1982).

The science writer should keep in mind that neither science nor science writing is monolithic. Acceptance in either group depends greatly upon individual, personal performances. You will do better with some stories than you will with others. Some scientists have expressed admiration for your nerve in setting out to write for the mass media about science in general. A scientist, they point out, does well to know one segment of a large discipline. Science writers are asked to write stories about many fields of specialized knowledge.

A more serious distortion threat to an individual science writer's acceptance could be the trend toward what may be called the "New Sensationalism" in American and perhaps world journalism. This is modeled on the British tabloid style of presentation, some Rupert Murdoch papers and the *National Enquirer*, or others of the "supermarket papers," which use lots of science-based stories. On advice from such consultants as Professor Stuart Schwartz of Georgia State University, some smaller city papers are adopting a strident, personal-address, "lively" style of reporting and headlining. "Nipples Cause Cancer" is often cited as the most memorable headline from an Ohio newspaper redesigned by Schwartz (Holder 1983).

This style, plus colorful graphics, contrasts greatly with the generally modest approach of scientists toward publication. Schwartz advocates a "Gee Whiz" style of writing and display and praises the *National Enquirer* approach for newspaper features. While better, clearer graphics and use of color may indeed make many science stories easier to understand, newspapers in this style have been criticized heavily by scientists for distortion. Recognizing the criticism, the *National Enquirer* has installed a very tough fact-checking procedure. Schwartz's position holds that the writer's contract is with the readers, not scientists or fellow journalists, and that ordinary readers do not like dull stories. This is true, but liveliness should not outweigh the writer's responsibility to present a story as accurate and distortion free as possible (Holder 1983).

Hoaxes and frauds

Hoaxes and frauds in science pose an entirely different problem in distortion for the science journalist. Unless the writer possesses all the skills of a good research scientist, it is unlikely he or she will perform the watchdog function of the press effectively. More likely any fraud by a scientist will be found out by fellow researchers, and the writer may hear about it through a friend in the laboratory or from a notice in a scientific publication. When fraud is discovered, the conventions of science call for a public retraction of the suspect scientist's published research papers by the journal. Journal editors, like their counterparts in the popular media, are reluctant to print such corrective notices. It is a sign that the peer review system has failed.

The extent of fraud in science, medical, and engineering research remains in dispute. Science writers William J. Broad and Nicholas Wade of *The New York Times*, formerly with *Science* magazine, say there is a lot of fraud. In *Betrayers of the Truth* (1983), they discuss more than a dozen cases of deception in science. Some of the deceptions were revealed only after a century of acceptance. In theory, the self-policing mechanisms of science should have rejected these swiftly. Piltdown Man had an accepted place in science for nearly thirty years after it was supposedly unearthed in 1908; it was not conclusively marked as a hoax until the advent of radiocarbon dating in the 1950s. Leaders of the science community claim that cases of fraud are few, relative to the size of the community, and result from mistakes of technicians and from individuals cracking under the pressure of their demanding tasks and ambitions.

Nonetheless, the study by Broad and Wade suggests there are questions the science writer can pose when skeptical about a scientist or a report that may help reveal something of the quality of research.

1. Does the paper or publication contain all results of all experiments? Science calls for complete reporting. Support for a hypothesis has sometimes been made to seem stronger by selective reporting of experiments, including only the data that most closely fit the theory.

2. To what extent has the data offered as evidence been smoothed from the raw data? Does it look too good? Experimentation is a messier business than many scientists admit. It is not unknown for researchers to clip and round data to make them fit the predicted results of their hypotheses. Obviously a course in statistics and research methods will help the science writer recognize unusual patterns.

3. Have other scientists cited this researcher? Citation in other scientists' research indicates that the work has been duplicated or used in new experiments and that it has held up. Most research work is never tested again; it lies in the literature and sometimes is resurrected. Citation means that other researchers trust the person's work. The number of published papers reported by a scientist sometimes may not be relevant because of techniques for increasing the numbers of publications and sharing credit for

work actually performed by others.

4. How long did it take to complete the series of experiments? Research is time consuming. Faked research may betray itself because the scientist physically lacks the time to complete the work claimed and resorts to "magic-pencil" or "dry-lab" experiments—faking the data. Broad and Wade cite instances of numbered rabbits appearing and disappearing and appearing again in research. Some data turn out to have suffered the "Andrea Doria Phenomenon"—lost by accident and reconstructed.

5. Has the work been published or accepted for publication? One complaint about science reporting has been that stories are written about papers that never appear again in the science reporting system; suspicions hold that these papers may have been written from shaky work that has been abandoned.

6. Is the report sufficient for someone to repeat the experiment? Has anyone else done it? Sometimes researchers may find essential steps or ingredients left out or that only the original researcher can make the experiment work, although science reporting calls for giving all the essential information needed to repeat an experiment. Few scientists will make their raw data available for inspection.

7. Was the researcher looking for this phenomenon or for something else, related or unrelated? Science is filled with incidents of serendipity, accidental discoveries that researchers recognized as indicating something new. Some of the great discoveries, including X-rays, fell into the laps of people searching for something else. The answer may provide a new approach to your story.

8. What was the listed researcher's contribution to the work? Enough examples exist for Broad and Wade to conclude that theft of credit for discoveries is a risk for scientists. Lab directors may claim credit for work done by others or appear as senior author on papers without having done any of the research. Scientists have appropriated data from others' experiments.

When discovered, errors have been blamed on assistants, job pressures, faulty memories, and unrealistic expectations, among other factors.

Among the causes of fraud, aside from outright deception, are self-deception and power politics. Scientists see what they want to see in the results, one reason for peer review. But the peer review system occasionally lets unsupported conclusions slip through, and there has been some indication that powerful members of the research community may receive less scrutiny than others. Papers from traditionally strong research institutions may inhibit critics, according to Broad and Wade. Politics is a subtle factor in the scientific community as in other communities. Some of its possibilities are only now being probed by sociologists and historians of science. The meetings and journals of science historians and sociologists of science offer science writers another source of stories about the culture of science and, on occasion, material to correct distortions from the self-reporting of scientists.

Corrective measures recommended by those picked to investigate cases of alleged fraud include opening and sharing records on collected raw data, asking outside laboratories to check experiments, using more coded studies, discouraging scientists from working alone, stressing quality in research over quantity of publications, and posting detailed standards for analysis and preservation of data in all laboratories.

Science amid politics

Scientific credibility approaches its greatest peril when tangled in the making of public policy. Science writers need to be aware of some of the distortions of science introduced by scientists when they testify as witnesses in public policy debates. As mentioned earlier, the data alone may not be strong enough to give a clear indication of policy directions. Or scientists may attack the credibility of other scientists' research, claiming the interpretation or the procedure itself is faulty. The American political system is adversarial, which may be ill-suited to the idea of scientific concensus. Since most research scientists depend upon federal grants and upon industry consultancies, legitimate questions may be raised about their independence from pressures or special interests within an agency, from industries associated with an agency they work for or from which they receive research grants. As with the Environmental Protection Agency, under the Reagan administration, a change in politics may produce orders cancelling some research or changing its directions.

The adversary system pits scientists against each other in congressional hearings called to elicit testimony for senators and representatives considering legislation. One should not be naive in thinking witnesses are called to these hearings by an impartial committee staff. Staff members come with partisan affilliations. Some witnesses are called and some request to be heard because of their interest in the laws under consideration. Distorted science news reaches the public because this adversarial system fosters the existence of partisan science, and journalists need to provide background information in this area. Often the witnesses actually heard are called because of their prestige, connections with prestigious institutions, or their public opinions on the subject rather than research experience in the relevant area. It is not unusual for political, economic, and emotional factors to override scientific objectivity in interpreting data.

Conflicts of interest are generally economic, although they may carry moral or ethical burdens. The federal government, for example, moved in 1983 to remove the choice from parents and their doctors on sustaining the lives of infants born so deformed that the quality of the babies' existence, their parents' existence, and their financial survival seemed at stake. These "Baby Doe" policies of the federal government were to be enforced through shutting off all government funds to any hospital whose doctors failed to adhere to new federal guidelines. When formaldehyde, used to make insulation for houses and mobile homes, was suspected of causing severe toxic or allergic reactions in residents of those houses, the Environmental Protection Agency, the Occupational Safety and Health Administration, and Consumer Product Safety Commission were unable to summon enough support for their data to get this insulation withdrawn from use. Industry lobbying efforts in Congress prevailed to keep the materials on the market. Obviously industrial scientists have their own survival issues.

Survival issues

Distortion of scientific and technological information occurs most easily in "survival" situtations where nutrition, energy, or environment are at issue. The distortion can be positive or negative—optimistic about the implications of the discovery or stressing its life threatening aspects. However the writer should find a scientific source who can make extrapolations about any discovery or confirm suspicions the writer may have about the meaning and implications of the discovery. Some discoveries obviously will touch universal "survival" keys.

Take the conflicting reports on research into the effects of food upon human behavior. A Texas sheriff read stories about the calming effects of health foods on people's dispositions and ordered his jail's vending machines emptied of potato chips, candy, and the like. But despite numerous stories about the malign effects of high carbohydrate, high salt, and high cholesterol "junk foods" on behavior, a conference of nutrition researchers concluded that the principal effect of "junk foods" was sleepiness (Kolata 1982). Few stories balanced this with scientists concerned with more long-range health effects from cholesterol-laden foods. Then a general campaign to change the Ameri-

can diet was launched in 1984 by the American Cancer Society and the American Heart Association, with almost no one looking into potential exceptions—people who might be harmed by the recommended diet. Obvious ties between bread and pasta and possible cases of chemically induced schizophrenia were drawn from findings that wheat gluten reduced the effectiveness of treatment in a group of schizophrenics (Singh and Kay 1976).

Distortions can arise in such fields as nutrition, energy, and environment when the writer focuses on one aspect rather than finding sources to sort out the potential positive and negative developments from policy decisions. A "bad" pesticide in terms of long-lived impact on the environment may be replaced with one more dangerous to those who apply it, creating a new occupational health problem, or unexpected risk to those who may be accidentally sprayed with it. Lower or stable energy costs may lead nations to future energy shortages because exploration for new oil reserves, production of more efficient electric devices, or development of alternate energy sources may stop for economic reasons or because people become more complacent.

Volcanic explosions, earthquakes, and other releases of giant natural forces, also touch primitive survival fears. Predictions about them put science writers in a dilemma. To ignore a scientist's prediction is to risk being left behind on news breaks and endanger the public. Californians have been put in a state of unease several times by predictions that a major quake will occur along the San Andreas Fault within a specified time frame, although at the time of the predictions, most earth scientists did not believe they had enough knowledge to make a confident prediction. Most news organizations will report such predictions; the better ones will ask researchers if the predicting scientist is qualified in his or her field or if the state of knowledge makes valid predictions possible with a small margin for error. This information will become part of any story.

Warren E. Leary of the Associated Press encountered another dilemma when reporting a study linking a drastically lowered sperm count in young men to the traces of toxic chemicals found in their semen. He obtained from the scientist a list of alternate causes for a low sperm count, and that provided a background paragraph to put the researcher's study in perspective (1979).

In writing about survival issues you may find it helpful to ask researchers to outline specific areas where more knowledge is needed. The source can be the scientist who announces the discovery or someone working in the same or a related field. It's important to ask the source to delineate between fact and his or her interpretation, opinion and speculation. Ask what evidence supports this view.

Distortion in service stories

The "service" story has a long history in the media. This type of article aims at telling readers or viewers how to improve aspects of their lives: health, nutrition, beauty, safety, education, occupation, and so forth. Care must reign here because you expect people to act on your recommendations. The medical column written by doctors, sometimes in collaboration with a journalist, is a good example, as is the personal advice column such as that of psychologist Joyce Brothers. One of the serious possibilities for distortion lies in dealing out obsolete and misleading advice. In the mental health field, two nonprofessionals (Abigail Van Buren and Ann Landers) get high marks for accuracy because they have built up a network of scientific and medical contacts willing to share the latest information with them. The writers also are very willing to recommend that their readers seek professional advice. Their performance does not support the myths that such columns offer obsolete or misguided directions (Tankard and Adelson 1982). The effect of service articles cannot be underestimated; media information ranks with peers as sources of sexual information for teenagers, for ex-

ample (Courtright and Baran 1980).

Concern over survival issues also brings out charlatans. Witness the proliferation of vitamin, mineral, and other health supplement vendors. The American Medicine News Service offers media subscribers a "hot line" for checking sources or getting additional information beyond its coverage of medical and scientific meetings as a source of stories on medicine, health, nutrition, child rearing, fitness, and lifestyle. Such stories also can be checked with local physicians, since many new ideas may take several years to become generally accepted medical practice. Calling local physicians on new techniques will let readers know whether or not such services are available in your area. Often the local doctors can be the springboard for service stories reminding readers of diseases common to an area, such as sun induced skin cancers in the South and West, and as reminders to seek professional treatment for symptoms.

Service articles risk distortion by omitting discussions of risks (fire hazards associated with new plastics, for example) usually because the writers are concerned with only one aspect of the story. One study of magazine stories about insects failed to find a single example of a writer offering anything but ways of destroying insects (Moore et al 1982). In truth, most insects are either beneficial or neutral in their relationships with man and his property. The Austin, Texas, daily newspaper, on the other hand, found high reader popularity in a long series simply identifying and explaining the habits of numerous local insects, birds and mammals. The sources, of course, were scientists at the local university.

Distortion in human interest

Some scientific efforts, in spite of protests about distortion from scientists, may be valued mainly for their conversational potential among mass media users. Actually it is hard to understand why this should bother either scientists or science writers, although trivialization of their work is often cited by researchers. Perspective in the larger meaning of science is good, but when people talk they are open to learning, and it need not be all as serious as it is to the scientists. A neglected story in this category is the debate over whether ancestors to birds developed their ability to fly through gliding out of trees or running along the ground (Lewin 1983).

Stories such as those about rings of debris circling the solar system, attempts to rescue beached whales, the slow, multiphasic processes of aging, and the discoveries of ancient cities may be more interesting for their specifics than for their place in the overall scheme of the universe. For Sandra Blakeslee, writing in *The New York Times* (1983), the human details of ancient diet revealed through a new method of detecting plant isotopes in fossil bones clearly outweighed the elegance of the method. Or consider an extreme, a story about the barber beetle, which kills millions slowly in South America by infecting them with Chagras disease, but which may be better known in the United States for biting people on the face and defecating in the wound than for the misery it causes, thanks to a Reuters story (Reuters 1981).

The writer also may find a useful paragraph, or a story, in clarifying why certain animals are used as stand-ins for research to aid the human condition. Rats, ubiquitous in science, have a reproductive system that provides a close analog to that of humans. The cardiovascular system of pigs offers acceptable responses for testing procedures ultimately destined for humans. Explaining these relationships can help understand science. Often there is temptation to take an easy shot at scientists by ridiculing their research because of the animals used as research subjects; the better procedure is to ask about the reasons for the choice and where the research fits in a larger scene.

Distortion in public documents

Courts and regulatory agencies, such as the EPA, offer public records a science writer can use for information. Environ-mental Impact Statements offer just one example of such a public record. Although these analyses of possible effects from such things as major construction projects are supposedly objective, data may be slanted or omitted. Progress reports and investigatory reports should be examined critically for similar faults; these have turned up in files of the Nuclear Regulatory Commission, for example, as well as in other agencies. Most state and federal agencies have the equivalent of an inspector general or an accounting office responsible for monitoring internal affairs of an agency. These offices can be a source of such documents.

Journalists often will get news of scientists' violations of society's norms or standards through court or police records. Most often this involves individuals or companies accused of law-breaking, violating a .trust, or not complying with a contract or regulation. Where they can, companies will agree to a settlement by which they plead neither guilt nor innocence. The science writer is limited by legal privilege to what is reported in open court or in documents filed in the case. This may produce distortion through omission because there is seldom any libel-proof record that reveals the entire story, as in the case where Mobil Corporation agreed to pay more than $100,000 and conduct an educational campaign after the Environmental Protection Agency charged the company with violating the lead-content rules for gasoline ("Mobil will pay" 1983). Such consent decrees and negotiated settlements commonly do not give details of alleged offenses or concede guilt.

All sorts of accusations may be made when a civil lawsuit is filed. Although such a filing is a public record, libel laws in many states will require you to wait until the other party files a substantial reply before this material is safe to print. Since a reply may take several weeks, journalists can attempt to get the other side of the story by calling the accused. Sometimes it is sufficient to point out that a lawsuit gives only one side of a story.

Such a limit does not apply in a criminal accusation, which is brought by the state. Fairness says you should make every effort to give the accused a chance to reply to the charges.

On the other hand a privileged document, such as one offered as evidence in a full trial or the official transcript of sworn court testimony, may be used without fear of libel as long as you are accurate in reporting. Court proceedings may offer the science writer the only opportunity to see or hear data needed to produce a story without risking financial peril from the libel laws. Such was the case when scientists of Industrial Bio-Test, Inc., were accused of faking studies used by companies to obtain product safety ratings on food, drug, and chemical products (Marshall 1983).

Court documents and trials offered similar views of the darker side of science and scientists in the dispute over whether or not radioactive fallout killed sheep during nuclear bomb tests in Nevada and in the accusations that Kepone, a pesticide manufactured by Allied Chemical Corporation, had damaged fishing in Virginia's James River (Smith 1982; Cotiaux and Darling 1976). Trials, public hearings, and their associated documents offer both direct and indirect evidence and data that may be unobtainable and unpublishable otherwise. Often they reveal facts about a company or individual while addressing other issues. This is privileged material, but it is subject to distortions because'of

the adversary system. Both sides of an advocacy issue tend to overstate their own cases and use selective data. Judges and juries determine the facts as well as guilt or innocence. The system does not encourage balanced presentations. In cases where public safety is at risk, science writers find increasing pressure for them and their media to strike the balances.

Experiments

1. In the role of the "Skeptical Science Writer" go back over science stories you have read or stories in current newspapers or magazines. Pick out one or two stories that need answers to some of the questions posed in this chapter. Prepare to discuss these in class.

2. Prepare a list of contemporary issues that need some scientific commentary to put them in perspective. Go through your university catalog or faculty directory and select names of people you think might shed light on these issues.

3. Are there additional questions you can raise to test the credibility of science, medical, and engineering stories? Prepare a list of them for class discussion.

4. Ask a graduate student or an instructor in the sciences to suggest other tests of how to gauge the worth of a scientific report.

5. Examine newspaper or magazine science stories for examples of possible distortions that should have been corrected in the story. Can you suggest ways of checking for distortion?

Chapter 6
Telling your science story

YOU ARE READY TO WRITE A FIRST DRAFT of your science story or your script. You have passed these decision points:

1. *Selection* of a subject from a journal article, a meeting, an interview, a press conference, a press release, a tip, or other sources,
2. *Verification* of your idea as newsworthy through documentation (journals and papers), interrogation (source interviews), observation (visit to sites), participation (own experience).

It is also assumed that your information is accurate, that you took care in your note taking or recording to get correct figures and quotations, and that you feel you have enough information to understand your story. This information should include sufficient background to connect the new developments in a significant way to older information. Know how this new information changes our understanding. It should not be necessary for your editor to ask, "Why is this important?" or "Why should we run this?"

The significance paragraph

Why your story is important should be clear in your story. Professional writers put this meaning into a "significance paragraph," even when it amounts to only a short phrase or a sentence. This makes the connection between you and your readers: why you are writing the story and why they should read it. The significance paragraph gives your editor and the headline writer, if you write for newspapers, the peg on which to hang the headline or title and to decide how prominently to display the story. The lack of such a clear, brief, unequivocal statement contributes to inaccurate, misleading, and overly sensational headlines. Too frequently the absence of a significance statement or the presence of a fuzzy one results from the writer-reporter's failure to understand the story. In an earlier, simpler time, descriptive reporting of what scientists said may have been enough, even if the meaning was not self-evident. Now you are writing in an analytical age. It is important to push sources to answer the question, "What does it mean?" You will have a very useful, direct quotation or one for paraphrasing. Admitting confusion causes no permanent damage to your reputation. Even if you think you know the significance, check it with one or more of your sources.

You can also develop an original significance statement. Sometimes the notes, interviews, and tape recordings do not yield a coherent, clear significance statement, or it may be couched in meaningless or technical jargon. Develop your own plain English version and test it against the scientists. "Can I say it this way ..." is a decent way to start a paraphrase of the scientific statement. "How can we tell this in English?" is a workable beginning also. Generally speaking, according to attitude studies, the scientist, the reader, and the reporter will be more in agreement on story accuracy and significance than will be editors and copyreaders (Tannenbaum 1962, 1963). A scientist's article or paper may not contain a significance statement; he or she depends on the audience's knowledge to grasp the meaning. However, there will come times when you, as a writer, disagree with a source on the meaning of the research, development, or application. Trust your knowledge, your insight, your instincts—but check them out with qualified people.

Significance statements belong at the top of your story or near there. They can be the lead. This logical point of organization often gets lost, however, when writers subconsciously get tangled in the details they report. Too often a significance statement may be omitted or buried deep in a story. If it is buried far away from the lead of your story, readers may quit in confusion or boredom because they cannot see why they should spend their time with you.

Choosing a story form

Writers, and science writers in particular, have more choices about how they do their work than many believe. The whole process is a series of choices or a consensus worked out with editors. Never did a story "write itself," as some reporters claim. If a few stories come easily from your typewriter or word processor, probably it is because the content makes your decisions easy or you see a workable beginning quickly. You may be quicker than some of your colleagues in making a decision. However, it is easy to forget that there is no one right way to organize a story. All stories represent a series of creative choices.

The gatekeeper role of editors makes their agreement essential, especially for the beginning science writer. Recent research indicates this is the point where "sensationalism" usually enters science stories. In his study of newspaper editors and science reporters, Carroll J. Glynn of Cornell University defined sensationalism as "placing exceptional emphasis on unique aspects of a situation." Editors give this element more weight in evaluating a story than do reporters, and the reason well may lie in editors' longer associ-

ation with newspaper journalism, an institutional bias toward excitement for its own sake. Illustrative of the consensual nature of story selection, Glynn reported that editors believe they assign a large percentage of the science stories while reporters say the percentage coming from editors is very low. Each apparently believes their bargaining produces two winners (Glynn 1985, 70).

Usually the first choice lies between a "hard news" and a "feature" or "delayed lead" approach. Some newspapers and a few radio-TV stations insist on hard-news leads for virtually every story. Obviously the choice is important because the opening shapes the way the entire story unfolds. Hard-news leads generally are summary leads, ranging form the traditional news story (who-what-when-where-why-how) that produces the inverted pyramid story, with facts arranged in decreasing order of importance, to more informal summaries that place key, but often routine, facts slightly deeper into the story. The latter are known as "soft news" or "feature" or "delayed" leads. Virtually all magazine articles are a form of the feature. The magazine article usually is formed around a "theme" or central idea of which the significance statement is a part.

NEWS SUMMARY LEADS.   Here are a few examples of summary leads to "hard news" stories:

> Fewer new cases of acquired immune deficiency syndrome, or AIDS, were reported in the United States in the second half of 1983 than in the first half of the year, Federal health officials said yesterday. However, they cautioned that it was too soon to draw conclusions about a long-term trend (Altman 1984, 6).

> MIDDLETOWN, Pa., Jan. 5 (AP)—Workers cleaning up the damaged nuclear reactor at Three Mile Island could be exposed to six times more radiation than previously thought, the Nuclear Regulatory Commission said today (Associated Press 1984b, 6).

Such summary leads for events include, often in one sentence, (1) who said or did the action, (2) what happened: a description of the event/action, (3) when and (4) where the event/action occurred. "Why" and "how" in such a descriptive or "objective" story come later and usually are attributed to one or more news sources. Skillfully done, such leads convey information quickly and even rhythmically. However, they suffer from lengthiness and often hide the point of a story in extraneous data for the reader.

Here is another type of a summary lead—the conclusion—which leaves routine data to a later paragraph:

> ALBANY, N.Y., Jan. 6—A report today to Governor Cuomo concluded that psychiatric services are in a chronic state of crisis throughout New York City and are able to work with only the most sick, violent and suicidal patients. (Barbanel 1984)

Readers found the "who" integrated into a paragraph giving perspective on where the release of this report fitted into the running political controversy over mental health care. In a strictly scientific article, Walter Sullivan of *The New York Times* put the routine three paragraphs deep in the story, giving more weight to "what" was said, a warning of the uncertainties and the significance:

> Five experimental groups, with detectors in India, Ohio, Japan, Switzerland and Utah, say they have recorded phenomena that could possibly be interpreted as occasional decaying of protons, the building blocks of all matter.
> But they are quick to point out that the observations could be explained in other ways.
> The actual proof of such decay would have sweeping implications, for protons exist in the nuclei of all atoms, and their decay would gradually destroy all matter in the universe. The destruction would not occur, however before the passage of billions upon billions of years (Sullivan 1984, 6).

All of the examples would be improved if their essence could be condensed into fewer words, but technical material works against this. This is one reason many reporters and editors like a featurized approach.

FEATURIZING LEADS.   Feature leads take many paths. Always put the significance high in the story. The difference, however, lies in using dramatic or literary approaches to story telling and applying them to both news events and to full-blown features, situation reports, or analyses that may not be tied to any specific event or time. Patrick Young of Newhouse News Service started his story about discoveries at the Gerontology Research Center this way:

> BALTIMORE — Why do we age?
> The answer remains unknown. But in a quarter-century of exploring that timeless question, researchers in the Baltimore Longitudinal Study of Aging have more closely defined what aging is and demolished some myths and stereotypes about the aged (1983, sec 1, 30).

Because of the powerful social pressure on leprosy sufferers, an Associated Press writer started a story this way:

> LOS ANGELES (AP)—Carlos immigrated from Mexico in 1969, married and fathered two sons, now 6 and 11. But he keeps a secret from his boys—Carlos has leprosy (Associated Press 1983, 32D).

From this humanized, personalized beginning the story moved through background sections dealing with an increase in leprosy with the arrival of people from other countries, the number of victims worldwide and nationwide for background, assurances from doctors that the disease is not contagious, and that new treatments are being developed.

Jerry E. Bishop and Michael Waldholz of *The Wall Street Journal* made the significance paragraph their lead:

> Spurred by major advances in genetic engineering, researchers are splicing together a host of new vaccines that could prevent illness in millions of people.

The new vaccines may be the biggest payoff yet from scientists' new-found ability to manipulate genes and transfer them from one organism to another. The vaccines, which could provide safe and inexpensive weapons against many infectious diseases, represent the first basic change in vaccine technology in almost 200 years (1983, 31).

The story permitting this layering of dramatic statement builds up to a minor climax before starting a new story-telling structure in the body of the story. This form has been likened to an "hourglass" in structure because after the introduction you can switch to point-by-point organization or follow a chronological development. This "hourglass" structure is amenable to a news event lead also. After the conventional 5-W-&-H lead, you can switch to a chronology of events or a detailed account of key events in a logical sequence, building toward a planned ending. Thoughtful writers will plan their ending at the time they fix on their lead or beginning by deciding upon a key fact, quotation or other material with which to close the story. This avoids writing yourself into some corner that you escape with difficulty. Remember, also, that the basic science story is the "how-to" story.

Developing the body

Developing the body of your science story often becomes an exercise in making nonscientists appreciate objects, ideas, processes, and events outside common sensory experience. While setting the course of your story through the choice of a lead, you may consider the realistic constraints of the writing time needed to meet your deadline. Another real limit involves space allotments that set the length of your story. More than six hundred words in a news story or newsfeature may call for special arrangements except for very dramatic events. Space and time limit the fullness of your reporting of details and dramatization.

Another factor to consider is the readability of your story. This is a combination of two elements. In spite of scientists'

claims of sensationalism, science stories, when measured by communications researchers, tend to rate as dull. Surprisingly, newspaper science stories are rated as duller and more difficult to read than those of newsmagazines, which use more technical terms. The general newspaper science story rates as suitable for college-level audiences, although it is aimed at a less-educated reader's level than newsmagazine stories (Levine 1981; Pitts 1980; Kwolek 1973, 225).

One element of readability is sentence length. It is only too easy to write sentences, especially summary leads, that run on forty, fifty, even one hundred words. (There is an example in the preceding text.) This is one reason college texts sometimes put you to sleep. Stories having an average sentence length of seventeen to twenty words seem to have the easy-reading scores for most audiences. This does not mean you cannot use longer sentences. It means you mix sentence lengths to reach a level where people with a high-school education or less can get your meaning more easily. This is also useful when members of an audience may have higher reading skills but are looking to you for help when they are tired, when seeking diversion from worrisome affairs, or simply when easy comprehension of difficult material is desired. Unless you are conscious of the problem, it is very easy to find yourself writing a story that only a college professor can understand. So, the longer the sentence, the longer the words, the greater the risk of losing the train of logic and your readers.

The other main element in readability of science stories involves translation of technical terms. Specialized vocabularies in scientific and medical fields make it impossible to avoid all use of jargon. However, the writer can define the scientists' words before or after their placement in a sentence. This calls for planning the construction of each sentence so the translation, explanation, or definition seems natural, not awkward. Take care in building the translation to avoid talking down to your audience. Being awkwardly obvious offends even those who feel they need the explanation. Slip such definitions into your story as deftly as possible just before or after you first use the technical word.

Here are some other tips. Use short words when you can, write explicitly, give examples of practical applications and analogies. Use "personal" words when you can. Write "her (or his) experiment" instead of "the experiment."

Numbers, the language of quantitative science, give science writers fits. Editors intuitively hate numbers. They think numbers give readers pain. Numbers give editors pain. This pain may afflict editors more than readers, since many readers deal with numbers routinely. However, the reader does not usually choose a math text for recreational reading. So use numbers selectively. include only the most important figures. Explain their meaning.

This maxim applies differently to each audience. *Scientific American* editors seldom flinch from precise numbers, even unto the billions and trillions. Most in the magazine's professional, highly educated audience can grasp the idea of 10-to-the-sixth power equalling a million. Most other audiences outside the scientific, engineering, and business communities likely would find such scientific notation bothersome if not puzzling. Unless the precise number makes a critical difference in understanding the story, rounding the numbers eases the reading.

Where relative size is a factor, comprehension can be increased by familiar comparisons, such as distances between landmarks, speeds, stacks of coins, grains of wheat or sand. (Comparisons with the size of a period in your newspaper or magazine offers a handy reference by which a reader can visualize relative sizes.) Ratios offer another useful tool for comparison. That a planet is four times larger or smaller than earth or that a temperature is hotter than the sun offers the nonscientist some mental and physical connections to scientific reality.

To give lay readers some understanding of the small size of a single atom, Gary Zukhav used this analogy:

> To see the nucleus of an atom, the atom would have to be as tall as a fourteen-story building! The nucleus of an atom as high as a fourteen-story building would be about the size of a grain of salt. Since a nuclear particle has about 2,000 times more mass than an electron, the electrons revolving around this nucleus would be as massive as dust particles.
>
> The dome of Saint Peter's basilica in the Vatican has a diameter of about fourteen stories. Imagine a grain of salt in the middle of the dome of Saint Peter's with a few dust particles revolving around it at the outer edges of the dome (1979, 32).

Granted that not everyone has visited or could visualize Saint Peter's, but local landmarks, including a familiar domed stadium, will substitute nicely. Such structures will give graphic artists a base against which they can draw illustrations to tell part of the message of your story.

Fortune magazine's science writers have excellent graphic artists to support their words with drawings, tables, charts, and other pictograms showing numerical relationships visually. Prodded by *USA Today* and other national newspapers, more newspapers and magazines separate numbers out of the stories and into illustrative charts and tables. Writers must think of their stories as "packages" of words and illustrations. Occasionally your scientists will provide sketches and tables or rough drawings to guide your artists. They might provide more if you ask. Distortion in the proportions of your graphic devices will be taken as seriously as with your words.

Both numbers and drawings offer many pitfalls and chances for misrepresentation. Where possible, the science writer should double-check them with the researcher. Keep illustrations (tables of numbers, drawings, and photographs) as simple as possible for mass audiences. Let the illustration emphasize only the key details that fit with your story.

Literary devices

An arsenal of literary devices can help you tell your science story and make the invisible come alive to readers, listeners, and viewers. All have been used by scientists themselves in attempting to describe the unseeable. These devices include scene setting, anecdote, analogy, description, specific sensory detail, paradox, metaphor, simile, narrative, chronology and so forth.

SCENE SETTING.   One of the most popular literary devices is scene setting. Examples abound because of its value in drawing an audience into the story. Mendel sorting his peas, for example. See how Richard D. Lyons of *The New York Times* carries you into tomorrow:

CORCORAN, Calif.—Imagine the farm of the future. Such an operation might fight insects less by bombing them with huge doses of chemicals than by blending sex attractions into insecticides to halve pesticide use.

This farm of the future would have many crops that would be sown, cultivated, fertilized, harvested, packed and shipped untouched by human hands. Photoelectric cells would spot which fruit was ready to pack so that only ripe fruit reached the market . . . . Futuristic as these ideas may be, they are being used today here in the San Joaquin Valley (1983, 1).

Judith Randal of the New York *Daily News* uses scene setting to sharpen the paradox of the imaginary become real:

WASHINGTON—It seems like science fiction: to suppose that being hired or promoted could depend on scoring well on a battery of blood tests for having suitable genes.

Yet 59 companies—most of them on *Fortune* magazine's list of the 500 major U.S. corporations—recently told the Congressional Office of Technology Assessment that they plan to make genetic screening a part of their personnel policies within the next five years (1982, 8A).

Richard D. Smith, a New York-based former editor of *The Sciences*, uses scene

setting to place readers in a darkened auditorium where a scientist is explaining the mysteries of Acquired Immune Deficiency Syndrome (AIDS):

The first slide on the screen during immunologist John Hadden's presentation was neither a chart nor a diagram nor an electron micrograph. Rather it was a Japanese woodcut of an elephant surrounded by blind men . . . . More than any image projected during the four days of the November conference, this one illustrated the glaring gap between what we know and what we need to know about the epidemic that the U.S. Public Health Service has declared its first priority (1984, 8).

ANECDOTES.   Another device is use of anecdotes. Anecdotes are ministories, stories within the story that illustrate a point in a your article or serve as the lead. The elephant story in the preceding section is both a scene setter and an anecdote that characterized scientists' knowledge of AIDS's cause or etiology. Both the Bible and *Reader's Digest* use them as attention getters and as props to enliven tedious parts of a story. Anecdotes, such as what happened when a new idea was first offered in public, are difficult to obtain because they must be appropriate to the story, fitting it exactly. To get them, you likely will have to ply your interviewees with open-ended questions, such as, "How did you ...?" "Where did you ...?"

OTHER DEVICES.   Within the story, you can use other literary devices to portray the unseeable for the nonscientist or the science-trained person from a very different discipline. Some of these devices, which also enliven copy, include metaphor, simile, and analogy.

Metaphor attempts to describe an event, experience, or thought in terms of something else. You are speaking and writing figuratively, letting this stand as an equivalent of the other for purposes of comparison. Metaphor implies rather than states exact comparisons. When scientists talk of the "cathedral of science," they bring to your mind a beautiful structure, soaring skyward and built with bricks and stones of knowledge.

Simile is that figure of speech that English teachers tell you is introduced by "like" or "as." Short and compact, the simile implies congruity (or near congruity) instead of spelling it out point by point. "Electrons, moving like firefires to lower states of energy" is a simile evoking the familiar to describe the release of a photon of energy when an electron moves from an outer, higher energy state to a lower, inner orbit around the nucleus of an atom. The steady rain of cosmic dust upon the earth can, for example, be likened to the film of dust that collects upon your car. Earl Ubell used a double-barreled approach to describing the appearance of components of the atom:

> Great excitement yesterday at the Hotel New Yorker ... Upshot is that proton looks like a peach. Neutron like a lichee nut. Description may reveal in long run what holds universe together. Story starts with discovery of proton half century ago; neutron found thirty years ago (1961,3).

Ubell poked no fun at the scientists' efforts, but this stripped down parody of Chinese linguistic style extended a metaphor through the story. With less than five hundred words, Ubell gained a distinctly different way of describing the essence of a new view of atomic structure. Do not underestimate the power of writing with novelty and with a strong, active voice. A readability experiment by Professor Lloyd Bostian (1983) showed that even college students read science stories faster and find the subjects more interesting when you write in the active voice. There are indications in his studies that less literate readers appreciate active writing even more. The "nominal style," that abstract form of writing found in texts and scientific papers, is the dullest and hardest to comprehend. Besides, it makes you write more words.

Analogy requires you to make or imply a long comparison between two situations in which you draw many points of similarity. For example you might illustrate the enormous scale of geological time before humans appeared on earth in terms of cities along a transcontinental walk or drive from New York to Los Angeles.

Seek out such figures of speech to enliven your stories. Ask scientists for comparisons, for analogies, and similes. Look for figures of speech in the casual conversation of the scientists. Create your own figures of speech, but test them against the concepts of the scientists you interview to ensure the comparisons are valid. Avoid the mixed metaphor; consider what you are saying should you be tempted to have "oceanographers digging deeper into the sea of knowledge."

Remember also the narrative, that faithful companion of the storyteller; you start at the beginning and quit when you reach the end. Usually the organization is chronological. By building the story on a time-ordered sequence of events, much of your organization problem solves itself. This makes the narrative one of the most popular forms. Almost all professional writers will tell you to plan how you will end a story when you plan the beginning, no matter what the form. Key steps leading to a discovery may be used alone or linked to the chronology. In the narrative, the ending takes care of itself.

State the problem—plainly

Your own skill with language and literary usage will determine how much you play with the fancier techniques of drama and literature. Know, however, that few writing tricks are better than a plain statement of the problem at the heart of your science story. While this may lack some qualities of grace (or pretensions thereto) in writing, it is first-rate communication. Blunt may not always be better, but it is effective. Harry Nelson of the *Los Angeles Times* cuts across centuries of medical technology with this:

> False teeth, eye glasses and wigs may not sound like medical breakthroughs, but hundreds of years ago they were the beginnings of Bionic Man.

Today, new synthetic materials and electronic technology have greatly expanded man's capacity to build a variety of artificial organs and spare parts that modestly mimic nature's creations (1984, sec. 5, 90).

Business Week and other industrial or trade journals favor this type of lead because of the ease with which it reaches the economic interests of their readers, as this example shows:

> Every fall a natural disaster strikes U.S. farmers, causing hundreds of millions of dollars in agricultural losses. Until now, farmers have not been able to do much about the annual killing frost. But some scientists now believe they can get around the problem. They have identified the culprit, and it is not Jack Frost.
>
> Instead it is a group of lowly bacteria that have the curious ability to cause ice crystals to form when the mercury dips just a couple of degrees below freezing ("Warming Up ..." 1983, 138).

Freelancer Bill Cromie, also director of the Council for the Advancement of Science Writing and an oceanographer, laid out the essential problem this way for *Mosaic*, a popularized science publication for the National Science Foundation:

> Hydrogen burns cleanly. Properly oxidized, it produces only heat and water. Since water is also a source of hydrogen, the cycle should be repeatable, the fuel inexhaustible.
>
> The catch is that the energy required to extract hydrogen from water is greater than the energy produced by burning hydrogen. But if the input energy for splitting water into oxygen and hydrogen by hydrolysis could be solar, the hydrogen could effectively concentrate and store sunlight for later use (1981, 7).

Personalizing the story

Telling your story through the people involved offers another way to increase attention. People like hearing about other people, especially if they are famous, talented, unusual, or colorful. You can weave information about their science

into the background and supporting material of the story. In a personality profile, the focus of the story is upon one person, sometimes told through the eyes of his or her friends and, sometimes, enemies:

> NEW YORK—Bruce Alperts met Barbara McClintock about 13 years ago, when he took a course she taught at her home base, Cold Spring Harbor Laboratory on Long Island.
>
> Alperts is a microbiologist and McClintock is a plant geneticist, so there is not all that much overlap in their work. But McClintock has the kind of mind that pays no attention to classifications. The whole world of biological science is in her grasp.
>
> This was about the time the biological community began to realize that it had an unappreciated genius in Barbara McClintock. That assessment reached its proper conclusion in early October when McClintock, at the age of 81, was awarded the 1983 Nobel Prize in Medicine for work on "jumping genes" that she had done more than 30 years earlier (Edelson 1983, J1).

The personality approach, beloved by newsmagazines, allows the writer more freedom for leisurely, informal openings. Here is Tracy Kidder for *Science 83* interviewing one of Harvard University's most outspoken scientists:

> Mike McElroy likes the big questions. The origin of life, for instance. He's dabbled in it on and off for the past 10 years. McElroy sits in one of Harvard's prestigious chairs of chemistry and enjoys the enviable freedom—the research money, the apprentices, the autonomy, to indulge his eclectic tastes. Listening to him muse about the beginnings of life is a marvelous way to pass a quiet afternoon in the dead of a New England winter.
>
> About three billion years ago, relatively suddenly, and, most scientists agree, because of the blossoming of life, oxygen appeared in the Earth's atmosphere (1983, 59).

An opening that mixes several elements, as this one does, promises readers you will discuss each aspect in the story. It is a device to capture readers and lure them through the story until you have covered each item. (One of the lapses of writers and editors—and not just in science writing—is to omit one or more elements when you write; this stacking of elements is one way of organizing your story. But you must deliver each to your reader.)

In other variations, you may concentrate on a group of scientists, such as a team of heart transplant surgeons or the entire staff of a laboratory or business, and how their combined skills and personalities make the institution unique. Developing an analysis and description of the interactions of the scientific skills and the personalities of the team can show how science works. In the period of big science, the lone scientist is a rarity. But that's another story.

Another approach to humanizing science is to personalize your reactions, although this carries some risks if you are sensitive to criticism. Unease in writing a personalized account of a laboratory visit may tempt the immature to poke fun at the occasion. On the other hand, an accurate, sensitively written, intelligent, serious account might be effective. More powerful would be your personal report from observing or participating in an experiment or field expedition. Remember the writer's dictum: show (describe), not tell. Be specific, concrete with your details. Avoid the abstract, unless you follow closely with an example that illustrates the abstraction.

Writing in a crisis

The foregoing implies a leisurely, thoughtful approach to science writing. That is misleading because even under the lightest of deadline pressures, journalism means composing a story faster than the scholar's pace. One of the things a science writer brings to journalism is some depth of background knowledge about the natural world and how to find the people who can extend the science writer's expertise. Never is this knowledge tested more stringently than when you must write amid the crisis of breaking news. Learn to think actively to write actively in anticipation of the day. A wide-ranging reading program is perhaps the only way to prepare.

Although few journalists admit it, there is very little "breaking news" in the newspapers and magazines or on radio-television newscasts. Most of the events reported daily can be anticipated, at least in their broad outlines. "Breaking news" means the unexpected. An example would be the attempted assassination of a head of state and the need for science or medical writers to report on his or her injuries, their seriousness, and the course of emergency treatment. Other examples include threat of a meltdown in the core of a nuclear power reactor, such as happened at Three Mile Island power plant on March 28, 1979, a volcanic eruption, or the outbreak of a new disease, such as AIDS or Legionnaires' disease. Disaster such as a massive power failure, earthquake, tsunami, or the like afford other examples. Routine as manned space flight may seem, each one for the journalist is an ongoing crisis waiting to occur. A space capsule fire that killed three astronauts in the U.S. Apollo program and an explosion during a lunar mission illustrate how swiftly the routine can deteriorate. Hints of similar crises in the Russian nuclear and space programs escape from time to time.

These situations call upon the science writer for improvisation and speed. Depending upon the nature of the news, the numbers of dead and the extent of property damage, the event itself likely will override the science as the major story. The science writer, however, will be called on to make the events intelligible to laymen and under the tightest of deadline pressures, in all probability. Indeed, from a journalistic standpoint, editors may look upon such a moment as justification for having a science writer on the staff. The writer is a bank of instant background and information sources.

You will be expected to draw upon

your own knowledge, on any library or computer research you can perform in a limited time, and on any experts who can offer additional information. Few occasions bring out such a single-minded pursuit of information and such a host of competing media as a crisis. Even the announcement of a singular event, such as the first transplant of a heart or other major organ, can bring on a crisis atmosphere. When dentist Barney Clark received the first mechanical heart, hundreds of print and electronic journalists from around the world, with medical knowledge ranging from zero to professional, flooded the hospital with information requests in person or by phone.

It is understatement to say that such events offer the worst of conditions for information gathering. Often information is lacking. In the case of the Three Mile Island nuclear power accident, specialists in nuclear energy were unable to establish immediately the cause or the extent of the accident. Finding the cause of Legionnaires' disease, so-called because it surfaced after a convention of the American Legion in Philadelphia, took months of laboratory and field research.

Although information and public relations specialists may be on the scene, their own access to competent sources may be limited. No truly applicable public relations or public information plan can be written in advance to cover all contingencies. Even when a rough plan exists, too often public and private managers lose their nerve or shift their priorities about full and open discussion of events. Their own sources of information may prove inadequate or incomplete. Competition grows fierce among the media representatives for any scrap of information. Rumors will fill the void, and the science journalist—no less than any other—faces the possibility of going on the air or into print with unverifiable information.

In crisis, you are on your own to improvise as best you can. Senior scientists offer good crisis sources, particularly if you have dealt with them or them or their colleagues before. In more normal situations, you may follow conventional, bureaucratic communications paths. A study of the communications preferences of scientists says they much prefer talking directly to the journalists. Younger scientists will use the public information office more than older ones, most of whom contact the media directly. Only a little more than half of the scientists contacted said it was important for scientists to make their knowledge available to the public, so cordial relations in the past may be more important to the writer in a crisis than the scientists' sense of responsibility. Journalists initiate most of the contacts, and only about 15 percent of the scientists would abolish public relations offices at the university under study. While a large percentage (66 percent) of scientists thought the public information office sometimes hindered communication, 72 percent said public relations staffers made dealing with the media easier (Dunwoody and Ryan 1983).

In response to the problem of getting information in a crisis, one space writer attempted to keep as much independence for himself as possible by building a portable reference library on wheels. He moved this technical library to each launch by booking an airline seat for the cart. In most instances, however, the science writer must improvise, building from background reading, past experiences, and whatever qualified sources can be reached.

These are occasions when the faiths of science and journalism collide, often to the detriment of both in terms of public respect. The solution in Russia and some other authoritarian countries is simply not to report disasters until after full reports and investigations are complete. Sometimes major disasters never are reported in public. Some scientists and political figures would like similar circumspection applied in the West. It is, however, a futile expectation of a media designed as a source of information independent from the government or other established sources. Science journalists must be as persistent as any others in defending their access to information.

Science journalists also face advertiser pressures. In one dispute the *Journal of the American Medical Association* lost $250,000 in advertising when a drug maker objected to a story about a competitor's product. One of the *JAMA* editors told medical writer Howard Wolinsky she was fired in the debate over articles the magazine printed about the competing products and their favorable or unfavorable presentation (Fitzgerald 1984). Media organizations vary greatly in their willingness and resources to resist such pressures.

Experiments

1. Read articles in an issue of a popular science magazine or science stories in a newspaper. Analyze the literary devices used by the writers.

2. Read through several articles in magazines such as *Science, New Scientist, Nature* or other scientific or medical journals. Can you find instances where scientists use these literary devices?

3. Go through several issues of *Science* magazine or other journals. In the *Science* Reports section you will find scientists reporting on results of their work. Write several combinations of leads and "significance paragraphs" from your reading. Bring your lead-significance paragraphs and a copy of the original article to class for discussion.

4. Read through several scientific or medical articles to find one around which you can develop a "scene-setting" opening. Medical journals are especially good for this because doctors often use the case study method for reporting their results.

5. From your reading so far, you should have found an article you would like to make into a popularized science or medical story. Write the story for your local daily newspaper.

Chapter 7
Science writing
and public interest

SEVERAL AREAS OF SCIENCE WRITING present journalists with special reporting problems. These areas include politics and public policy, business news, public relations, and such trans-science subjects as agriculture, environment, energy, nutrition, national security, toxic waste disposal, health, and medicine. While scientific sources and information play critical roles in stories on these subjects, the writer must go beyond science to give the audience an adequate report.

Stories on such topics contain elements heavy with news values: conflict, survival, money, power, impact, and personality. They affect and are affected by the scientific community, as well as almost all other communities or special interests. Government leaders and agencies play active parts in the interactions of these groups, as mediators, supporters, targets, and protectors of the "public interest." Scientific and technological data, when convenient, are marshaled for collisions between players of the games. Eminent and not-so-eminent scientists and engineers go into the public arena to offer their interpretations of the data and urge "rational" public actions favoring one side or another. Because scientists and engineers are not reporting to their peers, their disclosures and interpretations have been found less than complete on many occasions. None of the scientists or their employers has drawn censure from the scientific community for such public policy activities.

However the confusion generated has been great among journalists, public officials, and the public. Policymakers and journalists do not know who to believe in the conflicting testimony. So great has been the confusion that about twenty years ago Dr. Arthur Kantrowitz, chairman of the Avco-Everett Research Laboratory, Inc., proposed creating a "science court" in which panels of expert judges would render a decision on the validity of the technical arguments. Judicial traditions permit courts, with or without juries, to determine both law and fact.

The idea of a science court almost reached a test in 1978 when Governor Rudy Perpich sent 150 state troopers to control Minnesotans protesting constant exposure to possibly dangerous electromagnetic radiation from a 400-kilovolt electricity transmission line. Governor Perpich was willing, and the Ford Foundation and the National Science Foundation of the U.S. government agreed to pay the costs of the experiment. However, neither the environmentalists nor the two power cooperatives, who had won in the regular courts, could agree on this form of arbitration.

Many disputes like these now go to the regular judicial system for resolution, and a number of judges doubt the courts' ability to achieve a fair settlement. To some, it appears that technology has outrun the ability of society to understand and control issues raised by it. One example is the legal status of frozen human embryos. Are these clumps of cells human beings? How far through their growth stages can scientists do experiments on them? Can they inherit property if one or both parents die before such embryos are transplanted into a mother and carried to birth? This situation occurred in when a wealthy couple died, leaving a pair of embryos with an Australian fertility research clinic in 1984. Who owns the embryos? Does someone inherit the embryos along with other property? What are the responsibilities of inheritors to these bits of living matter?

Another example: the first Swedish citizen to receive an artificial heart became legally dead when his own heart died, by the definition established for his country.

As Daniel S. Greenberg, one of the few journalists who specialize in science and public policy, observed, the idea of a science court was neither all that good nor all that bad. Its biggest flaw was the assumption that scientific and technical facts can be isolated from their social, political, and economic settings. "As it turns out, in most scientific-political controversies, less at issue are the scientific facts than the values attached to them," said Greenberg (1978).

Reporting political, public policy, environmental, business-economic, and societal issues carries the science writer into more aspects of the realities of worldly affairs than the "reality" of science. It is a world of power, political and economic, that historically lies vulnerable to manipulation for private and personal ends. Those ends include gain as well as avoidance of economic damage or damage to personal reputations. It is a world in which scientific study may be asked to produce answers on which government and social policy may be based. It is a world in which answers may be demanded before science develops sufficient data for policy guidance.

Politics and public policy

Science writers dealing with public issues must remain aware of the politics affecting basic and applied science and of the key players in this game. Politics involves ordering the relationship between individuals and between institutions in a society. It also is the art of compromise. Politics is the art of using power, personal and institutional. Because of the values attached to issues involving government power, issues tend toward compromise or trade-offs as engineers call them. Everyone gets something; no one gets all he asks . . . usually. Trade-offs may be made on factors other than scientific facts or their validity. Emotion, jobs, votes, money, friendships, and institutional values are a few of the bases for resolving political conflicts. The primary involvement for science and scientists with government comes over money and differing concepts of the general welfare.

BUDGET AND FINANCE. Federal tax money, collected from all of us, fuels science in most industrialized countries. It was not always that way. Before the 1940s and World War II, pure science was a small enterprise, paid for almost entirely by university budgets, private foundations, or donations from individuals. Only agricultural science, as part of the Department of Agriculture's commitment to land grant colleges and improving farming in the United States, received steady and substantial funding from government. Only the chemical industry, led by DuPont, maintained substantial research programs. The aircraft industry financed its own new models, with some War Department (as it was then called) encouragement. World War I demonstrated the practicality of chemical and aircraft science. World War II demonstrated that even more exotic sciences could be pushed, with large sums of tax money, to practical discoveries: nuclear energy, electronics, medicine, optics, jet-rocket propulsion, and others. Combat, the ultimate in survival issues, has always been an incubator for new science and technology. Wartime success with innovation led most countries to adopt government financial subsidies for science and technology in peacetime.

Government budgeting and spending are sticky issues to write about. In 1984 the Battelle Memorial Institute, in its annual report, estimated that $94.2 billion would be spent in the United States for research and development. More than half of that, $48.8 billion, would come from industry, a change from early post-World War II days when government money overwhelmed private industry's contribution. The U.S. government research and development budget spending was calculated at $42.7 billion. U.S. budget estimates placed the federal contribution in 1984 at $46.7 billion, which included money to be committed to projects but not actually spent.

Science writers must be careful when analyzing financing. Federal budget years start in October. Budgets usually get less funding than agency managers request. And there are two federal and state budgets: one involves money designated or authorized for research and development; the other budget deals in money actually appropriated to be spent in any given year. Because large applied technology projects take several years to build, as in the case of a new aircraft, money may be committed or authorized for projects but appropriated and spent over several years. Mixing both authorized and appropriated figures in a story can confuse writers and readers. Pick one or the other set — or use very clear tables to show the differences.

Science writers should remain sensitive to shifts in allocations of research and development money. In Fiscal 1984, the official $46.7 billion research and development budget was divided this way: basic research — $7.2 billion, defense research — $28.1 billion, other agencies — $11.4 billion. Of the $7.2-plus billion for basic research, about half goes to colleges and universities, with roughly ten schools getting most of the money. The Office of Science and Technology Policy (OSTP) estimated that the basic research spending was almost evenly split between agencies supporting the life sciences ($3.3 billion)

and the physical sciences and engineering. However, the financial edge of physical science and engineering was nearly $600 million — $3.9 billion. These funds are spent through the various cabinet departments and agencies. A central office for monitoring them exists in the presidential Office of Science and Technology Policy. A counterpart exists in the congressional Office of Technology Assessment. In spite of official claims to rationality, the distribution of this money is very politicized.

Contacts in each office afford the writer listening posts for most issues that arise in government. Other sources include the staff and elected members of various committees and subcommittees of the House of Representatives and the Senate who have responsibility for budget authorization, appropriation, and oversight for each agency.

Even if you are not in Washington, get on the mailing lists for reports and the hearing transcripts of these offices and committees. They can provide you with background information and sources of information for specific projects. If your local college or university library is an official depository for government documents, these documents will be available there. Getting them from the committees and agencies usually is faster. The National Science Foundation and the National Institutes of Health fund most basic science and medical research. Allocation of funds between the various agencies and even inside them is very much a function of political lobbying.

Major players in the politics of science and its fund allocations are the various nonprofit "disease" foundations. They supply many of the witnesses arguing for increasing or shifting appropriations each year. The many National Institutes of Health are the product of lobbying by these special interest medical and health groups for their favorite diseases. Writers should look also for political influence from powerful legislators for facilities in their districts. University administrators and prominent scientists will be found lobbying their representatives as hard as any other special interest.

REGULATORY AGENCIES. Federal and state regulatory agencies offer science writers other insights into the politics and policies of science, medicine, and high technology. In addition to making news by the laws they enforce or fail to enforce, they fund data gathering that supports regulation as well as some research that adds knowledge to the store of science. The Environmental Protection Agency is typical of the regulatory agency with heavy research activity in addition to regulation and enforcement responsibilities. Sometimes regulation is linked with promotional responsibilities, as at the Department of Agriculture. This amounts to a conflict of interest in many cases, since such agencies generally become captives of the clientele they also regulate. The old Atomic Energy Commission was broken up on these grounds, with the research and development of atomic energy devices given to the Department of Energy and the operating safety and supervision functions assigned to the Nuclear Regulatory Commission. The top management of the Environmental Protection Agency went through a complete reorganization in 1984 after it was revealed that agency policies favored the companies EPA was to regulate. Journalists have learned to be wary of appointments to regulatory agencies during changes in administration. New political appointees may or may not experience success in shifting the direction of agency research programs that define the need or extent of regulation. The technical nature of the data that supports regulation lends itself to the skills of the science writer.

Often regulation lies with cabinet departments, such as the U.S. Department of Agriculture, because of political influences of the special interests they regulate. The USDA supports a whole range of research projects by its own scientists and labs and by scientists in land grant universities and colleges. The goal of USDA is to make farming more profitable, which makes it a friendly regulator.

The relationship of an agency to the industry it supports and regulates often makes some of the research findings suspect and puts agencies in conflict. For example, when ethylene dibromide (EDB) contamination was found in grain-based foods in 1984, science writers found the EPA trying to write stricter laws for the pesticide use — and eventual abandonment — while the USDA worked to keep the carcinogenic poison in use for citrus growers to control insects (Sun 1984). However, ending the use of EDB signalled an opportunity for the nuclear industry because irradiation of grains and fruit to kill insects and their larvae emerged as a strong contender to replace chemical pesticides. The nuclear industry would profit from greatly increased sales of equipment to process the farm products. However, in a fashion typical of these questions, there were few, if any, questions raised about the desirability of spreading nuclear radiation sources into the equivalent of every grain storage terminal in the United States, Canada, and Mexico. These are questions that science writers, and especially those in environmental reporting, should raise. Look for solutions that raise new problems.

Such interagency conflicts are far from rare. They make up another aspect of science politics. Science writers will search in vain for a central, rationalized science policy for the nation. There are policies within each agency as to the nature and funding of research to serve the "mission" of each agency. Thus agency or institutional bias may lead to conflict. Agriculture, for example, may fund research on how to increase the yield of tobacco fields while the Department of Health and Human Services tries to discourage the use of tobacco, supporting research on its deleterious effects.

Even though there has been an official science adviser to each president since John F. Kennedy, the plurality of interests working through Congress and the While House sometimes produces conflicting policies. For example, at one point the Reagan administration was advocating reducing the costs of medical care and the intrusion of government into private affairs. Then, in conflict with its previous stand, the administration entered the so-called "Baby Doe" controversy to force a lifesaving operation upon a retarded infant with spina bifida (a condition where the spinal column does not close, leaving the spinal cord exposed) and other birth defects. The parents and their doctor had agreed to let the infant die rather than have her confined for life in institutional care, paid for by federal medical care and welfare funds.

Enforcement of such policies goes back to the federal dollar. Institutions and individuals receiving federal money agree to abide by prevailing guidelines of the granting agency or risk having that support withdrawn. In the case of "Baby Doe," any hospital or doctor refusing food or treatment would be considered violating the infant's civil rights and jeopardizing federal support. It is a tactic available to government in almost any controversy.

Regulatory agencies are the most neglected of government organizations in terms of the mass media. They move slowly in a quasi-judicial process. Their work is often highly technical and their regulations written in legal prose almost too thick to decipher. An agency generally favors those it regulates. Getting a story often means understanding decisions that hinge on small but significant changes in the level of permitted statistical risks.

Journalists' fear of numbers often blurs their effectiveness in reporting regulatory actions. For example, in the EDB controversy, which drew front-page headlines for weeks because of the survival issues in contaminated food, only William Hines of the *Chicago Sun-Times* produced useful data for readers in a citrus-growing state when the final regulations were issued.

Six daily papers studied published news stories about EDB being forbidden after nine months, but only Hines's story gave consumers and growers a reading on the amount of EDB allowed to remain in fruit until the ban went into effect (1984).

Another consideration in the reporting of public policy issues is that the United States operates on two governmental levels: federal and state. Often they conflict. The State of Mississippi, for example, once took over an abandoned pesticide plant to produce a long-lasting fire ant poison that the EPA said should be banned. Generally, federal law overrides conflicting state law, but until state rules are tested in court both may prevail. Where there is no conflict, the systems operate in parallel, with disputes, especially over environmental matters, going to court in one or the other — or both. When cooperative enforcement agreements have been worked out between federal and state agencies, the state agency will enforce both sets of regulations.

At the same time, these agencies are sources of stories, many publicized by the agencies for their own benefit. Reports and studies conducted by agency scientists, contractors, and review panels usually need updating and checking carefully against other sources of information. It is generally a good policy for the science journalist to ask, "Who benefits?" when examining conclusions of such studies. In many cases the agencies will ask the National Academy of Sciences to act as a "science court" in studying problems where the scientific evidence is unclear, the political problems very touchy, and the economic issues conflicting. Such was the case when the National Academy of Sciences studied data on the acid rain question and concluded that there was indeed a connection between the burning of coal in the industrial Midwest and acidity in the lakes of the Northeast and Canada. This report conflicted with Reagan administration contentions that more research was needed before such a connection could be made (Pasztor 1983)

The general neglect of regulatory agencies by other journalists allows the science writer to carve a professional niche here. Howard Simons, former science writer and later managing editor at THe Washington Post, said that one of his techniques for getting exclusive stories was to go to these agencies that few other reporters touched and dig until he came up with a science-based story he could sell to his editors. The power of the regulatory agencies and the economic interests they affect support a nearly hidden field of journalists. These are the science and business writers for industrial and trade journals and for specialized newsletters whose subscribers expect accurate, technical coverage of the interaction of science, technology, and politics affecting the subscribers' business.

For journalists covering these agencies, understanding the intermixing of science, technology, and economic interests and the governing legislation of the agency is essential. All the elements should be present in a story. Part of this job is made easier for the journalist since economic impact data have become a required part of many regulatory proposals. Calculations of economic impact are vulnerable to agency biases, so the science writer should be skeptical of such predictions. Science specialties such as environmental and energy reporting will cover several federal agencies and their counterparts (in water, air, and land regulation) at the state and sometimes city or county levels. Local congressmen and state legislators, in some instances, can pry information loose from these agencies. It may be necessary to use state and federal Freedom of Information and Open Records laws to obtain records of decisions, research data, and other information.

Science, business, and economics

Science writers for business readers must concern themselves with the interaction of science and technology with money, power, jobs, and other socioeconomic factors. If the focus of the publication or program is on the business community, the economic factors probably dominate science in the writer's approach to any story. In The Wall Street Journal, Forbes, and Business Week, for example, a writer must seek an economic angle that justifies printing the story. Exceptions are made, usually, only if you can demonstrate an effect, such as health or financial, upon the personal lives of the audience. Examples of some of the most thorough science-technology-business stories appear in a British magazine, The Economist. Its slightly different perspective on the world as well as its value in showing how to integrate business background with science journalism make it worth reading.

Several reasons make science and technology reporting a primary component of much business news coverage. (1) Business organizations produce and consume most of the world's new technology and provide related jobs. (2) Applied science that creates and solves societal problems likely will come from business groups. (3) As business organizations grow larger, they may surpass the power of governments in national and international influence. (4) For the general and business reader, understanding commercial applications of science and technology will help understand social, political, and economic trends. (5) There is an increasing crossover and merging of the business and scientific communities as a result of business use of science and technology.

Some of the best and worst aspects of science and technology show up in business and technology reporting. Certainly it is good for science and technology writers to report the economic benefits inherent in new applications of knowledge. For example, consider the promise of the science-art of genetic engineering and the selective breeding of organisms. This potential application of science produced for Steven J. Marcus of The New York Times a major business section story on the possibility of breeding microbes to clean up specific types of agricultural wastes, a troublesome environmental problem, and excrete useful chemical by-products (1984). Too often, however, the science-business story tends to focus solely on the potential benefits in terms of jobs and profits. Too often the stories fail to explore negative possibilities, especially those effects a new technology may produce when applied widely. The litter of near-indestructible plastic items, for example, nearly overwhelmed conventional methods of dealing with trash.

The drug industry offers many examples of new products with unfortunate outcomes. On that same day the microbe story appeared in *The New York Times* on the hopes for genetic engineering, the paper also reported the statement read by a federal judge in Minneapolis, Justice Miles Lord, to three drug company officials as part of an estimated $4.6 million settlement of lawsuits over sales of a birth control device. Said Justice Lord:

> Your company, without warning to women, invaded their bodies by the millions and caused them injuries by the thousands. . . . Your company in the face of overwhelming evidence denies its guilt and continues its monstrous mischief. You have taken the bottom line as your guiding beacon and the low road as your route. This is corporate irresponsibility at its meanest (Associated Press 1984a,9).

A medical doctor for the drug manufacturer was singled out for special attention by the judge who accused him of violating "every ethical precept" of the Hippocratic oath. An appeals court had the judge's statement in court stricken from the record as being too strong for the occasion.

Companies, often led by U.S. firms, turn out many useful new products. Most cause little, if any, disturbance in the market place or in society other than profits. Yet the potential for nationwide and even worldwide good and harm goes with each product because of the rapid and efficient marketing and distribution systems of modern business. Sometimes effects can-

not be foreseen; it took nearly fifty years for the mass produced automobile's potential for air pollution to be recognized. Sometimes effects are already known, and ignored, when they are negative. Business managers have been known to suppress adverse data (including fatalities) about products, attempt to use political influence to win scientific and governmental endorsement of spurious products, and to obtain dismissal of court decisions assessing company liability for death and injury. A known level of risk may be accepted as merely the cost of doing business. Special interest influence may be exercised through promises of votes or campaign contributions.

Thus the business-oriented science writer will look for scientific and technological developments with significance to industry. Science-technology writers also should probe company sources for the possibilities of misuse of new products, the effects of those products when multiplied by the millions, and for the results of "risk analysis" studies. It is an imprudent company management that does not attempt such studies, considering the potential losses in a product liability trial. Copies of such analyses often find their way into the hands of journalists. Sometimes insurance companies and independent testing laboratories can provide such material. *Consumer Reports* magazine runs its own testing laboratories.

Another source of technology analysis may be government laboratory reports. A large number of the people trained as scientists spend their time testing and analyzing products, monitoring the environment, and collecting and analyzing data. Most government projects involving research, development, and engineering are done under federal contract, and analyses may be found in such sponsoring agencies as the National Aeronautics and Space Administration, the Department of Energy, Environmental Protection Agency, Department of Transportation, and the Department of Defense. These agencies also operate their own national laboratories. Because information in some of these agencies is classified or at least "closely held" by policy, science writers may get their first critical view of new technology through scientific papers at meetings of scientists and engineers or from an agency's internal report. In most cases a visit to the private or federal laboratories can be arranged to report on a particular project. In other cases, media and industry may be forced to use the Freedom of Information Act to obtain data critical of a product or industry from federal sources.

Accompanying the growth of science-related industry in the United States is the growth of newsletters and trade journals devoted to each branch and subbranch of an industry. The science journalist who learns a specialized field well may find it profitable to work for — or to start — one of these publications. These industry publications serve, also, as sources of news and background information on the industry. Obviously a proindustry bias or viewpoint will prevail in most cases, but this will be easy to spot and discount, if necessary, as you become familiar with the field.

JOBS, ENERGY, AND PATENTS. Another side of business-science reporting will be more controversial than covering the marketing of new technology or the jockeying for one government contract or another. Scientific and medical aspects of occupational health are much neglected topics in most countries. Reporting on occupational safety and health offers the science writer problems because of the difficulty of obtaining reliable and libel-free information. The manufacture of many products involves exposure to powerful chemicals. This includes birth control pills, pesticides, electronic components, and others. Some industries, such as coal and uranium mining and textile milling, expose workers to conditions that produce disease, such as the debilitating "black lung" of coal mining. Liability for work-related diseases and injuries, like product safety, will be denied by most companies

and fought in court. For example, faced with lawsuits alleging liability for exposure to asbestos products from workers and customers, asbestos manufacturers were accused of using the bankruptcy laws as part of their defense strategy. Much of the information to be obtained in this area will come through unions, court documents, or sometimes from the National Institute of Occupational Safety and Health (NIOSH) or the Occupational Safety and Health Administration, both federal agencies. The vigor with which these agencies investigate working conditions may vary from administration to administration.

Energy reporting is another science-related specialty whose focus is primarily business-oriented. Although there exists a large and complex research and advanced-engineering establishment in government and industry, the questions of energy availability generally revolve around the question: "For what price?" The myriad of energy sources and technologies offers the science writer the ultimate trade-off equation in sorting out the questions of how much energy, from what sources, at what prices and, in the case of nuclear power, at what ultimate risks. Realistic estimates of comparative energy costs must include the long term cost of storing radioactive waste.

Patents, and the proprietary right to make money off new inventions, are another aspect of business-science reporting. Obtaining information that is considered patentable becomes difficult because premature disclosure can cost an inventor or a company patent rights if patent examiners consider the information, application, or technique common knowledge. Patent information may surface in one or two ways. One is award of a patent, affording the inventor or the owner of the patent commercial rights. Patent stories also may surface in court when ownership of a patent is challenged. One story began about twenty years ago when a former Columbia University graduate sued his Nobelist professor and Bell Telephone

Laboratories over credit for a key concept in the invention of the laser. More than a patent story, this is another aspect of the scientists' continuing battle to establish priority for first discovery. With such widely used devices as lasers or photocopiers, fortunes are at stake. Some of the hardest fought court battles in the future will involve patent rights on biotechnology and genetic engineering processes, part of the open literature of the scientific world. Rights to such processes will be bought and sold between companies.

One of the continuing problems of reporting on business and its involvement with government regulations designed to protect the health and safety of workers and consumers has been reliance of regulators upon industry data. In at least one instance, EPA's scientific credibility in approving pesticides was challenged when it was discovered that EPA scientists were merely taking industry-supplied data for tests on pesticide toxicity and passing them off as independent work. Similar use of oil company data has been found in the Department of Energy. Industry reporting is unlikely to stress "worst case" aspects of a product, and science reporters should ask about the sources of data used in reaching decisions. One way special interests work in the political system is to cripple the effectiveness of an agency by persuading administrators or legislators to keep the numbers of trained personnel below that needed to do a thorough job of regulation and testing.

Trade or industry associations may supply you with data, but you should be advised that these industry-sponsored groups play a role in balking potential regulation. The Lead Industry Association once threatened to sue the U.S. Centers for Disease Control if its scientists did not call off a meeting aimed at telling doctors how to prevent lead poisoning in young children (Marshall 1984a).

Public relations and information specialists

Science writers are employed by business or government as public information officers at research facilities and in advanced-engineering establishments in government, industry, and nonprofit institutions. These science writers and public information specialists probably make up the majority of those who call themselves science writers. There are more men and women working in science public relations and information than are employed as science writers for newspapers, magazines, and radio-television broadcasting. Many worked as media science writers before taking jobs with industry. Often these public relations people are the first contact between journalists and a company, agency, or a scientist. Many of these institutional science writers also communicate directly with nonscientists through their companies' own publications and broadcasts.

"In-house" science writers have as their targets the employees and staff of the institution. Others produce newspapers, newsletters, and magazines for "external" audiences, including customers, stockholders, contributors, public opinion leaders, and the media. Their primary job is explaining the institution and its activities to people who have or can be persuaded to have a direct interest in the organization, including its financial and technological progress. Other public relations people place stories directly with journalists or answer their queries about stories. In a small organization, one person may perform all these tasks.

Shrewd information specialists operate like journalists to build up their own series of contacts and informants, especially inside a large corporation, such as IBM, or a major university. Unlike journalists, who seldom show their copy to their sources, the public relations science writer expects to have his or her sources read the copy for accuracy and the tone or wording. Ideally this increases the level of accuracy, although the science writer may not enjoy quarreling over exact wording with scientists, legal departments, and managers of the institution. Sometimes these battles act to obscure, from the public relations person and from employees and outsiders, facts about the company's operations.

In the normal course of events, companies try to follow the precept that the best public relations is the truth. However, the attachment of public relations personnel to corporate and marketing organizations indicates clearly that their job is to sell products, services, and images. Sometimes companies will attempt to withold information from the public relations department. So public relations science writers will do well to ask as many questions as the journalists about research and development projects. Likely the journalists will ask the same sort of questions, and the public relations office may find it wise to counsel against publicity, or even to counsel that some cleaning up may be in order lest the company or institution find itself in embarrassing circumstances. One of the functions of public relations personnel is to anticipate or predict media reaction to an organization's activities.

Many science journalists indicate they think public relations people have too often sold the media stories that did not represent genuine advances in science or technology. So the mass media journalists are especially sensitive to a barrage of calls, press releases, and other materials touting products that are only marginal improvements over other companies' wares. Writers can achieve a measure of protection against being fooled by asking for the generic or chemical name of any "new" drug and checking this name against chemical reference books for other producers. On occasion, critical stories have been written about news conferences called to trumpet duplicative or questionable research and development.

There are also many steps a public relations science writer can take to assure a good outcome, if internal research indicates a project is worth publicizing. One of these is making up for the deficiencies of the media writers, including providing well researched background information. This information can be provided journalists through press kits given out at the news conference or as supporting infor-

mation attached to a news release. Because the announcements usually come at the convenience of the institution and its public relations office, there should be a sufficient time to insure thorough research and accuracy. In many cases where research or contract work is funded through a government grant or contract, the institution is required by the agreement to check the release and clear any news conferences with the agency paying for the research. In other instances, the contracting agency will make the announcement itself to receive the benefits of publicity.

Not all business announcements are based solely on seeking free advertising through publicity. Securities and Exchange Commission regulations call for companies whose stock is traded on the public exchanges to announce new developments likely to have significant effect on a company's operations, primarily its profits. Canny public relations personnel should also have answers to financial and related questions where these are parts of the announcement. Most company managers prefer to tell as little as possible about hazards, costs, and potential profits. But there are other sources outsiders can use. Journalists may obtain independent estimates from industry analysts at stock brokerages or from competitors. The Securities and Exchange Commission, keeps in-depth information on companies whose stock is traded on the public market. Libraries and business magazines offer other sources of data. More and more journalists check the quarterly and annual company reports and the more detailed financial reports filed with the SEC. Journalists also use the Internal Revenue Service 990 forms to obtain income information about nonprofit research organizations.

Suspicions exist that many dubious scientific and technological achievements announced at industry press conference stem from management's desire to add a little zip to the price of the company stock.

Industry trade journals offer alternative

and informed sources of information for journalists. Such trade journals also are a major outlet for stories about companies and their activities. Some journals operate aggressively and maintain independent sources of information inside companies that make up the industry they cover. Public relations science writers need to become familiar with these alternative information sources to avoid conflicting statements and to protect themselves from situations that can cause a loss of trust by journalists. Companies have been known to sacrifice public relations people by putting them into compromising circumstances. If the public relations person cannot dissuade the company from releasing misleading information, resignation probably is the best course when the public relations officer has given the best possible counsel and had it rejected. Once destroyed, trust among media journalists is difficult to rebuild. Word of ethical performance travels swiftly in the small world of science writers in public relations and the media.

Following all the same verification steps the journalist uses is self-protection for even those who produce internal publications, which occasionally go to journalists and become "news tips" for the mass media. If a company publication carries false or misleading information, it is unlikely the organization will shoulder the blame for any controversy that results, even if it circulated as management policy. On the other hand, public relations science writers have several factors working in their favor. Not many science writers indulge in investigative reporting. Some of the reasons were outlined by Dr. Rae Goodell (1981).

1. Science and scientists intimidate much of the press.
2. Editors and writers lack confidence for science investigations.
3. Science writers know of the science community's sensitivity to criticism and fear losing their sources.
4. Because science writers share scien-

tists' enthusiasm for science and its values, they are easily co-opted.
5. Most science writers lack interest in covering political and economic aspects of science.
6. Both science writers and scientists tend to focus questions on the technically possible rather than what is desirable.
7. Daily newspaper editors misunderstand the nature of science, and withhold time and flexibility for in-depth stories.

If you write for a publicly traded corporation, university, or nonprofit organization, you may attend scientific meetings to widen or maintain your contacts with science journalists. These meetings also offer insights into the workings of competitors. You can expect to pay a registration fee at the meeting, although some information people receive courtesies of the pressroom without charge, as do most journalists. It is bad form to use the occasion for more than discreet promotion of your organization. It is possible, however, to have copies of your scientists' papers placed in the pressroom or to arrange interviews. The managers of the pressroom at a scientific meeting may ask an industry science writer to help corral the company's scientists if they fit the society's press needs, but organizing a separate company press conference breaches protocol. The public relations science writer usually can arrange interviews for individual journalists attending the meeting without infringing on the society's territory.

The industry science writer may also have to deal with a new figure showing up at scientific meetings. This is the securities analyst, who either works independently or for one of the stock brokerage houses. These analysts will be looking for signs of research that can drive company stock up or down. Some financial journalists attend scientific and medical meetings for the same purpose. Often such information will not come from a company report but from a university or government researcher who has tested the product for efficacy or safety. These analysts, who may be former science journalists or public relations people, also attend press conferences to make their assessment of the effect of new products upon a company's fortunes. The independent analysts often publish newsletters with advice to stockholders, increasing the need to prepare for economic questions as well as those dealing with science and technology.

SOME NEW QUESTIONS. Companies making prescription drugs or materials that must be administered by doctors pose some new problems for scientific public relations and marketing practitioners. This is the practice of advertising and promoting brand name drugs, medical devices, and other materials directly to consumers. In the past, doctors were the sole targets of this kind of promotion, on the theory that the doctor alone would choose treatment for a patient. In 1980, however, Collagen Corporation, maker of a material that could be used to smooth scars and fill acne craters, set out through advetisements in women's magazines to encourage people to request the treatment. Some drug manufacturers also sought Food and Drug Administration permission to advertise their prescription products in consumer publications. Robert P. Charrow, law professor at the University of Cincinnati, warned that this increases the exposure of a company to liability lawsuits. When medical products are marketed only to doctors, the legal doctrine of "learned intermediary" requires the manufacturer to warn only the doctors of possibly undesirable side effects or consequences of such treatment (Charrow 1983; "Smooth Selling" 1984). Although this is an issue likely to be decided in the courts, public marketing may require science public relations managers to include similar warnings in all public presentations. Many journalists fault public relations people for being less than candid about risks now associated with new drugs.

Part of the pressure to advertise brand name and patented medications directly to users stems from increasing requests for "generic" drugs. These medicines are sold under their chemical names rather than brand names. Generic medications sell for considerably less than their brand name or "proprietary" counterparts. As long as there are these competing economic pressures, there will be competing claims over whether or not generics are as effective as brand names, even though a consensus of medical authorities accepts the use of generics. The corporate science writer may be pressed to defend the more expensive company product in news and advertising copy without appearing to defy scientific convention, although some scientist, somewhere, can be found to provide research data favoring a brand name product.

Also at issue for both industry and media science writers is the possibility that decisions on scientific developments will tend to concentrate research in the hands of what David Dickson, a science reporter in Washington for *Nature*, calls a "class of corporate, banking and military leaders" without being subject to considerations of the larger democratic process in society (1984). Dickson assumes that university scientists, getting more of their support from industry, will find it harder to maintain independence and open discussion in the face of this political and financial power and the temptations of new fortunes possible in such emerging areas as genetically engineered life forms. A more benign view holds that businesses are buying into university research to learn sooner of new developments, not to control them.

However, debate over the supervision or control of such man-made life forms as bacteria that have been altered to achieve various commercial ends will continue. The National Institutes of Health hold informal approval power over such microbes designed for use in laboratories. But later experiments will require outdoor testing, which environmentalists see as risking the chances of escape from test areas and alterations to the balance of nature. It has occurred with the introduction of other organisms, such as fire ants, into regions where they have no natural enemies.

Risk assessment

Influencing how the media report these and other questions will be an issue for science writers. Expert "help" will be offered in the guise of educating writers and readers in the "proper" way to view technological risk. This poses a problem for all science writers because it touches on withholding information from an audience, on one hand, or perhaps raising unnecessary fears on the other. In addition, the science, art, or technique of estimating risks to society and to individuals is new and highly speculative. The methods and difficulties of predicting such risks merit articles.

Some scientists would, like former astronaut and New Mexico Sen. Harrison H. Schmitt, withold estimates of danger from journalists or ask journalists to censor themselves by not reporting on possible dangers in technology (Schmitt 1984, 17). This is an old request, going at least back to instances when mayors have asked newspapers not to report sharks at beach resorts because it would hurt the tourist business. Cost-benefit or risk-benefit analysis asks society, in a cold-blooded way, to accept a certain number of deaths, for example in airplane crashes, because guaranteeing 100 percent safety from death or injury would make the cost of air travel prohibitive. We live in a statistical world where we take our chances. But journalists have been criticized for alarming readers over technological risks that are far lower than the risk-of-injury in crossing a metropolitan street, driving a car across town, or other common and accepted "risk" situations.

Part of the controversy lies with whether people choose the risks they take, such as driving or smoking cigarettes, or have the risk imposed on them by others. An example of such an imposed risk could be living downwind of a plant where the managers begin production of a chemical suspected of causing disease. An issue in occupational health is whether or not workers in an industry should accept higher exposure to chemical risks because of their job than the general public must accept. Another factor in acceptable risk levels lies in full knowledge of the risk. For example, firemen in the author's hometown were willing to fight a chemical fire at a paint factory — until they learned the building contained nitrocellulose, guncotton, an explosive used in its liquid form as an ingredient in certain paints. Science journalists will have plenty of opportunities to write about this new field of risk assessment as research in it grows over the next several years.

Behind the objections to mass media reporting of risks — even exaggerated and sensationalized — lie economic and professional interests that may find it more difficult to meet their economic goals because of adverse public opinion. The industrial calamity at Bhopal, India, in 1984 increased public demand that companies disclose the presence of all dangerous substances on their premises. An increase in the number of highway and railroad accidents provoked similar pressure in the 1960s and 1970s and forced chemical companies to label tank cars carrying dangerous chemicals. The companies did so reluctantly, just as many resist frank disclosure of on-the-job hazards. However, a National Academy of Sciences committee has held that informing workers about hazards in their workplaces is an ethical action rooted in the benefits to society generally from an individual's right to self-determination.

Sociologist Dorothy Nelkin, a student of science in society and a member of the AAAS board of directors, holds that media access to information about the risks as well as the benefits of technology is central to the existence of an informed citizenry able to engage knowledgeably in political choices. Timely communication of information on risks to the public also has practical importance. Media coverage may exaggerate the problem of risks, but by increasing public awareness, it may also elicit the support that is necessary to bring risks under control. It may force public officials to be accountable to their constituents. And it may help bring critical problems to the public agenda (Nelkin 1984a, 21). Actually, those are the results desired by special interest groups when they solicit media support, often with overblown data, for their side of an issue.

Sources of information

Here are some sources of information that will help you research trans-science subjects. Most can be found in any library, although some are specialized references available at most colleges or universities and many business libraries.

Business: *The Wall Street Journal Index* (companies, general topics), covers 1957 to present. *Business Index* (newspaper business sections from 1979). *Standard and Poor's Corporation Records* (updated annually). *Moody's Industrial Manual* (annual). *The Stock Market Directory*, 1982 (covers 1500 companies). *Directory of Corporate Affiliations* (annual). *America's Corporate Families* (annual). *Standard and Poor's Industry Surveys* (annual), covers 697 industries and leading firms.

Politics: *Congressional Quarterly* (weekly). *National Journal* (weekly). *Public Affairs Information Service* (PAIS), monthly and available through on-line computer service in some libraries.

Medicine and science: *Index Medicus, International Nursing Index, and Index to Dental Literature*, monthly and annual printed cumulation by National Library of Medicine and also on-line computer index MEDLINE. *American Men and Women of Science* (directory).

Computerized data bases: Pharmaceutical News Index (drug industry news). Science Citation Index (life and physical sciences). MEDLINE (medicine, nursing, and dentistry). CENDATA (Bureau of Census demographic data). Access to these may come packaged with subscriptions to many commercial data services.

Call-up services: Scientists Institute for Public Information; 355 Lexington Ave., N.Y., N.Y., 10017; phone: 1-800-223-1730; in New York state call: 212-663-9110.

Experiments

1. Examine the business news section of a metropolitan newspaper. List stories that have a strong science or technology content. What is different from other science stories you have read?

2. Go through an issue of *The Wall Street Journal*. How many stories required explaining some aspect of science or technology?

3. Look at recent copies of *Business Week, The Economist*, or *Forbes* magazines for stories whose economic or business significance rests on science or technology.

4. Search the *Readers' Guide to Periodical Literature*, the *Business Index*, or *The Wall Street Journal Index* for stories indicating lawsuits over product liability.

5. Can you find stories involving business and science-technology in which there are clues that public relations people from government or industry helped get these stories into print?

Chapter 8
Medical and health science news

MOST MEDICAL REPORTING DEALS WITH trans-science news. Nowhere else are threads of scientific enterprise more tangled with economic, political, personality, and social values than in medicine and the related health sciences. Stories of life and death, the survival values, are specific and personal yet also broad and general. Cancer and heart disease, to seize obvious examples, are individualized; we suffer and die one by one. These diseases also claim millions of lives each year in faceless, nameless statistics that brand them the most frequent causes of death. Yet most doctors and dentists earn their positions of respect and their livings through daily care of lesser ailments: fevers, sore throats, broken bones, ailing gums and teeth, hemorrhoids, infections, ulcers, acnes, colds, influenzas, pulled muscles, appendicitis, high blood pressure, etc., etc., etc. Hardly the stuff that makes news. Or does it? Its impact is universal.

Science writers need to understand the culture of health and medicine to write effectively in this area. Important as news sources are in other fields, the cooperation of people in health and medical fields is vital for the writer. This chapter on medical and health science news will help writers avoid some of the pitfalls that may alienate sources and guide writers to some aspects that insiders discuss only reluctantly.

Within the last half of the twentieth century medicine developed from an un-

certain art to something approaching science. This is not to underrate the prior centuries of hard-won medical knowledge before the discovery and production of antibiotics as much as to point out to the science writer how much more, relatively, has been the product of recent decades and how very many unknowns remain. One dreaded disease, smallpox, has been eliminated. Many people survive once-fatal injuries and diseases. Longer life for all of us is but one result of this revolution in effective medical care. Nearly forgotten is the fact that in the early 1900s most men and women died before the age of fifty. Life expectancy exceeds seventy years now. From this one fact branch dozens of changes in society that affect job opportunities, career choices, care of the aged, politics, allocation of resources, leisure activities, and social services.

Health care professions employ millions of people worldwide in what is known as "health care delivery." Supporting them are others manufacturing drugs, medical supplies, and medical devices. Hospitals and clinics by the tens of thousands across the United States give physical, institutional representation to the idea of health care. Such institutions often bestow identity to the towns that harbor them, as does the Mayo Clinic to Rochester, Minnesota, or the Menninger Clinic to Topeka, Kansas.

Medicine is money. Economic impact of the health care industry is pervasive.

During the 1970s and 1980s, the rising cost of medical and health care and drugs led the indices of inflation and presented national economic dilemmas. The national medical bill exceeds $350 billion a year, more than 10 percent of the Gross National Product by estimates of the Department of Health and Human Services. That's nearly $1400 per person. In 1984 the American Medical Association asked their doctor members to stop raising fees for a year. Incomes of many doctors rose to surprising numbers. Some doctors and medical suppliers achieved wealth through boodling among federal, state, and private health care insurance plans. And the perception of doctors as kindly father-figures shifted toward that of elite technocrats, effective but aloof. A minor industry sprang up to show doctors how to manage their lucrative practices, invest their money and engage in political activity, usually in opposition to national health care programs. From a shortage of physicians at midcentury, the United States government and governments in other advanced nations began asking if more than enough doctors had been trained, even though their distribution into metropolitan areas left many rural towns with neither doctors nor hospitals.

Access to first class, comprehensive medical treatment — discussed into the 1960s by the AMA — became an issue of national policy as federal Medicare and Medicaid funds for the aged and indigent were threatened with depletion. Actions of doctors to slow down rising medical costs brought no similar response from hospitals, also leaders in the inflation of the 1970s and 1980s. In fact, hospitals offered so much potential for profit that large companies, such as Humana and the Hospital Corporation of America, were formed for the business of owning and operating hospitals. This reversed a trend of nearly a century in which ownership of hospitals moved from private hands, usually those of a doctor, into those of public, nonprofit, or religious organizations. The remaining publicly owned city and county hospitals were forced into competing for paying or insured patients to help defray the hospital costs of those both ill and poor that they, as public institutions, were obliged to take. Corresponding increases in private medical, dental and health insurance led businesses to resist providing the cost of coverage for their employees and dependents as a fringe benefit. Disturbing questions were raised over whether or not the price of treating illness had moved beyond the means of all but the wealthy?

In the latter part of the century, new forms of health care sprang into general usage, encouraged by economics and public policy. One was the Health Maintenance Organization, pioneered in the 1940s as Kaiser Permanente in California for employees of what was then Kaiser Industries. The HMO aimed at providing prepaid medical care, sometimes in the HMO's own clinic, not just insurance to pay a portion of the hospital and doctor bills if you became ill. In theory, the HMO offered both doctors and members advantages over medical care through independent practice. Another recent development in the United States is the privately owned "minor emergency clinic." Located in neighborhood office buildings or shopping centers, it supplants family doctors, who long ago had dropped house calls, and dwindling numbers of hospital emergency wards. "Day surgery" facilities appeared, also, for patients who needed the protective services of fully equipped operating rooms but only a few hours of postoperative nursing care during recovery. Then it was off to home for them, to recuperate in less expensive beds with the aid of family, friends, or visiting nurses. The 1970s also saw rejuvenated interest in two older medical practices: midwifery and home birth.

Another new development was a wellness movement in which the concept of preventive medicine expanded beyond vaccination against disease and beyond public health legislation aimed at ensuring safe food, water, and medicines. This development found support in the medical community which encouraged people to take more personal responsibility for their own health rather than expecting doctors to restore and repair. Ironically, the movement drew part of its strength from distrust of the existing, science-based health care system. The movement emphasized diet, exercise, clean environment, and for some, an almost-mystical faith in an array of vitamins, "natural" health foods, appliances, and other paraphernalia believed to build fitness and mobilize the body's natural defenses against disease and aging. This is an area of health care often plagued with quackery and misleading claims as charlatans, including some with medical degrees, prey upon the fears of disease victims and their willingness to try almost any avenue to a cure. The meat and dairy industries faced decline as millions of adults switched away from animal and milk products to poultry, fish, and grains.

Media's role in health and medicine

Medicine involves a lot of media use and employs most of the science and medical writers. Hospitals and medical research centers employ writers, editors, photographers, and artists for staff, patient, and medical community communications. Part of the output, especially for photographers and artists, involves documenting surgical procedures and preparing research reports. Some research reports are polished and edited by medical writers and editors from rough accounts prepared by the researchers. Other medical writers, some on staff and some freelance, prepare educational materials for staff, patients, and the public. These include brochures, pamphlets, and scripts for films and tapes. Some science writers serve as educational specialists to translate and amplify medical instructions for patients. A few science writers report encountering public relations counsel hired to promote individual doctors or members of group practices.

Medical institutions also use science writers and editors to develop media press releases, employee publications, magazines, and other materials that inform staff members, community leaders, patients, former patients, and potential donors about the needs and activities of the institution. These writers usually work in the community or public relations departments and write general news and promotional material as well as popularized science and medical articles.

Other science and medical writers produce a large array of medical publications aimed at every segment of the medical community: doctors, nurses, administrators, technicians, manufacturers, and so on. Many of these publications originate with the professional associations for each medical and occupational specialty. Almost every sponsored journal is matched by a commercial publication, such as *Medical World News*, usually privately owned. Both sets of publications rely upon support from advertisers of medical supplies and drugs. Many of the commercial publications are "controlled circulation," sent free to the health practitioners. Writers on these publications will be involved with stories of the science and the politics of science and medicine in the state capitals and in Washington, D.C. Changes in federal programs, appropriations, regulations, and administrators affect members of the professions and their pocketbooks. Almost every branch of the medical and health sciences has legislation before Congress each year. The *Journal of the American Medical Association, Medical Tribune,* and *Medical World News* offer examples of magazines mixing science, medical, political, and professional information in each issue.

Other magazines, such as *Medical Economics* and *Dental Economics*, attract professional readers and advertisers with articles showing the professionals how to manage their offices, their time, and their investments. Because of the high incomes of doctors and medical administrators, magazines have been published to show them how to manage their spare time and recreation, how to have fun. Almost all of these professional publications limit their circulations to licensed or registered members of the profession or a specialty. *RN* aims at registered nurses, for example, while *Today's OR Nurse* slants its material toward operating room nurses. *Hospitals* is for those who manage a variety of health care institutions. As you might imagine, writers for these publications do less translating of technical jargon because they write for professionals who understand the details of their business and demand a high degree of technical and financial accuracy.

Other major employers of science and medical writers and editors include government, at the federal and state levels, and volunteer organizations, such as the American Heart Association or the American Cancer Society, associated with specific diseases. In addition to serving as outlets for science writing, these agencies and associations offer major sources of information for science and medical writers who publish in the mass media. With the medical professions, the medical institutions, and the specialized medical publications, they form the basis for a medical communication system transferring knowledge about health and medicine to the general public.

Medical popularizers also find their outlets in consumer publications of all varieties, including newspapers and magazines. Most of the women's publications carry a regular column of medical news relating to females, the home, or to children. When a newspaper expands its news staff to include science specialists, it usually picks a medical writer first. *American Health* typifies several general audience publications that offer news of developments in medical research, nutrition, clinical medicine, fitness, and other aspects of the "healthy lifestyle." Because of the high popular interest in medicine and in the people who make medicine and develop its research promises into practice, medicine has been a staple of the consumer magazine. This brings both those who write for the medical community and those who write about the medical community into a unique skein of relationships. Understanding this as a communication system will smooth your way through medical writing.

Writers popularizing medicine will bump into the "Ingelfinger Rule," which discourages premature disclosure of research results. Therefore writers may have difficulty persuading some research physicians to talk freely before publication of their research in a journal. Dr. Arnold S. Relman, editor of the *New England Journal of Medicine*, the most stringent enforcer of the rule, has attempted to clarify his policies of refusing to print a story that has received what he considers premature publicity. Dr. Relman counsels medical researchers against giving science writers the actual paper presented at a meeting and supplying too many details, including figures, before the NEJM's peer reviewers have seen the material and NEJM has published the research (1984). The Ingelfinger Rule is discussed further in chapter 9, but one of its effects is to increase the chances for error when you cover medical research meetings unless you can double-check figures in your notes with the scientist.

Working with doctors

As members of one of the oldest and most closely organized professions, doctors move in a sensitive web of relations with patients, other doctors, hospitals, nursing staffs, the law, and the public. The most sensitive area is that of confidence and confidentiality between the doctor and patient. As a writer you may need patient information. But because mistakes in medical information about specific patients falls into the realms of both libel and privacy, reliable information is almost unobtainable without the cooperation of the doctor. Some are more cooperative with journalists than others and will help you obtain patient consent for stories as well as making time for interviewing. Cultivating professional friendship with these doctors pays many dividends. Because the medical community is so close knit, your reputation for accuracy, knowledge, and consideration will spread rapidly. If it is good, you may find an increasing flow of story suggestions coming your way. This can build up your personal list of contacts for information and evaluation of potential stories.

In a news gathering crisis, such as major surgery on a world leader, medical journalists need this network of news contacts to get both specific and general information quickly on surgical procedure, chances of recovery, and so forth.

Because of their often limited time, doctors appreciate the time you spend researching the specific story topic before starting an interview. This research includes broad, medical-encyclopedia reading as well as specific journal articles or case studies. One of the most useful courses a beginning medical writer can take is the medical terminology course available at most campuses for premedical and nursing students. It will be of enormous help in conversing with doctors and in translating medical articles.

Medical doctors write up many reports as case studies, and these lend themselves easily to dramatization and anecdotes. Restraint in such dramatization is a good rule, however, even though many specific clinical details, such as the size of tumors, degree of disfigurement, and loss of blood or body functions, are spelled out in excruciating exactness. Sometimes use of a pseudonym or false name will be in order for a patient because of the nature of the case or the possibility of invading someone's privacy. Such use of a false name should be made very clear to your readers. Although this moves into one of the sensitive ethical areas of journalism, writers use pseudonyms regularly. Identification may be accomplished with only a first name. When a Texas youth called David died in 1984, he had lived twelve years as "the bubble boy" who was born without immunity to disease. He spent his entire life inside rooms draped with plastic sheeting to provide a sterile atmosphere. Science writers entered a conspiracy with doctors, nurses, friends, and David's parents to withhold the family's last name to protect his identity, privacy and his freedom to participate in schooling and other limited contacts with the outside world. In return, the writers got the cooperation of the family in providing access for stories and information about the child as he grew up. A pseudonym does not automatically protect you from libel or invasion of privacy, however. True identity can emerge simply because the case is unique.

In dealing with physicians, medical writers should remember that no one person can "speak for medicine." Opinions are strictly individual in medicine as they are in politics and public policy. A consensus among doctors may develop about accepted medical practice, but individual cases may call for exceptions to generally accepted procedures, and each physician accepts responsibility only for his or her own actions and opinions. Medical actions are subject to review both by the doctor's peers and medical review boards. Such peer review may take place at the local level or at the state level where the state medical association generally takes responsibility for licensing of physicians.

Doctors will tell you about standard procedures, and you can use the *Merck Manual of Diagnosis and Therapy* as a brief guide to these. *Physicians Desk Reference*, commonly referred to as PDR, will disclose many facts about drugs and their effects. Because much of the information in both references comes from drug manufacturers, many science writers seek more information from teachers of medicine and pharmacology. In this context, science writers should always inquire about specific side effects of any drug therapy. No chemical powerful enough to have significant effect in neutralizing a disease or its symptoms will be without some unwanted effects.

Beginning science writers need to be

wary about mistaking treatments aimed at the disease itself and those aimed at alleviating the symptoms. Treatments of the common cold, for example, relieve symptoms but do not attack the viruses that cause them. Only a few medicines, at this stage, affect virus-caused diseases, and they are in limited, experimental use. There is also a respected tradition in medicine that relief of the symptoms, particularly life-threatening symptoms, of an untreatable disease may give the body time to heal itself or for the disease to run its course, as happens with the cold.

Science writers also should moderate their enthusiasms for new treatments and new drugs when discussing them with doctors. Stories in popular media about new procedures are one of the frequently cited aggravations to practicing physicians and researchers. Such stories can be embarrassing if the doctor has not yet heard of the procedure. More importantly, doctors fear they may raise false hopes in patients for whom a new treatment or drug is unsuited or offers no better prognosis (a medical term for forecasting the likely outcome) than other treatments. With some exceptions, and sometimes tragic results, physicians are very conservative about adopting new treatments.

Doctors and hospitals

Almost as sensitive as the doctor-patient relationship is the doctor-hospital relationship. Hospitals are very politicized places with strict "pecking orders" and complicated power relationships between physicians, administrative staff, registered nurses, vocational nurses, technicians, secretaries, and volunteers. Doctors, almost without exception, need formal approval at each hospital where they practice to care for patients they order into hospital. Permission can be revoked. Doctors' patient records, particularly those of surgeons, are reviewed regularly against expected performance in that particular hospital and records for all cases of a specific disease. Some hospitals are more strict than others. One hospital took

years to acknowledge and remove a heart surgeon who was legally blind in one eye. However, the necessity of doctors to practice in a hospital redounds to the benefit of the medical writer, particularly one beginning a career. The need of the hospitals for publicity helps secure cooperation from doctors on occasion.

All hospitals need to encourage community confidence in them, and seek to do it through publicity about their successes, equipment, facilities, people, services, and patients. Most hospitals have someone who promotes the hospital's cause, and in the smallest hospitals that person may be the hospital's chief administrator or board chairman. Others have professional public or community relations staffers. Those in charge of public relations can help arrange news or feature coverage. When doctors, patients, and hospital staff agree that the story will help all of them, story arrangements offer few problems. But there are many stories to be told. The hospital administrator will have a point of view different from the medical staff. This involves mutual manipulation by press and source, or course, but all parties enter this with their eyes open. Other help in arranging stories can come from officers and public relations people for associations that provide money to fight specific diseases, especially near the time for the annual fund-raising drive. Because competent hospital and association officials are inside the medical community, they often are privy to evaluations about the organization and its various members. They can, if the science writer is alert to what they say, steer you away from trivial stories and from the occasional doctor or administrator seeking personal publicity from very thin material.

Hospitals themselves are legitimate story subjects. Each has its own personality and politics and style. You probably should risk losing some of your accumulated good will and inquire about such statistics as the mortality rates and staphylococcus infection rates of patients inside the hospitals themselves. There are a couple of the guideposts for estimating quality of care. Comparing prices for rooms and other services among local and regional hospitals produces well-read stories. More records will be available, of course, at public hospitals, but any hospital accepting patients for tax-assisted Medicare and Medicaid file public financial reports with the agencies that pay the bills. Blue Cross also makes available analyses of charges. Such records allow you to compare costs between profit-making and nonprofit hospitals in your area. In some instances, these costs may be 25 percent or more higher for patients at commercial hospitals.

A medical reporter needs familiarity with the various hospital "codes" or policies governing the release of public information about patients. The medical reporter can expect to be used frequently by news editors to support general reporters in gathering information about those injured in accidents and disasters. Good personal relationships with the medical, nursing, and administrative staffs of local hospitals will help speed this process. Such contacts cannot be developed in a crisis; they are the subject of ongoing TLC by the reporter so that they can be used in emergencies.

**Doctors among doctors
and others**

Physicians make up one of the more complex subsets of the medical community. THey are gossiped about, watched, enticed, envied, admired, and so on through the whole range of emotions. They practice solo and in groups, subjects that can make fascinating reading for an audience dependent upon them for life itself. Jealousy may run high in the medical community, and some city or county medical societies may still have strict rules regarding self-promotion at the expense of other doctors, although these strictures have eased. In earlier years, physicians like lawyers were forbidden to advertise excpt through telephone listings and an office sign. Some local medical

societies prohibited listing of specialties. In some towns, the president of the medical society may be the only one permitted to speak on medical subjects.

Doctors run grave risks of drug abuse, alcoholism, and other perils of high-stress occupations, as does the entire medical community. Regularly medical societies and hospitals find impersonators among community physicians. The disposable incomes of doctors, well over $80,000 on the average, according to *Medical Economics* surveys. Neurologists take home more than $90,000. Incomes like this makes doctors attractive markets for advertisers and for confidence schemes. Jealousies exist between the specialties and between branches of the healing arts, as in the ongoing competition between osteopaths and medical doctors and chiropractors.

Doctors regulate their own professions, although licensing is done through state governments in most cases. Most doctors find it politic, though not mandatory, to belong to the American Medical Association. Each state has its own medical association, with varying amounts of control over doctors practicing under its aegis. Abuses of this self-policing system in favor or against individual physicians surface regularly. Associations of physicians are among the most powerful collectors of campaign money for political action committees of various sorts. Profiles of these organizations and their operation offer writers an opportunity to explain important segments of our society to readers. Election of doctors to head city, county, or state medical associations affords you the chance to profile these medical leaders because of their offices. Other doctors will enter the public eye through politics, business, and sometimes crime. Court records and trials — including malpractice trials — often give the medical journalist a different look at the practice of medicine in the community. Because of the potential of damaging the reputations of people to whom reputation is a chief professional attribute, no warning should be necessary about strict adherence to the highest standards of accuracy and fairness when dealing with the medical community.

Medicine and the law

Your state medical association probably offers the best route to locating digests of the laws governing the practice of medicine in your state. Going through these laws may suggest stories worth developing. Some states have found it necessary to monitor the way doctors prescribe narcotics in an effort to control drug abuse in the state. States vary, also, in the way they permit delivery of medical care to the indigent and to the incarcerated. Reporting on how these health care delivery subsystems operate offers readers more knowledge of their community in dramatic settings.

State and federal laws govern the release of medical information about individuals. According to studies by Alan F. Westin and M.A. Baker (1972), computerized record systems allow illegal access to personal data whose protection is one of the physician's most sacred obligations. This is less the fault of individual physicians than of hospitals, clinics, and insurance companies. Insurance companies pool information from health claims, and the releases that patients must sign to get insurance payments allow the swapping of individual data. Copies of medical histories sometimes show up in the hands of credit bureaus and employers. Computerization also allows almost anyone who knows the access codes to make and sell unauthorized copies of medical records from hospitals. The protection of such records in your state is a story topic of high interest.

Malpractice lawsuits alleging wrongful death or injury as the result of a doctor's mistake offer another area worth exploring for medical writers. Insurance against malpractice claims costs the medical profession more than a billion dollars a year, by some estimates. Medical research and new techniques for determining the con-

dition of babies in the womb have spawned new legal questions for doctors and judges. There are also the questions of "wrongful birth" and "wrongful life" for children with severe birth defects that may be traced to medical practice. Periodically settlements of such claims drive insurance premiums to levels that cause doctors to announce they will no longer deliver babies.

The law raises other disturbing questions. The Washington state supreme court ruled in 1984, for example, that two retarded children should not have been born. This decision places doctors in the position of playing God, physicians say. Similar cases have arisen in New Jersey and California. More undoubtedly will arrive as genetic screening for potential birth defects becomes more widely used. Wrongful birth suits may arise also from births after sterilization operations. Because infants can become plaintiffs through their parents, they are, legally, protesting their own birth. Such cases will add to the ethical, moral, and political conflict that already revolves around abortion.

Literal life and death questions involve laws and policies regulating when people are legally dead, since heart-lung machines and other devices can sustain physical life long after heart and brain activity ceases to register on monitoring instruments. Science writers will get involved in stories over whether or not people can choose to die, requesting that life-prolonging treatment stop for reasons of cost and the quality of their remaining life. Such choices, often forced on grieving relatives, are among the issues medical writers can illuminate.

Medicine and public policy

Science and medical writers will report on medicine as public policy at several levels. The U.S. Department of Health and Human Services controls much of the federal money and policy, although in the United States public health is decentralized.

Each city or county of any size will have its public health officer, usually a physician working full or part-time to oversee and enforce laws and policies affecting all residents. Chlorination and fluoridation of water is an example of a public health policy. Local public health officers may also oversee and operate public health clinics, well-baby programs, and other medical service projects. The numbers and mix of services vary from state to state and are very sensitive to local political climate. Inspections of public eating places may be run from such an office. In cases of epidemics of influenza or more serious diseases, the public health officer may have authority to close schools and public gathering places. Much of the office's function is educational. For science and medical writers this office often proves an uncertain news source. Much depends on the political vigor of the person who holds the position. Some officers have been known to underplay the existence of health problems to avoid local political disputes.

Because counties are creatures of the state, the public health officer may also answer to the director of the state department of public health. Florida's state health department first spotted the high levels of the pesticide ethylene dibromide (EDB) in packaged cake and other bakery mixes and banned their sale. New York and California have strong state health departments. In other states, public health officers may not have the legal power to take such actions. Public health officials live in a state of tension with private physicians and local hospitals because they practice medicine on a large scale and because they work as employees of government rather than as private practitioners. Because they are public officials, doctors in public health need not be quite as reticent in talking with journalists as other physicians. However local politics makes some very timid.

State health departments are good news sources for science writers. These departments provide testing activities and data gathering on a statewide or nationwide scale. Figures on the incidence of diseases are compiled here from data sent by doctors and hospitals; often first warnings of increases in illnesses surface here. Western states, for example, issue warnings about rabid animals and bubonic plague through state health officials. Some states arrange supervision of hospitals and nursing homes through the state health officer as well as the organization of large-scale public health programs. Statistics gathered here provide the science writer useful background information for stories on almost any medical problem.

All phases of public health focus on the federal Office of the Surgeon General in the Department of Health and Human Services, which provides much of the financing for state programs. Statistics and analyses flow from the local and state levels to the Centers for Disease Control in Atlanta. CDC doctors and technicians are the epidemiology shock troops sent into areas of public health crises, such as outbreaks of encephalitis and meningitis, to find sources and causes and to suggest remedies to local health officers if needed. They deal with disease on a large scale, and take seriously their responsibility as public spokesmen in critical health situations. Often these federal health officers will be more candid with journalists than local health officials.

Medical research policy

Medical research receives its major funding through a branch of the Department of Health and Human Services, the National Institutes of Health. The NIH is located in the Washington suburb of Bethesda, Maryland, along with a gaggle of other federal health organizations. NIH provides more than $4 billion a year for basic and applied health research. This money is spent in its own research centers or as grants to research scientists (who may or may not be physicians) in universities, hospitals, and independent research institutions.

Founded after World War II to fund basic biomedical research, the NIH has been unable to resist political efforts to divide its funds among subinstitutes focused on one or more diseases. Driving this atomization are the national volunteer organizations who wield political clout through Congress and the subcommittees overseeing the NIH budget. This division of resources has become known as the "disease of the month" syndrome among science writers. Actually, there were in 1984 only eleven separate institutes. However, the lobbying efforts of the Arthritis Foundation (thirty-six million sufferers estimated in the United States) appeared certain to produce the twelfth — The National Institute for Arthritis and Musculoskeletal Diseases. The older institutes are National Cancer Institute; Heart, Lung and Blood Institute; Dental Institute; Arthritis, Diabetes and Digestive and Kidney Diseases; Neurological and Communicative Disorders and Stroke; Allergy and Infectious Diseases; General Medical Sciences; Child Health and Human Development; Eye; Environmental Health Sciences; and Aging.

At issue is whether or not research, training, and equipment money dispensed through the Congress to each institute's budget dilutes basic research that could be used to attack more than one disease. Each institute, however, has a powerful clientele of voluntary health organizations in the home districts of each U.S. representative and senator. These organizations are capable of exerting large and emotional forces on elected officials. There is, of course, competition for money between basic research scientists and doctors and those researching in a disease-specific field.

For the popular science and medical writer, each institute is an information source. Each has its own public information staff, coordinated through the office of the overall NIH directorate. For the medical press, every move in the NIH system is an important story. The institutes can provide lists of their grant recipients and background information on the status of research in their various fields. The institutes also can arrange interviews with experts in their specialties. The NIH operates the U.S. Library of Medicine and computerized data bases such as MEDLINE and *Index Medicus* for full-scale literature research by medical personnel and medical writers.

Drugs and medicine

Another major news source in health research and applications is the Food and Drug Administration. The FDA also has ties to state health departments, but its major impact comes through its direct licensing of new prescription drugs and most medical devices for use in the United States. Through its Bureau of Biologics, the Food and Drug Administration also licenses, conserves, and encourages the production of vaccines against a host of diseases. As preventive medicine, vaccination is now less in favor because antibacterial drugs, such as the sulfas, penicillins, and tetracyclines effectively cure most diseases at less expense and trouble. But because antibiotics work only on bacterial infections, vaccination before infection is the most effective strategy for dealing with viral diseases. Confusing the effectiveness of antibiotics against bacterial diseases with possible treatment of viral infections is one of the pitfalls for the beginning science writer. Many viral diseases have no matching vaccine. In fact, effective medicines for rare diseases may not be produced because their development and production are unprofitable. For some of these conditions, the FDA runs an "orphan drug" research and development fund.

The concept of mass vaccinations against disease received a setback in 1976 as health officials perceived a threat of deadly swine flu sweeping the United States. A vaccine was rushed into production and administration. But a potential for the act of vaccination to produce a disabling condition known as Guillain-Barre syndrome was revealed. Analysts of science reporting often cite news coverage of the swine flu vaccination program as an example of government manipulating the media into support of a premature mass innoculation program only to see the media turn opinion against the project because doctors and public health officers did not warn against the risks to sensitive individuals.

A fallout from this discovery has been a reluctance of many parents to give diphtheria-pertussis-tetanus (DPT) vaccinations to children. While the chances of a fatal vaccine reaction are far less than the risk of death from any one of the diseases, the uncertainties of the decision paralyze a large number of parents. An additional issue lies with the reluctance of vaccine makers to follow in the paths of those medical pioneers who discovered innoculation against disease. Where vaccines were blamed for injury, huge legal judgments made vaccine makers rethink the profitability of vaccine production.

Drugs and safety

Drugs, almost by definition, are poisons. Among the truisms of medical practice is "giving something" to a patient brings results. Sometimes that "something" is a placebo, a sugar pill with no demonstrated curative potential that, nevertheless, seems to help the patient. Why doctors and researchers think it often works is a story worth developing. Investigation will take you into one of the nearly mystical areas of medical philosophy in which doctors invoke the marvelous powers of the body to heal itself. But humans have a fascination with drug taking as do most physicians. The drug industry is founded upon this search for a "silver bullet" that, in the mythology of pharmacology, magically shoots down specific diseases. Until recently most drugs were derived from plants either directly or through identification of the effective chemicals that could in turn be manufactured. These plant chemicals are the basis of useful folk medicines. Now chemistry linked with computers promises the ability to design chemical molecules that meet the specifications for combating disease.

The FDA's Bureau of Drugs, in theory, monitors drug safety. In fact it looks at data from a series of laboratory tests, animal tests, small-scale human tests, and large-scale "clinical" field trials. This data is supplied, in the main, by the drug manufacturer. These prelicensing tests may cost a drug maker millions of dollars, incentive enough to get new drugs and medical devices onto the market. Sometimes the FDA contracts for independent tests to check the manufacturer's data or to explore where the maker did not go. Until the first drug safety laws in 1938, drug makers could market anything. The government had to prove it was dangerous to get a suspect drug removed. Laws since then make the manufacturer prove safety and effectiveness before approval. The FDA monitors the data and analyzes the research design to see if the trials will yield the right data.

The 1938 law grew out of tragedy. Sulfanilamide, the first wonder drug, required large doses, pills too big for children to swallow easily. Because sulfanilamide would not dissolve in water or alcohol, the most common medical solvents, the companies began selling an elixir (liquid) of sulfa mixed with diethylene glycol, better known as antifreeze. About one hundred people, mostly children, died from kidney destruction that could have been detected, and later was, through animal tests. That incident produced both the law requiring demonstration of safety before marketing and the medical subculture of industries devoted to drug testing and rat breeding. Suspicion abounds that some testing is manipulated to produce results favoring the manufacturer. Maintaining quality control of testing and test management remains a constant concern at all laboratories.

The record of the FDA and the drug industry is mixed, at best. So the medical reporter should not be surprised to see drugs removed after being placed on the market. All government agencies receive criticism for relying too much on industry-supplied data. With millions invested in developing and testing, pressure builds on drug company managers to begin selling the product and recovering their costs. Government and industry investment in the drug interferon, which seemed to promise immunity against a broad spectrum of viruses, has been estimated at $500 million without any useful product. If the FDA finds companies submitting false test data, it can take legal action. However, the potential for earning billions through sales may justify the risks, in the eyes of the drug company. Fines are commonly accepted as part of the cost of doing business.

Testimony reported when a drug's victims take a company to court indicate that manufacturers may routinely accept the possibility of a certain number of deaths (another example of risk imposed on consumers by outside agents). Medical journalists may well add to their repertoire of questions some about the expected number of deaths predicted for any new drug. What number is acceptable? An arthritis drug was linked to twenty-nine deaths in Europe when Britain's Committee on the Safety of Medicines banned it. Testimony taken when survivors of an American who took the drug sued the maker indicated the manufacturer's research director considered this not unexpected. Few, if any, drug companies have gone out of business for making bad medicine.

The classic story of prevention in drug marketing lies in the thalidomide case. Dr. Frances D. Kelsey of the FDA received the government's highest civilian award for her action in blocking its sale in this country. Because some reports on the tranquilizer mentioned instances of peripheral neuritis, a numbness in fingers and other extremities, she held up approval under tremendous pressure from the drug's maker and distributors. As she waited, European doctors began reporting thousands of children born without limbs, along with other defects, or with flippers instead of arms after their mothers took the drug during pregnancy. The case had two effects, one journalistic. The FDA began requiring testing for potential birth defects. The other effect was to prod the *London Times* into nearly open defiance of Britain's press laws against printing pre-trial stories about a case in court. The newspaper's staff risked censure after finding that the British manufacturer was using very tough tactics in negotiating settlements with parents of the children deformed by thalidomide.

Writing about testing

As a result of this incident in the 1960s, which has not been completely settled, drug companies faced longer and more complicated tests and a reduced pace of new drug introductions. Many new drugs will be coming onto the market between now and the end of the century. Some, like the arthritis drug, will be withdrawn for cause. Science journalists can expect, also, to write about charges of the manufacturers covering up deaths from some drugs. There also will be complaints that the companies are overregulated as manufacturers push for easier testing and faster marketing. Most science writers accept such testing at face value, seldom inquiring deeply into the methods and techniques. Among the most meaningful tests for efficacy or effectiveness are variations of the "double-blind" test. One part of a test group gets the product; the other part, the control group, does not. When the test is managed by a neutral third party, even the experimenter does not know which members of the group get the drug being tested. This minimizes placebo effects, where people show improvement simply because they think they are getting the medicine or because someone is paying attention to them.

Journalists should accept as valid no test without a control group unless the researcher offers acceptable reasons for not using a control. Some conditions are so rare that assembling two groups to test may be impossible. Medical statisticians work with small-group numbers, with acknowledged limits of validity, for this reason. Ethical questions surrounding giving medical treatment to some and withholding it from others may sometimes call for sacrificing test validity. As a gauge for how far a test may deviate from acceptable minimums, some experimenters believe that no test with fewer than one hundred samples from one hundred subjects will suffice. Clinical or field testing of food, drug, and medical products will involve thousands of people. Quite often these tests may be conducted in foreign countries where drug regulations are much more relaxed. Science writers should seek details on how tests are conducted.

Animal tests precede and sometimes replace human tests. You don't deliberately give humans a cancer, for example, to see if you can cure it. Also animals can go through several birth-death cycles to approximate human cycles that would outlast the experimenters. Extrapolating from animal tests is never exact. This is the first counterattack launched when a commercial product manufacturer is wounded by test results. The other counterclaim is that force-feeding extremely large amounts of a product, a food additive, for example, gives false readings. This position contains both truth and misleading hyperbole.

Depending on the animals chosen for the tests, substances that disrupt human systems — as indicated by the early animal tests on sulfa drugs — will tend to disrupt similar animal systems. Much of the confidence in animal testing has developed through backtesting chemicals that were first suspected as the source of human illnesses. Backtesting involves giving animals substances linked to human diseases and seeing if similar conditions result. Researchers also examine animal data retrospectively when unexpected reactions to drugs appear. Conventional logic boggles at the idea that feeding animals unrealistically large doses of a substance, an artificial sweetener for example, proves that the substance causes cancer in humans. The attack goes, "Why

you would have to drink fifty barrels of soft drink to get that much."

That is true, as far as it goes. Cancer, as an example, is a disease that develops slowly over a long time and at unpredictable rates. The simplified philosophy underlying such animal tests holds that if some animals get cancer or another disease with short-term force-feedings, predictable numbers of subjects, including humans, will develop similar cancers over a longer period with lower dosages. And in fifty years, you might well be exposed to the equivalent of several barrels of a substance. This does not mean that you, individually, will or will not be a victim. As an individual, you may not be susceptible, just as some heavy smokers do not develop lung cancer. But this is one way of developing some concept of the increased "risk factors" when large numbers of people or animals are exposed to the suspect chemical. When compared with the known incidence of a general population or a control group contracting a disease, researchers may find the numbers indicating a risk factor of 1.3 or 1.5 for animals receiving the substance. This means a 30 percent or 50 percent greater chance of contracting the disease through exposure to the substance being tested. Scientists will feel more comfortable with science writers who approach the reporting of risks cautiously, carefully.

Ask scientists for more details on such risk factors. It will help increase credibility of your stories. It may be good practice to seek details on the experimental model used since one particular test scheme may yield a lower or higher disease rate than other models for the same disease test. Part of the validation of the connection between cancer and smoking, posed more than twenty years ago in the first U.S. surgeon general's report, for example, is being played out in the increasing rate of lung cancer among women, more of whom smoke than when the report first appeared. However, these and related studies show "association," not clear-cut cause and effect, so there will always be plenty of room for specialists to argue about the quality of both the experiment and data interpretation. Consensus and acceptance by the medical community of such results should be probed by the reporter.

All of the suggestions on how to monitor "good" science apply to medicine. The science writer should invest in any of several good medical dictionaries and in one or more laymen's books on medical care. Obviously they are no substitute for organized courses in physiology or medicine, but you are not a doctor and will not be making diagnoses. You only write about disease. You are seeking to communicate as accurately as possible what medical authority tells you. Formal courses will help your understanding if you have the opportunity and time to take them. Public health and hospital management courses are common in many colleges. Medical writers are always in a learning process.

Almost everyone is familiar with journalistic accounts of various diseases, either dramatized and focused on a single victim or summarized. Possibly it is the medical story most often written and broadcast in the mass media. Some research indicates that these are not the stories that most interest readers. Stories about specific health problems and diseases may have little impact on individual readers, concluded Hugh M. Culbertson and Guido H. Stempel III (1984) after surveying readers of a group of Midwest newspapers. Medical costs and insurance matters occupied the attention of 74 percent of those surveyed, but only 12 percent of newspaper mentions. This concern with the economic aspects of medicine ran ten times higher than other health-related interests.

Experiments

1. Look through one or more medical journals for a case study report and turn it into a popularized science story.

2. Visit the laboratories of a city or county health officer and gather material for a story about what goes on there. Arrange to interview the person in charge of the office on its operations in your city.

3. Arrange, if you can, to have the president or executive director of the city, county, or state medical society visit the class and talk about both media coverage of medicine in your area and the most pressing medical problems including economics.

4. Select one or more local or area hospitals and gather material for a profile about the hospital, the services it offers, how it operates, its specialties, patient costs, its problems, and so forth. Gather samples of internal newsletters, bulletin board memos, press releases, and external magazines that would help you document your story. Tell what emergency room services are available.

5. Obtain statistics from your local public health officer that show medical conditions in your city. How many doctors do you have in relation to the overall population? Is this higher or lower than the state or national average?

6. Spend a day or night as a participant observer, if you can obtain permission, with a hospital emergency room staff, an emergency medical service crew, a minor emergency clinic, or a public health clinic.

Chapter 9
Controls on science news

MANY FORMAL AND INFORMAL CONTROLS surround the communication of information about science, medicine, engineering, and technology. Although some are common to all journalism, these controls and their application vary with country, subject, time, and occasion. It is important to understand the nature of these controls because they may delay gathering or publishing information at times when you can least afford delay. Knowing they exist, you may anticipate and thereby avoid situations that provoke confrontation and delay.

Some controls are unique to science and technology as a culture and as a business. Other controls, such as the laws of libel and invasion of privacy, affect all journalists but have special meanings when you deal with scientists, doctors, and engineers or with their work. Other controls, primarily those of outright censorship in the name of national security, have sharper teeth for both journalists and scientists.

Conventions of science

We talked earlier about the principle that data becomes "science" only after review by a scientist's peers and publication in a refereed journal. Thus you may encounter resistance to any detailed discussion of a scientist's most current research work. This is one example of how science writing can be controlled by the professional and ethical codes of another group. One of the most aggravating quarrels for

science writers has been such a dispute with Dr. Arnold S. Relman, editor of the New England Journal of Medicine. Under Dr. Franz Ingelfinger, Dr. Relman's predecessor at the NEJM, the journal established a policy that no research work that had been discussed extensively in the press or medical trade journals would be accepted for publication in the NEJM. This decision contributed the term "Ingelfinger Rule" to science writing. Few other journals follow this practice so rigidly. Part of submitting an article to NEJM is agreeing to minimum publicity while it is under review or in press. While Dr. Relman (1979) has said he has no objection to news reports of presentations at scientific meetings, he discourages granting interviews afterward, turning over copies of the paper to the press, or providing copies of slides and charts, since these may appear in NEJM. Such a chart precipitated a confrontation between science writer John Elliott of the Journal of the American Medical Association, and Dr. Relman and Dr. Sander Shapiro, one of two University of Wisconsin authors of a research paper given at a meeting of the American Fertility Society (Elliott 1979).

The Ingelfinger Rule is opposed by two groups of medical and science writers. Newspaper journalists maintain that NEJM policies can bottle up information doctors need immediately. If such information appears first in a paper given at an open scientific or medical meeting, doctors who did not attend could be alerted by news reports. The other opposing group includes writers and editors of commercial medical and health magazines, some popular and some aimed solely at physicians. While the general audience writers see their role as alerting the public, the doctors' magazines aim at telling physicians as much usable information as time and space permit. These commercial medical publications are in direct economic competition with the NEJM, although the altruism of both groups is tempered by self-interest in getting information to their audiences first.

Physicians, Dr. Relman holds, have the right to read of new developments first in the professional literature; and science writers should attend meetings for background information only, since much work presented at meetings is incomplete and unreviewed and may never be published. He also points out that NEJM needs fresh, original, and unpublished material to maintain its status. Although the focus of the debate is on material presented at scientific meetings, Dr. Relman has also told reporters the policy aims at curtailing the release of any unverified information, such as claims for cancer cures that raise false hopes (McDonald 1983).

Relman's arguments have been offset by counterarguments from other journal editors. Dr. William Barclay, editor of the *Journal of the American Medical Association*, says doctors do not treat patients on the basis of what they read in the popular press. Dr. Edward Huth, editor of *Annals of Internal Medicine*, says he relies on mass media and medical press to alert him to new developments. Dr. Michael Gregg, editor of *Morbidity and Mortality Weekly Report*, published by the Centers for Disease Control, says such a policy can inhibit a scientist from reporting promptly critical information bearing on public health. Mark Bloom, science writer for *American Health* and one of the rule's strongest critics, has presented evidence that the policy does not have support from British and Canadian journal editors ("Bloom vs. Relman," 1982).

The rigidities of the scientific information system may have delayed for several years the public and medical recognition that children were vulnerable to the acquired immune deficiency syndrome, AIDS. Dr. Larry Bernstein of Albert Einstein College of Medicine told science writer Rita Rubin (1985) that in 1981 he and other doctors tried to persuade editors of the journal of the American Academy of Pediatrics that since 1978 they had been seeing two or three more children each week with AIDS symptoms. Journal editors rejected the doctors' proposed report warning of AIDS and pre-AIDS in children. At that early stage in AIDS research, the disease was believed limited to adult homosexual men. Thus it was nearly five more years before the wider dangers of AIDS infection became known. William Stockton, former director of science news at *The New York Times*, has threatened to use the Freedom of Information Act to obtain information where the research is financed with tax money. "I am a journalist first and a science writer second," he told one group of science writers, saying that the job of the press is to inform the public, not educate it. Stockton said he had submitted one such a request for information held by *The Journal of Infectious Diseases*. However the requested article appeared in an issue distributed shortly after the FOI request was filed, and Stockton did not pursue the matter (Frenkel 1981).

Freedom of information

Although the Freedom of Information Act has been used to obtain scientific data, the efforts were not by journalists but by businesses. Jerry E. Bishop, science writer for *The Wall Street Journal*, holds the position that only when the research funds come totally from private sources do scientists have the right to decide when and where information is to be released. Says Bishop, "A paramount obligation of anyone who accepts public funds is public disclosure of how and where those funds are used. This disclosure can't be made whenever the recipient decides to make it. It must be made on demand" (1982,2).

Such a position has not received judicial support. The U.S. Supreme Court on March 3, 1980, ruled that a private group or individual working with federal funds could withhold information that had not been turned over to a government agency. The court held that Congress does not make a person an "agent" of the government by giving research funds. Earlier the court had said that data could not be forced from a private group for benefit of another group's financial gain (*Forsham v. Califano* 1980, 1978; *Ciba-Geigy v. Mathews* 1977; *Washington Research Project v. Dept. of Health, Education and Welfare* 1974).

One of the scientists' fears about using FOI and state open records laws deals with disclosing the names of patients or research subjects if raw data can be obtained. The holding of the courts leads scientists now to submit summaries of data to their agency sponsors since only material actually in the hands of federal agencies can be forced into disclosure. Before the Supreme Court ruling, a United Press International reporter did get data from the National Institute of Neurological and Communicative Disorders and Stroke before publication. The scientist was criticized publicly for releasing the data prematurely, when in effect it was forced out under protest from NINCDS, reported Dr. Donald B. Tower, head of the institute. Inaccuracies in the story caused baseless fears and anxieties about the effects of anesthetics on babies during birth, Dr. Tower told science writers (1979). Dr. Tower's complaint was echoed by Morton H. Alper, M.D., anesthesiologist-in-chief for the Boston Hospital for Women.

When forcing out information under the FOI or open records acts, science writers perhaps should consider a two-phase judgment. First, is the information worth having after you get it? Second, if this is raw data, can you get it interpreted

expertly? Then comes the decision on whether to print a story or not. In the NINCDS case or cases of incomplete research (which could block completion of a program), contacting the researchers as well as looking at their data might have avoided raising unwarranted fears about the dangers of anesthetics, of which there are several. Although all experimentation with human subjects requires a signed "informed consent" release that supposedly explains the project, some research may be biased by full or erroneous publicity about its purpose. On the other hand, a story that pushes readers to query their doctors more closely about medical procedures is hardly an imposition on the physician.

Reports and program recommendations in such applied science areas as defense, space exploration, transportation, and occupational health may be bottled up to hide embarrassing evaluations of the agency. National security often is given as the reason for secrecy. Where only agency efficiency, spending, or other decisions come into question, the need to inform readers about the official activity seems overriding. The application of judgment to the story remains in the hands of the science writer, but full disclosure of any phase of government activity seems more desirable than secrecy. That philosophy is not universally shared.

Copyright and trademark

Science writers can run into legal problems in two other areas. *Science* magazine won a judgment against *Science Digest* in 1980 because the cover and logo of a redesigned *Science Digest* emphasized the word "Science." While the court did not say the infringement was deliberate, it ruled that "Digest" was not equally displayed. Few science writers start magazines, but if you design column headings or newsletters (or magazines), know that publishers of established publications will fight hard to defend their property rights. Almost every writer has received a note from one or another company complaining about the use of a trademark name without capitalization and credit.

Because so much emphasis is put on basing science and medical stories on published journal articles or on papers delivered at meetings, risk of copyright infringement is very real. Facts are not protected by copyright, although it is only fair to credit scientists and journals in every story using their data. Such credit need not be so elaborate as to spoil your story. And if the journal has published an erroneous piece of research, its editor can share part of the blame with you.

Copyright infringement and plagarism involve using an author's exact words as published. There are no firm guidelines on how much you can republish from a journal or a paper prepared for a meeting, which is protected automatically as a creative work, as is a science writer's manuscript. A few quotes extracted from a paper or journal article, with credit, probably will not draw criticism or worse, a lawsuit. However, to print all or most of a paper as if it were written for your publication moves toward a clear violation of both the spirit and the letter of the copyright law. A paper printed in multiple copies and distributed at a meeting may be considered "published" in a limited sense, but ownership of the copyright remains with the author until he or she signs a legal form transferring ownership. If you want to publish an especially good, readable paper, you and your publication's editor should secure written permission and offer payment to the scientist. This is done regularly on technical publications, since ideas gain authority under the byline of the scientist. But your editors should treat the scientist-author fairly.

Administrative controls

A variety of administrative controls or mishaps can interfere with your work. Some are deliberate and some are accidental. Patrick Young, science writer for Newhouse News Service, discovered that government information people some-

times become competitors. He attempted to get what he thought was a more or less routine story on an eye research project funded by the NIH. The physician insisted on coordination through the NIH information office, which dragged its feet on answering Young's questions. When Young questioned the legality of withholding information, he found that NIH had its own press release moving through the clearance process inside NIH. Young broke his story loose from NIH's top communication office on grounds that media questions should be answered first, even if a formal press release is in process (1981).

This brings up a dysfunction in the information process. Stories sometimes get lost when one newspaper or station breaks a story. Because this is seemingly an exclusive of a competitor, other media may ignore the story unless it is a very big story indeed. This results in useful information failing to get into general circulation. Alert information officers often stage a press conference with the scientist or arrange some other media event to give a fresh angle to the story for writers who were scooped.

One way of evading a bureaucratic or administrative roadblock is to find how far up the agency's hierarchy the support goes. Frequently a lower-level employee misunderstands policy or the strength of his or her support for an action. Moving the question higher up the ladder may open negotiations that produce better understanding on the part of all persons as to what policy really is. Sometimes information people are merely timid about approaching a scientist for an interview, and sometimes they are told to stall a journalist. Some scientist-administrators will use someone else, if they can, to avoid discussing sensitive topics. Try calling the person directly if you are told he or she is "too busy to see you." Another ploy is to talk to the administrator's assistant or go to a superior. But try negotiation or other tactics before using the heavy artillery of an FOI request. This is faster and less damaging to relations inside a bureaucracy. Sometimes, however, you may have to use FOI or Open Records laws to convince administrators you are serious.

To repeat, science journalism is a judgment business, and you may find that good relations with an information officer will get you better results than going over the head of the information office. Some information people are swift and cooperative; others may need educating. The best can steer you through the bureaucracy and help you convince sources of the merits of granting interviews. Occasionally you may want to bring a situation to the attention of the local or national science or medical writers association officers and seek their help in securing release of information.

Another alternative is to find other sources of information. If you are aggressive and willing to risk disappointment, you often can make enough telephone calls to researchers doing similar work to ferret out the gist of the blockaded information. This is a tactic used frequently when a special commission or panel or an agency head withholds information while arranging a press conference for television. If the story is worth having, it is worth the extra work and expense to call any expert who might have an advance look at the information. Not many events deserve this treatment. It can be used to show that you know your beat and are not dependent upon staged events or hand-feeding by the information office.

Another administrative control is the "release time" on news releases or journals. The NEJM, for example, asks reporters to sign a letter agreeing to abide by a Monday release time in order to get advance copies of each issue. At one time, press releases routinely carried notices about the day and time when material could be used. This practice has been largely abandoned, although some special events may be coordinated this way. Few press releases are used intact by major media anyway, so such an embargo causes few problems. Before agreeing to or breaking an embargo, the prudent sci-

ence writer should check out the story and see why a release time is specified.

Release times often show up on press copies of papers prepared for a scientific meeting. Usually this time is keyed to the day and time the speaker is scheduled to deliver his or her address. On the chance that the speaker may withdraw the paper — which happens — it would be foolhardy to write a story based on what could be undependable research. A paper that is withdrawn may be worth a story, if the scientist will discuss why it was taken off the program. Given the routine nature of most papers and news releases, you should have very good reasons for breaking the release time. A reputation for aggressiveness is one thing; untrustworthiness or carelessness is another. If a story is embargoed for all journalists, you have extra time to work up a more thorough story than your competition. But when one medium breaks a release, the embargo usually is considered broken for all.

The right of access to laboratories, military bases, and other facilities poses difficult problems now. At one time, during the cold war of the 1950s, the author roamed all the unclassified areas of a Strategic Air Command base without an escort. It was a privilege won by insisting that as a citizen and a taxpayer, a reporter should be allowed to travel anywhere a beer truck driver or any other delivery person servicing the base could go. Leads to many interesting nonclassified stories were picked up just by talking to people, watching and listening. I became part of the scenery, in effect. By avoiding the classified parts of the base, I gave the Military Police no reason to suspect any security violations. That was before the Viet Nam war and the sometimes violent antimilitary protests, before two presidents were shot, and before the growth of that peculiar form of murder known as political terrorism. The privilege may not be worth the risk now.

Press escorts are a familiar administrative control by civilian as well as military sources. You may think an escort will cramp your interviewing style, but why let it? It may be physically dangerous, to move unescorted around some military or civilian research installations. There's hardly any question you would ask a scientist or administrator that you cannot ask in front of an information officer. You sometimes have to ask the information officer not to intrude his or her questions into an interview, but most officials genuinely are on the side of the journalists in obtaining release of information. But this is another form of administrative control that you as a science writer should weigh for its effect on your access to information. You need not give up your independence simply by being assigned to cover areas of sensitive information.

Access to private research facilities is a different matter. As a citizen and a taxpayer, you have some right to enter most government facilities. On private property, the right of access is controlled by the owner. You will get more cooperation — and more control over what is told you — when dealing with commercial research operations by working through information officers. If you distrust the information you receive, you cannot wander around the place without risking trespass. Some stories may be worth that risk, but a recent U.S. Supreme Court ruling, however, forbids trespass on private property even when covering a public news event unless the property owner gives you consent. This could prove very aggravating to writers who occasionally cover airplane crashes and industrial accidents at research facilities by crossing private property to reach the accident site. State laws may help in overcoming barriers to access since common law gives journalists some right to accompany fireman, policemen, and other public officials into disaster areas.

Exercise caution. Plane crashes are messy, including what happens to human bodies in addition to the mechanical dismemberment. Airplanes, hospitals, and industrial laboratories often contain exotic gases and liquids whose explosive force or poisonous effects can upset all your plans. Exposure to radiation is always a possibility around some military and civilian accidents. Watch out for your photographers. Some laboratories have pure oxygen and hydrogen around, as do hospitals, that can be touched off by the heat or sparks from a flash unit or the spark of an electrically driven camera. The same may go for your tape recorder, two-way radio, or other equipment. In some electrically sensitive areas, your portable computer terminal may be forbidden, if you carry one into an interview.

If your beat includes a government installation, civilian or military, it pays to get from the headquarters in Washington, D.C., a clear statement of access policies for aircraft accidents and other disasters. A similar understanding about what state or local police are allowed to do at a scene should be spelled out in a letter for you. Often official policies are not known at the field level or by local officials making up their own rules. It is not uncommon for state police to assume that they are under the direction of federal officials at a crash site when official policy may include access by the press. And military policy generally favors access for newsmen, with or without press escort. Because some military people harbor a bias against open reporting of such events, a letter or card spelling out the official access policy can be worth carrying with you.

Libel and privacy risks

Libel laws also pose very real threats to science journalists. The risks are especially high in areas of trans-science, charged with political and emotional juices. You can write yourself into a libel suit more or less innocently or carelessly. Doctors, researchers, engineers, nurses, and semiprofessional personnel in the scientific professions rely on their good reputations for their livelihood, their positions, and general well-being. Protecting that reputation is integral to practicing their professions.

Libel (printed defamation) and slander (spoken defamation) are injuries to reputation that can be redressed through civil court trial. Defending against a libel suit in court, even if you win, costs lots of money. A course and a book on communications law should be part of every writer's armament. However, a short, working definition of libel holds that a libel is a false statement printed or broadcast about someone, which tends to bring that person into public hatred, contempt, or ridicule or to injure him or her in his or her business or occupation. The key word is *false.*

Libel must contain four elements: *publication* including communication to even one third party; *identification* by name or as a member of a group small enough for ascertainment; *damage* or actual injury, including monetary loss, impaired reputation, mental anguish and suffering, ridicule and humiliation; and *fault* knowing a statement was false, entertaining doubts about its truth, or publishing in reckless disregard (*malice*) as to whether it was true or false. Truth is your best defense against charges of libel. Fair comment is another.

Wrongly implying that someone has a dread or loathsome disease offers one example of libel. Challenging professional judgment is another. One physician received a retraction from a science magazine that had questioned the course of treatment he had prescribed for a prominent patient. The possibility of libel may discourage writers from soliciting overly critical remarks about a scientist's work. You can be guilty of libel even when you quote someone correctly, if what they say contains libelous statements about another.

A company can be libeled as a corporate individual under the law. Implying that a company is in financial trouble is a unique form of corporate libel, unless you substantiate the accusation. Companies filing under Chapter 11 of the bankruptcy law are not broke but seeking legal protection to reorganize withour being forced

into bankruptcy; this distinction should be clear in any story. Wrong identification of a person or a company can libel, such as getting the wrong name of the manufacturer of a dangerous product. Therefore any story that could damage a reputation deserves thorough checking, perhaps with a lawyer. Remember, the facts must be provable in court, if necessary. This is not the same as your "believing" they are true.

How do these rules of libel apply to science writing? When actor Rock Hudson was hospitalized, reporters were very careful not to say he had AIDS until Hudson and his agents conceded the matter. Get consent from individuals or parents and guardians of minors, signed if necessary, for stories and pictures used in connection with medical stories. Make it clear you intend to publish the material you obtain. Do not get information by using false names or purposes. Get both — or more — sides to any story, and give people the chance to respond to attack. Make it clear in your stories that they had this opportunity. "Consent" and "opportunity to reply" offer defenses against libel and invasion of privacy.

THE PUBLIC FIGURE.   The idea of the "public official" or "public figure" has special significance in reporting on science, technology, and medicine. People who are nonpublic or "private" figures need very little proof of damage to their reputation if they sue for libel. The public figure must prove the libel was published with reckless disregard for the truth or with serious doubts about it. "Malice" is the legal term for this. But defining a public figure gets into uncertain depths. Not all public employees or people receiving public money are public officials or public figures as seen by the courts. In theory the U.S. Supreme Court has said public figures are people who "occupy positions of such pervasive power and influence that they are deemed public figures for all purposes" as are those "otherwise private persons who thrust themselves into a public controversy" of their own will.

The court has ruled that public employees are public officials if they have, or appear to have, substantial responsibility for conducting government affairs. This, so far, includes elected officials, candidates for office, police, judges, county medical examiners, and a psychiatrist at a state hospital. A high school chemistry teacher was considered a public official while a history teacher was not. Former governors and a government contractor doing environmental impact analyses have been judged neither public officials nor public figures.

Research scientists may not be public figures. Ronald R. Hutchinson, a behavioral scientist, was ruled a private figure when he sued Sen. William Proxmire, and a press assistant, who gave Hutchinson a derogatory Golden Fleece award for research funded by NASA and the Navy. Proxmire called the research, on why monkeys and other animals clench their fists and jaws under stress, a waste of money. Hutchinson successfully demonstrated its bearing upon analyzing how humans might perform under stress. The case, *Hutchinson v. Proxmire* (1979) set another precedent. Because the senator issued the charge in a press release — rather than from his privileged position on the floor of the Senate — and repeated it in a broadcast, the senator lost his immunity to suit under the speech or debate clause of the U.S. Constitution, the court ruled.

If you report from official documents or from the speech of privileged people, you have a defense from libel. Events happening in open court, for example, are privileged, if you give a fair and accurate report. Court documents and other public records carry privilege for you. Journalists and others are also entitled to use the defense of "opinion and fair comment," on a matter of public interest and/or on facts stated in the article that are true or believed to be true. This must be comment or opinion, not an allegation of fact, and identifiable as opinion. Even when journalists identify their writings as a "column," implying fair comment and opinion, a jury and judge may not agree. An *Atlanta Journal and Constitution* science writer was found guilty of libel in drawing a comparison between a Nobel Prize-winner's proposals for sterilization payments to people of low IQ and medical experiments in Nazi Germany; although the damages awarded were only $1, the journalist lost his case and the newspaper paid a considerable legal bill (Associated Press 1984c).

Public figures have been identified as including actors and entertainers, the author of a diet book, a drug abuse foundation, an insurance company, opponents of fluoridation, professional athletes, and a sportswriter. Fund raisers for a charity, the research scientist on a grant, an ex-convict, a jockey, and an attorney active in politics all have been ruled nonpublic. So determination of who is a public figure becomes very tricky, and the science writer should rely on other defenses where possible. Reporting on fraudulent research may await public repudiation after an official investigation, on a public hearing, or on published retraction in a scientific journal.

NEUTRAL REPORTING.   Because science journalists operate from published material, the newer concept of "neutral reporting" as a libel defense is important. It stems from a story in *The New York Times* reporting that the Audubon Society magazine had accused several prominent scientists of being paid "scientist spokesmen" who cited the society's annual Christmas bird counts as proof that flocks were thriving in spite of the pesticide DDT, a very politically charged issue in 1972. Although a district court jury decided the scientists were libeled, the 2nd U.S. Court of Appeals threw out the judgment against the *Times* and the Audubon Society. The Supreme Court refused to hear the scientists' appeal (*Edwards v. National Audubon Society*). This clears the way for reporting published accusations in a dispute on the grounds that you are merely conveying charges hurled in public debate.

Federal libel law is a relatively new and developing field. Most libel law is state law, and the writer also needs familiarity with the local laws for publishing and broadcasting. These vary from state to state in such things as the statute of limitations, the time beyond which you cannot be sued. Courts are also looking very hard at attempts by those who have been criticized to stifle criticism by suing. Some publishers are suing back, if they think the suits are brought to harass them and their staff members. In some states, timely retraction, correction, or apology may show your good faith and reduce the possible damages. Sometimes the retraction alone is enough to prevent a suit, which also means heavy expenses for the plaintiff. Writers should not attempt to make retractions without the advice of a lawyer, who can negotiate a settlement that includes an agreement not to sue if you run a correction. Badly worded or grudging corrections and such can make the situation worse. And some states offer the limited protection of shield laws, which can protect you from being forced to identify sources of information; this protection may be very weak and limited.

Sometimes writers need their own attorney and libel insurance. When libel damages were much smaller than multimillion-dollar judgments, which began in the 1970s, writers assumed the newspaper or magazine would pay the costs of libel defense. This is not automatically so any more. Free-lance writers often must sign contracts binding them to pay or share libel expenses. In addition, the interests of the writer and the newspaper may be different. A newspaper and its libel insurance company can leave the writer stranded by agreeing that it is cheaper to settle a libel case out of court and pay damages. Part of those damages may be assigned to a writer personally; and the writer may want to defend his or her reputation in court rather than settle.

Invasion of privacy.

Persons involved in newsworthy events give up some of their right to privacy, whether they are voluntarily or involuntarily caught up in the event. Generally courts defer to the writer's judgment on what is news or not. Therefore you usually can write about matters of legitimate public interest with safety, even if the topic is not a spot news event.

However privacy law also has some special pitfalls for science writers. Sometimes a story will provide the opportunity for both libel and invasion of privacy. Privacy law protects the right to be "let alone." In some ways, it is the other side of the libel law; the more truthful the statement, the greater the invasion of privacy. Like libel, privacy law applies only to living persons, but courts recognize privacy rights for relatives of famous or public persons, living or dead. Violations can occur through intrusion into private affairs beyond what is relevant to the news. Thus you may get onto shaky ground developing material about the families and personal lives of scientists and medical patients who do not cooperate with your project. Disclosure of sensational material on health, sexual life, or economic affairs may intrude through publicizing private matters. Reporting and photographing what takes place in public, such as on a public street or public grounds, does not intrude. Unsavory information dredged out of a person's history may constitute an invasion of privacy if he or she lives down the transgression.

Consent offers you a defense, but consent can be withdrawn. Science writers covering the artificial heart operations at the Humana Corporation hospital in Louisville encountered this problem. Dr. William C. DeVries told science reporters soon after he had implanted the third mechanical heart that he would limit the information he would give to the press about the patients or the experimental procedure. Until this point, science writers considered the information assistance given them a perfect example of press and physician cooperation, a textbook public relations example. DeVries called the operation "old news now . . . you just don't need to know as much as you did before." (Altman 1985, 6). He said recipients of the hearts were being affected by having to answer press queries and be photographed and that he wanted to preserve his data and analyses for scientific publication. His action followed public criticism from other members of the medical research community of the amount of data released daily at press conferences.

Occasionally a person will cooperate with interviews and photographs but change his or her mind about having the story published. This remains a possibility when you are focusing on an individual to represent a typical victim of a disease, for example. Unless you can persuade the individual to restore consent, you will need to find another example.

Appropriation of a person's name, likeness, or personality for purposes of commercial exploitation also violates privacy. A scientist's picture used with a news or feature story is one thing; even if it is taken in a public place, using that picture in an advertisement for a product, including your publication, can be a violation — without signed consent. You can also invade privacy, in some courts, if you disclose trade secrets or give away how the person performs some special skill so that it can be duplicated.

Putting a person in a false light is another legal trap in privacy law. It can occur when you attempt to dramatize or condense facts or events in a news or feature story or when you accidentally put a real person's name to a composite of several characters, as you might while personalizing an account of some far-ranging social science research. When you use a composite, say so. It is very possible, since privacy law is still developing, that science writers could so misrepresent the purposes of scientists or their research that you could get into a "false light" situation. Clearly, also, you should resist temptations to poke fun at scientific research

by individuals when the tedium of writing serious stories makes you yearn for something humorous to write about. Ridicule and false light are both actionable.

Commercial obstacles

Given the problems of libel and privacy, you can understand why *Science* magazine wrote most carefully and respectfully about an inventor who received a lot of publicity in New Orleans, and about the television journalist who had taken up the inventor's cause. The inventor claimed he had been injured by the U.S. Patent and Trademark Office's refusal to grant him a patent on a machine that seemed to generate more power than it took to operate it. This would seem to defy the second law of thermodynamics and to be the perpetual motion machine that science claims is impossible. Science writer Eliot Marshall (1984, 6) cited all of the impressive documentation supporting the inventor's claim, including statements by the technically knowledgeable engineers who made evaluations of it.

When a scientist or a company has a patent application under study, secrecy prevails because admitting exclusive information into general knowledge may invalidate claims for a patent. Documentation in scientific literature is part of the legal evidence for establishing the rights to invention and patent claims, which usually are assigned to the scientist's employer. This is another reason that first publication means so much, even to basic research scientists. For more than twenty years after the research and development explosion following World War II, patent rights to inventions financed through government contract or grant went into the public domain. Gradually industry has been moving forward its request to have exclusive rights to patent such developments for commercial purposes, and has succeeded in some parts of the space and defense industry. Government still gets to use these without charge.

So you may be asked to refrain from writing about some things you see in industrial laboratories or manufacturing plants. In addition to potentially patentable devices under test, you may see valuable trade secrets, ways of doing things, that are not patentable. Some companies will forbid your cameras inside plants. The better companies will offer to take pictures of you.

Scientists in private industry may be close-lipped about what they discuss. In some companies, merely talking about research fields of interest is forbidden by managers as disclosure of company plans for the future. Other firms are more open and put a lid on research discussions only when a clear product development appears economical. Scientists also muffle their criticism of competitors or industrial practices to avoid trade law complications. They can, however, supply you background material if you develop the kind of trust that permits this sort of exchange with or without attribution. Research and development companies may also allow you to use their technical libraries. And stories developed out of plant tours can give readers a better understanding of the community, even if the company does not lay out all its secrets. It may be useful to you later in understanding the company or some new products.

In many large corporations, managers of field research or production facilities have limited authority in dealing with the media. Requests for a plant or lab visit may need approval from the corporate headquarters. It is only fair to give some idea of what kind of story you are seeking so that people can prepare answers for you. And it is a good idea to keep contacts in the corporate headquarters, even if it's with public relations people, against those times you need some information or a favor in a hurry when dealing with the local managers.

Life scientists may become more reluctant to discuss research with the media as it becomes increasingly possible to use living organisms, such as bacteria, in production processes for medicine, pure protein, or other valuable products. Scientists see these processes, including cloning and genetic engineering, as ways to the kinds of personal fortunes made earlier by scientists in chemistry, plastics, computers, and electronics. Harvard and other universities with highly skilled research biologists have started commercial subsidiaries devoted to such bioengineering and technology, which could affect the flow of information to scientific meetings, the literature, and the media.

Another commercial obstacle to obtaining scientific and technical information can surface with government contractors. This is a clause found in most contracts between a company and the government agency. The contract binds the company to get agency approval before releasing any information about the contract. One purpose of the clause is to minimize the publicity the contractor receives and to assure the agency it is notified of any release of information. Sometimes agency officials want to ensure that they, not their contactor, get credit for the new developments. Government and industry information officers wrestle regularly with each other and with their technical management supervisors to clear release of such information. Media science writers often do best requesting access and interviews from both the agency and the contractor.

Because of the sordid history of government contracting (going back as far as the Roman legions at least) the open, competitive bidding process exists. Thus science writers have access to scientific and technical information as well as to price and time-for-performance specifications. This bidding process is designed to keep contractors honest and prices low. It does not always work, but anyone can use the "Bid Boards" at government installations to get information about proposed contracts and the specifications for equipment, performance, installations, and so on. Some national security purchases are kept secret or details of the proposal restricted to persons with a security clearance. Unclassified bid notices usually are posted near the contracting office. You can look at the proposed and actual contracts, too, unless they are classified. Progress reports on most projects are also public record. Find the Bid Board, where contract notices are posted, and learn to use it.

Security and censorship

Unfortunately, in the eyes of many scientists, war and technological advances go together. This means you will encounter efforts at outright censorship and at classification for national security and defense. You will be surprised at how easily "Top Secret" material can be declassified when a government project manager thinks you will write a favorable story. So ask for the information. Most of what is classified probably should not be, but classification is easier for timid government officials than risking a close call. One report on uses of the bow and arrow remains classified, at last report. In addition, classification is an easy way of hiding failures and other embarrassing technological or political problems from reporters and other outsiders.

Twice, at least, the federal government has attempted to censor stories about the science and technology of nuclear weapons. In March of 1950 the Atomic Energy Commission persuaded *Scientific American* to destroy three thousand copies of the magazine in order to delete several passages from an article by Nobel Physicist Hans A. Bethe about the development of the hydrogen fusion bomb. All of the material had been taken by Bethe from unclassified sources, primarily books available in public libraries. President Harry S. Truman had ordered H-bomb work to proceed, against the advice of many scientists, including Bethe, who worked on the atomic or fission bombs. The public rationale for the action was that the article might be taken more seriously because of Bethe's reputation. This is one of the few cases of successful prior restraint on publication in the United States.

In 1979, the Department of Energy and the Justice Department obtained an injunction to prevent *The Progressive* magazine from publishing an article titled "How a Hydrogen Bomb Works." The fight was long and complicated, and journalists beat the censors when a half-dozen other publications published the article, or ones similar to it, independently. Publication revealed just how much of the information was in the open library shelves or in textbooks and how few of the detailed workings of an H-bomb were disclosed. This was hardly enough by which to build a bomb; little, if anything, appeared that was unknown to any physicist doing minimal research in the topic. In fact, during the late 1970s, several physics students had put together research reports on how to build nuclear bombs. One of *The Progressive*'s mistakes lay in submitting the manuscript to the government for approval. Approval was naturally refused, touching off the debate. The U.S. Constitution, as interpreted by the Supreme Court, forbids restraint before publication, but that does not keep federal and even state officials from trying to censor if you give them opportunity.

This and other incidents indicate that the journalist's best tactic is to publish first. If you as a journalist can find out the information, it is almost certain that any espionage agent could also. Censorship is a technique through which a country's enemies often know more about U.S. strengths and weaknesses than the citizens. If you gain access to classified material and decide publication will not harm national security, do not brag in print that you have seen restricted material. Why provoke some bureaucrat with the idea that he or she somehow made a mistake? For a full account of *The Progressive* case, read Bruce M. Swain's "*The Progressive*, the Bomb and the Papers" (1982).

Under President Ronald Reagan many gains in public access to information slipped backward. Censorship for national security purposes and to inhibit exchange of commercially valuable technology tightened in many areas of science and technology. There were some indications that as much of the drive toward secrecy came from the Department of Commerce as from the military. So national security was not involved. *Science News* discovered that nearly a third of the six hundred unclassified papers on the program of the Society of Photo-Optical Instrumentation Engineers meeting in San Diego were canceled on demand of the departments of Defense and Commerce (Greenberg 1982). Visits by Russian scientists have been canceled, and universities and scientific societies have been pressured to restrict meeting attendance to "American citizens only." And there have been reports of some universities restricting enrollment in certain engineering and computer science classes to American students.

Erwin Knoll, editor of *The Progressive*, compiled a list of other censorship efforts: a warning to Scripps-Howard News Service that it could be prosecuted under the Atomic Energy Act of 1954 for receiving documents indicating that enough uranium was missing from the Oak Ridge nuclear plant to build eighty-five bombs, warnings of espionage law violations given two former Air Force intelligence specialists who challenged official explanations of how a Korean Air Lines jet was shot down, and 9 of 175 academic research papers on cryptography challenged by the National Security Agency (Knoll 1984). Some proposals would keep foreign nationals from coming to the United States to take certain certain types of physics and electronics degrees. The actions in 1983 were enough to cause the American Association for the Advancement of Science to set up a special research project on the potential effects of secrecy upon the conduct of scientific research (Chalk 1983).

Press conference control

Two other potential control mechanisms over what gets reported pale beside the security restrictions, which can have limiting effect on what science or medical information is reported to scientists and to the public. Science writing analysts Rae

Goodell of MIT and Sharon Dunwoody of the University of Wisconsin have focused on the use of press conferences and pressroom access rules to limit what and how data are obtained by the press. A select group of journalists were invited to what has become known as the Asilomar Conference where scientists worked out early guidelines for minimizing dangers in research on recombinant DNA, the method by which new genetic material is put into bacterial cells to produce insulin. An embargo, which most reporters accepted passively for the privilege of attending, kept them from seeking alternate and conflicting views to those presented by the conference organizers. Thus the risks from escaping mutants were emphasized over the views of scientists less concerned with the dangers of runaway bacteria. Guidelines from the conference were virtually abandoned by NIH and universities when commercial products appeared possible from these bioengineering techniques. Goodell concluded that journalists too often take the easy way out by writing from what is made available to them (Goodell 1981).

Dunwoody reached much the same conclusion after analyzing eight hundred stories from an annual meeting of the American Association for the Advancement of Science. Most reporters covered topics presented through the press conferences (Dunwoody 1979b). Jerry Bishop of *The Wall Street Journal* conceded Dunwoody most of her points and that the practice makes for a more comfortable life, but called the practice more of the reporters' making than of the scientists'. What is reported, Bishop said, is less news of science than what is the best story out of a particular day's meeting. On another day a similar story might be ignored. Without the press conferences, often called at the request of the reporters, few reporters would go to meetings, said Bishop (1980).

Hospital codes

Another control over what science writers publish lies in hospital codes setting policy for releasing information about patients. Both the Colorado Hospital Association and the South Carolina Hospital Association, and related health services professions, abide by uniform information rules adopted in their states. In the spring of 1981, *The Denver Post* heard of a baby being operated on in its mother's womb in an attempt to prevent hydrocephaly, a condition where fluid pressure on the brain may retard mental development. The newspaper wanted full details of the operation. The Denver medical center information office was ordered by hospital management not to answer questions.

Doctors also refused cooperation, but the newspaper obtained a copy of the doctors' report, which had not then been given to a journal for publication. The doctors refused to give more information. An appeal to the Code of Cooperation Committee of the Colorado Hospital Commission brought a ruling that the patient had become a public person because of this pioneering operation and had lost the right of privacy. Because the commission had only advisory powers, doctors and hospital managers ignored the ruling. The physicians' paper appeared in the NEJM thirteen months after the surgery. This incident offers a spectacular example of what can happen when journalists seek hospital information beyond the routine.

Usually the information will be about patients with more common medical problems: gunshot wounds, burns, automobile accidents, and such. Science and medical writers should obtain copies of each hospital's guidelines for the release of information. These usually are based on American Hospital Association recommendations. They will be adjusted to meet various state laws regarding privacy and the kind of information that can be released on so-called cases of public record. Specifics vary, but you usually can get the name of the patient, nature of the accident, general location of injuries and their nature, a statement of condition, and name of the physician. Information be-

comes much more restricted where sexual assault, intoxication, or mental illness is involved. Where the case is not of public record, written permission may be sought from the patient on any release of information.

Science writers should also get copies of each hospital's plan for information release during natural disasters or accidents that involve many people. Science writers are almost certain to be pressed into such general news coverage because they are more familiar with hospital personnel than other staffers.

Experiments

1. Obtain copies of hospital codes in your area and prepare a story on the information policies of hospitals for your readers. Find out if a uniform code exists for the state hospital association and what it involves.

2. Interview or invite as a guest speaker a scientist or doctor who will discuss the Ingelfinger Rule and its advantages and handicaps. How would he or she respond to the situation in Denver? Would the thirteen-month delay in publication affect many ill children? How would you find out how many?

3. Contact your city or state police and/or a nearby military base for a copy of the regulations dealing with access of journalists to disaster areas, including airplane crashes and industrial accidents. Military hospitals may have regulations on information release that differ from civilian hospitals. Perhaps you can arrange a speaker from your contacts.

4. Select a story subject and call laboratories or research center managers in your city or on campus. Do you encounter any problems with industrial secrets or classified information?

5. Universities have differing rules about classified research projects on campus because of potential difficulties in getting faculty research published. What are the guidelines on your campus? Can you locate scientists who have encountered difficulty, including prior review, with publishing their research?

Chapter 10
Ethical issues
in science writing

AS A SCIENCE WRITER YOU FACE MORE than the usual number of ethical choices that bedevil journalists. These can involve bribery for example, offers of money to plug a drug. Alton Blakeslee, a respected science writer at the Associated Press wire service for many years, reported that he was offered $17,000 to mention the name of a commercial drug in one of his stories. The money would have been paid indirectly and secretly by the drug's manufacturer (Communication 1964, 60). You will find some lapses on the side of the media, as did Elizabeth M. Whelan (1984). Material from the American Medical Association and the American Academy of Family Physicians convinced her that *Time* and *Newsweek* editors downplayed the dangers of smoking in stories for the magazines' special health supplements to avoid conflict with cigarette advertisers.

Generally ethical practices develop to help keep writers and their media out of real or apparent conflicts of interest that might compromise the accuracy and truthfulness of their reports. For some writers, ethical choices will be guided by codes of ethics adopted by their newspapers, radio-TV stations, magazines, and networks. Some of these codes forbid accepting free travel, lodging, and food from a news source. One of the strictest codes, that of the *Louisville Courier-Journal and Times,* will not let reporters accept even a courtesy meal. Writers must make some payment. At other publications, editorial managers feel no mature writers will al-

low a few dollars worth of free food and drink to influence what they write. But to avoid the appearance of undue influence, more science writers and their publications are picking up their expenses for a yearly seminar sponsored by the American Cancer Society for a select number of writers from the major media. The seminars are held on the eve of the annual cancer fund drive and local chapters often pay part of the expenses of sending a journalist from their home area.

These gatherings, where the ACS brings science and medical writers together with experts in cancer research and treatment, have been a tradition for decades with the ACS. Alan C. Davis of the cancer society defends the practice for putting writers and scientists together in comfortable resort surroundings at the start of new lines of discovery. Social and professional exchanges take place in a relaxed atmosphere. Jerry Bishop of *The Wall Street Journal* considers the occasions extended press conferences and holds that they now contain less science news than in earlier years. Says Bishop, "I have never been at a press conference that was called for the benefit of the press, whether it was called by the White House, Merck, Harvard, UCLA or the volunteer fire department." He does not feel obilgated to go or write a story unless there is something new presented. Benefits to the ACS are irrelevant. The late Pat McGrady, who started the seminars, has said that the seminar speakers originally were chosen for their newsworthiness, but their success moved ACS administrators to take over more direction and to specify which speakers could be invited. As news content went down, McGrady said he asked to step out of organizing the annual seminars (Davis et al. 1978).

One risk of extended contact may be to lull writers into uncritical thinking and cut them off from additional viewpoints. Dr. Osler L. Peterson and Dr. H. Jack Geiger (a science writer before entering medical school) called attention to this risk of uncritical acceptance several years back in objecting to ACS claims that "one in three who get cancer are cured." Geiger pointed out that writers and editors should ask for more explanation when such claims are made because they give the average reader the idea that victims of any cancer have such a chance of surviving five years to be considered cured. In fact, cancers come in many forms and types, Geiger observed, and that survival statistic is the product of averaging all survival rates. Averaging the very high survival rate for one type of skin cancer with the very low rate for lung cancer, for example, misleads. Because such statistical quirks continue to be exploited on various occasions, good ethical and professional practice calls on you to ask for details anytime someone gives you an "average" figure. Probably it's misleading you and your readers (Peterson and Geiger 1962).

Conflicts of interest

Accepting a trip and paid expenses often means the difference between getting a story and not getting it for some writers. Large media organizations have the expense money to pay for any coverage. This does not hold for smaller newspapers, magazines, and radio-television stations, where most beginning journalists start. Many freelancers also would lose story opportunities and the chance to gain new experiences without sometime assistance from the sources of the information. These sources, obviously, have an interest in getting publicity in return for paying all

or part of the writer's expenses. And a few writers have a reputation for living well and taking anything they can get on such trips. Other writers have said that they react with hypercriticism, sometimes, to show their independence. And public relations people, whose budgets support such junkets, may not invite a writer again if a story upsets his or her bosses. The writer cannot erase all thoughts about these possibilities. However the social contract lies between the writer, the editor, and the reader. Getting the reputation for an easily bought journalist will hardly help your reputation or that of your publication. Practical considerations reinforce the idea that writing for publication always involves judgment and balance. One of the writer's guideposts has to be the advice of philosopher Albert Camus, that we should not lie about what we know.

Freelancers have more issues to decide for themselves than staff writers, who have the benefit of policies set by their editors and of ethics codes. Even staff writers face these decisions when they freelance part-time, as many science writers do. Few people can earn a living completely from freelance stories, even in science and medical fields. Some freelancers will do public relations work and write advertising copy. This takes a clear view of your own integrity as a writer and an understanding of exactly which job you are doing at any given time. Many writers refuse to touch advertising and promotional copy. Because of real or apparent conflicts, and competition, many publications will not allow their staff writers to do freelance work. Other companies limit outside writing to books or noncompetitive media.

Another delicate choice for science writers involves knowing just which publications to accept story assignments from. Pfizer, for example, has sponsored the distribution of *America's Health*, a consumer-oriented magazine from World Wide Medical Press, Inc. Although both Pfizer and the publisher disclaim any untoward influence over the magazine's contents, there is the possibility that a writer would be identified with a commercial interest. His or her reputation for impartiality could suffer.

The freelancer may also be offered two paychecks for the same story. A company or institution may offer a fee to research and write a story and allow the writer to sell the story to the magazine or newspaper editor. Travel writers run into this fairly often. In such a situation, your editor should know full details of the arrangement, including any bonus for placing such a story in a specified publication. Then the editor has the decision on whether or not such a story conflicts with the editor's ethics or company policy. Disclosure of such an arrangement should not come as a surprise to the editor after publication. A few editors and writers insist on including in their stories a paragraph explaining that the writer was the guest of the news source while gathering the material.

Some editors accept conflicting interests, if they are disclosed to the readers. However science writers criticized the Associated Press over a ten-part series about cancer, written by Alton Blakeslee, a retired AP staffer. Blakeslee wrote the series as a paid consultant to the American Cancer Society. AP Newsfeatures asked to see the articles and sold the series to newspapers without telling them that Blakeslee was paid by the American Cancer Society, source of most of the information. The decision was protested by both Blakeslee and the ACS, but the AP editors preferred to identify the author as "brought out of retirement" for the occasion (Bloom 1979). These potential conflicts demonstrate why many publications prefer having staff writers supply all their copy.

Personal financial gain

Staff science writers should also understand company policies on using information for personal gain while doing "work for hire" as a paid staff member. Some news organizations forbid retreading in-

formation gathered for a staff story, giving it a new slant, and selling the revised story to another publication, even a noncompeting one. This, as in many other situations involving these very personal ethics problems, strikes other writers as excessive. Facts, they maintain, do not become exclusive property of a company, and when writers do stories on their own time they should be free to sell that product of their creative effort. One *New York Times* writer fell into a dispute with his company because his book was accepted by a competitor to the *Times*'s book publishing division. These and other instances lead writers to wonder how deeply corporate policy should intrude into personal ethical and financial decisions. So long as the writer produces the stories requested by the company, should he or she have free choice in the use of outside time?

A stickier financial question afflicts both science and business specialists. This is using their opportunities to learn advance information about a company and profit thereby from business or stock investments. Science and business writers work on the leading edge of business and high technology planning. Wire service and national newspaper and magazine writers know that a favorable or unfavorable story will affect stock prices as subscribers buy or sell their stock after reading the story. Science writers know they are touted by some drug makers hoping to increase stock trading. Scientists and doctors investigating drug effectiveness face similar temptations. A bad report on a drug's side effects, for example, can send the stock tumbling. And the science and business writers have advance information and opportunity to call their brokers before the story appears. Bishop of *The Wall Street Journal* has spotted stock analysts at scientific press conferences and meetings. He also tells the story of $300 million in Merck & Co. stock changing hands on the day before an advance press release went into print. Often analysts are on mailing lists that enable them to get advance copies of scientific journals and other materials. Another *Wall Street Journal* reporter got from a stock analyst the full text of a favorable clinical research study two months before its publication date. Suspicions exist that the researcher and the analyst hoped for a good story to drive up the price of the stock (Bishop 1981).

Some publications forbid owning stock in companies you write about, and many writers voluntarily stay out of the market. Other writers consider guessing which way any stock will move is risky, at best, and see no problems with stock ownership and speculation. Recommending specific stocks, however, might force you to register as an agent under Securities and Exchange Commission rules. Buying and selling stock on such advance information could leave you open to "insider trading" charges, although the SEC is not a strict enforcer. Because any SEC controls or licensure over a publication, such as an investment newsletter, threatens to violate Constitutional guarantees of freedom of the press, personal ethics may be the only guide here. But there are potentially criminal temptations as well; one business writer wound up in jail for seeking payment to withhold an unfavorable business story.

Publications ethics

Publications managers sometimes need to look at their own ethical standards. *Science 83* (The date in the name changes with each new year.) has carried classified advertisements that promise college degrees by mail and degrees without classes. This seems an odd notice in a magazine sponsored by the American Association for the Advancement of Science, whose members are so careful about the pristine character of their own credentials and those of their colleagues. Carrying an advertisement is not necessarily an endorsement of a product, but the reader might wonder what else the publication would find acceptable. Ads for questionable medicines, therapies, and devices show up regularly in newspapers, for example.

Media frequently draw criticism for the slow speed and grudging spirit with which they acknowledge error. It is much easier now to get a correction than in the past, except in cases involving a potential libel. But most writers and editors seem to reluctant to admit they are human and err. The technical nature of most science stories make science writers especially vulnerable. *The New York Times* took more than three months to acknowledge an erroneous interpretation of a mathematics story, even though mathematicians called it to the *Times*'s attention. The mathematicians were upset, mainly because the story spread across the country through wire service distribution. When published at last, the concession of error was buried six paragraphs deep in new story whose thrust was that American mathematicians were now saying the math discovery was less significant than it first appeared. Except for corrections requiring the advice of a lawyer, such as in libel, there seems little reason to avoid putting mistakes behind as soon as possible. Reluctance to correct error is one of the reasons many readers say they distrust journalists. The possibility of framing a correction may temper some hasty leaps to conclusions. *The Atlanta Journal and Constitution* admitted error in linking radiation from the Savannah River nuclear plant to a rare and fatal blood disease, which had no known link to radiation as a cause. The writers confused the fatal illness with a less serious ailment whose incidence in the population was within expected norms.

Telling what you know

Every science writer is asked to bury a story now and then. Usually the request comes from scientists who warn you not to write about reports from one of their number. The writer does have choices, since there is more to write about science than most people will ever have the time to put into print. The occasion for such request comes, generally, when some new interpretation is put on old data or a new theory is propounded. There are no firm answers, but respected science writers tend to be libertarians. They will print it if the subject is interesting to general readers and let scientists pound out their consensus later. The truth generally will sort itself out and they will write about the battle as it rages. And if the issue fails the test of debate, they will stop writing about it. Science writers tend, on this subject at least, to go with Dr. Barry Commoner, the environmentalist, who urges you to remember that mother nature always bats last.

Scientists are not always right. Earl Ubell (*Communication* 1964, 36) recalls that the first scientist to propose virus as a cause of leukemia "was nearly flayed alive" at a scientific meeting. Ubell was pressured to ignore the scientist's report. Soon after the scientist's research won the United Nations' Kalinga prize, and most cancer researchers were following the virus path. Science and medicine frequently chase after fads, some of which, like leeching, may last a century or more. Sometimes scientists find they have built careers on discredited or outmoded ideas and theories that they defend until forced to give them up.

Why and how should you moderate this tendency to print? Doubts may remain even after determining a piece of research or an interpretation meets all of the tests suggested earlier. Predictions of disaster, for example, meet all the tests of news values. When a government agency issues a news release, as the U.S. Geological Survey did in 1979, about indications of a potential earthquake, you cannot simply throw the announcement away. Ask if the prediction lies in the field of the researchers' expertise, and further, does the field of science possess the techniques for reliable prediction? Posed to several scientists, this question should allow you to determine if such a prediction has general support or is the theory of only one or a few researchers. Thus your story can be weighted toward the consensus. But there is no chance that warnings about public health and safety will be ignored.

Some criticism is inevitable. John Lear, former science editor at *Saturday Review*, once drew a letter signed by seven eminent scientists, including a Nobel Prize winner, protesting the publicity given to the possibility that meteorites gouged the ocean basins aeons ago. Lear pointed out that while the other scientists might disagree, the researchers' credentials were as good as theirs and that the respected British journal *Nature* published the man's paper. "There is no one accepted theory," wrote Lear (1962, 41).

Similarly, anthropologists flailed *The New York Times* for writing about an article, taken from a scholarly journal, accusing Aztec experts of covering up the extent of cannibalism in the ancient society. One critic maintained that even if a reputable journal carried the article, it did not mean it was proper for the newspaper to pass these views along to the public. Debate in the scholarly journal was all right, but "not in the popular press where people are likely to believe anything they read," said one anthropologist (Rensberger 1977, sec. 2, 23). While willing to publicize other people's fights, journalists may not overly publicize their own ethical quandaries. Almost no one wrote about a research article indicating that newspaper stories publicizing murder-suicides by airplane pilots seem to inspire additional murder-suicides (Phillips 1978). Science journalists may have reasoned that there was no way they would suppress stories about any murder-suicide, so why torture the point.

Most journalists, without compelling reason otherwise, will side with Bishop of *The Wall Street Journal* when asked to keep science information out of print. "Science reporters have no business evaluating scientific research; it is not their role to be peer reviewers . . . . The reporter who attempts to make this kind of decision becomes a preacher, a moralizer, not a reporter" (1981, 20)

You live with your mistakes. Harry Nelson, medical editor of the *Los Angeles Times*, knew instinctively he should not have made a story from a Memorial

Sloan-Kettering Institute report saying that a suspect cancer drug actually showed some effectiveness. He checked all the indicators for legitimacy of the research and the researcher. His story was hedged with qualifiers. Later studies, however, failed to verify the results. He suspects the report was slipped to him by enthusiasts for the drug as a miracle cure (1978).

Columnist Bob Green (1982) will regret for a long time his failure to adequately disguise the name of a high school student whose true initials he used in a story about her drug problems. Her friends quickly identified her and ostracized her to her great personal despair. From this and other experiences, he says, he learned to help those who do not know enough about the effects of publicity to defend themselves. Sometimes writers follow other reasons for self-censorship. As a group, science writers granted the requests of sex researchers William Masters and Virginia Johnson-Masters for no publicity, even while they were publishing their reports derived from measuring and photographing human sexual intercourse. Sensational stories could have been written from the open literature, but the science writers evidently felt the need to protect the research from attack if the exact nature of the project became widely known. So science writers can and will exercise self-censorship, but they want to make the judgment, good or bad. It is part of learning to see yourself as a journalist, not an educator or a scientist. Sometimes you will be wrong.

Ethics in choices

Another ethics question concerns the pattern of your choices of stories to report. Regularly choosing to write on the bizarre, the unusual, the exceptional in science and medicine tells readers what you or your editors think is important in science. Whether or not these readers agree with you is something else. A case can be made that such choices misrepresent science.

Should you support community groups' in putting their viewpoints across for the good of society? Free-lance science writer David R. Zimmerman (1979) questions whether or not science writers should involve themselves and their publications even in such activities as educational stories involved with birth control, smoking, low-cholesterol diets, and all other campaigns by voluntary organizations. By nature these are like all public relations campaigns, uncritical, tedious, and dull. These reasons are enough for journalists to ignore them, says Zimmerman. In addition these campaigns use the media for a partially or completely hidden public relations client and represent promotion of a special interest as much as enlightenment. When you or your medium enlist in such campaigns, you may have been co-opted by the promoters for their purposes rather than sifting material for the general audience from self-serving material, a caution sign raised by John L. Hulting of *The Boston Globe* in his handbook on ethical principles for the American Society of Newspaper Editors (1983).

This can be construed as involving yourself in a cause where the purpose is more overtly political instead of for the general good. On the other hand, some press critics fault the media for lacking a clear philosophy or rationale for the kinds of stories they choose. These critics want the media to operate more for educational or social responsibility purposes. Dr. Gene Burd of the University of Texas at Austin analyzed one metropolitan newspaper for evidence of preventive journalism in medicine, stories giving readers educational stories on how to prevent problems or cope with situations such as stress. Although the amount of medical-health news space devoted to preventive health (17 percent) surprised Burd, most of this came from Jane E. Brody's health column, syndicated by *The New York Times*, or other outside writers. Very little preventive health copy came from the paper's medical-health writer about local issues (Burd 1981).

That offers a look at one philosophical approach to science-medical news coverage. Another writer, working with a different perception of science news, could explore the potential effects of Pope John Paul II's appeal in November of 1983 for physicists to abandon research on military weapons. Five months later, no secular publications had analyzed the effect. Did the possible effect of moral persuasion not register with science writers as a story beyond the event of the Pope's declaration?

Fakes in science writing

There are deep philosophical explorations available on what causes deception in science, but most science reporters will not encounter them in daily news coverage. A simple, perhaps innocent, deception is a more likely event. It can be on you, or on the reader in the rush to publication and broadcast. The July 1983 issue of *Omni* magazine carried a story purportedly tying prehistoric human use of the swastika symbol to research showing that such a pattern could have been formed in the sky by gas from a comet or other celestial object encountering magnetic fields in space. One of the two investigators credited with the discovery said their research did not indicate such a conclusion. In addition, the two men had not worked together for many years, implying that some very old work had slipped into print as fresh news (Osio 1983).

On the other hand, you can be hoaxed — and hoax your readers. Joseph Skaggs, an instructor in mass communications at the School of Visual Arts in New York, fooled an unwary United Press International reporter with a phony press conference and news releases about hormones from a super-cockroach that cured allergies and other conditions. A cursory check through the indicators discussed here and earlier would have turned up a nonexistent university as one clue that things were not as presented. But UPI was not the only one hoaxed. A clipping service collection showed that approximately a hundred newspapers used the story. One of the traps in science is that its discoveries have been so grand that almost anything sounds possible (McDonald 1981).

Journalism is long past the time in 1913 when Joseph Knowles and Michael McKeogh carried a proposition to the *Boston Post*. Knowles would live, practically naked, in the woods for two months as a "scientific" experiment in survival, clothing himself in animal skins and eating nuts, berries, roots, fish, wild duck, and venison. McKeogh would write the stories from messages Knowles would scrawl with charcoal on birch bark. Unfortunately, it was all fakery. Knowles's bearskin had two bullet holes and he was seen slipping into McKeogh's cabin where a guide-cook reigned (Carson 1981). This was a time when medical and scientific fraud also reigned. They contributed much to the distrust between science and the media, with the media often a willing accomplice. Be skeptical of stories that seem too good to be true; often they're not.

Both medical and scientific fraud are still around. The key to deception lies in secrecy. Science, journalism, and government conducted in secret, unchallenged, offer too many chances for abuse of trust. Rex Buchanan, a science writer and teacher of science writing, sees the necessity for journalists to maintain something of the adversary position with scientists without alienating sources of science information. That takes open and tolerant communication with the scientists (1979).

Are you involved?

Questions may be raised, also, about the ethics of noninvolvement for both scientists and science writers. This is the posture some scientists adopt that accepts no responsibility for the uses made of their discoveries. Journalists are under attack both for their neutrality in reporting and for being partisan. A society of readers and viewers feeling confused and unable to sort out highly technical issues can hardly be blamed for regarding the scientist as cold and the journalist as confusing and both, at best, as unhelpful when their reports lack material that could guide nonscientists in evaluating the impact of new discoveries. Sorting out the right thing to do in a democracy is going to take, as pollster Daniel Yankelovich advises, scientists reducing their isolation and learning a messier discipline, how to deal with making public policy in the open arena. It will take also journalists who are willing to learn and understand what these scientists are doing if the public is to make rational choices. Writes Yankelovich: "Sooner or later the decisions that determine our survival must be endorsed by the electorate" (1984,12).

Before accepting too eagerly the arbitration of public issues by scientists, journalists might do well to remember the cautions of the late Polykarp Kusch, physicist and Nobel Prize winner:

> Science cannot do a large number of things, and to assume that science may find a technical solution to all problems is the road to disaster. . . .Science, in itself, is not the source of the ethical standards, the moral insight, the wisdom that is needed to make value judgments, though it is an important ingredient in making value judgments. An apalling number of citizens believe that it is up to the scientist to make the judgment, as though he had an especially valid set of values (Kusch 1961, 3).

Pseudoscience in media

Of immediate concern to scientists and science writers is the large amount of false science occupying time and space in the media. Media managers fret about the credibility of the media while exerting very little influence over content that knowledgeable, educated readers and viewers hold to be of dubious value, at best. Daily horoscopes and other astrology material offer the most notable example of this sort of material. Its publication may be justified on the grounds that millions of people believe in horoscopes and demand them in their newspaper or they will buy another. Entertainment values also provide a rationale for publishing horoscopes. However this weakens the media's case when they seek to claim respect on the basis of accuracy and seriousness of purpose.

The media are vulnerable, also, on ethical grounds for publicizing a wide variety of health and medical fads without seeking additional, expert information. Periodically, for example, media will carry stories on people indulging in exotic attempts to cure any number of chronic diseases. Sitting in old uranium mines to absorb radiation or flying to some foreign country for injections of mysterious miracle drugs offer only two examples. General reporters as well as science writers should be skeptical whenever someone approaches them with claims of a "cure" through some secret and exclusive formula or device, a simple relief method, vague testimonials from people whose full identity cannot be established, or some special dietary or nutritional solution. Another clue to a confidence game is when the promotion rests on cleansing the body of unspecified poisons.

Writers should be warned they are about to take part in unethical practices if the news source claims approval of the Food and Drug Administration; federal law does not permit suggesting FDA approval in marketing. Beware, also, of claims that the FDA, the medical establishment or the well-known disease foundations are in some conspiracy to withhold recognition or approval of the so-called treatment. Often these promises are couched in a gobbledygook of vague, scientific sounding terms that on examination mean nothing. This helps the quack deny making any promises when the law begins to look at the scam.

Medical quacks prey on writers and the public by negotiating a transfer of trust, a task made easier by some of the well publicized medical and economic practices of hospitals and doctors. Tactics include cost comparisons, free introductory treatments, claims that all doctors butcher or poison patients, telling the gullible that conventional medical practitioners are "too busy" to give full attention to a condition, and a dozen other ruses to undermine your trust. These are well known salesmen's tricks, getting you to agree on one point and moving that agreement to other grounds.

Another favorite ploy of charlatans is to

rediscover from China, Africa, Tibet or other exotic land a "cure" known to the ancients and lost for centuries.

Testimonials are particularly hard to resist. Few offer documentation that the persons were diagnosed as actually having the named disease. However even people with the most devastating diseases sometimes feel better, if only briefly. Some diseases simply run their course, with or without treatment. Just enough spontaneous remissions of disease, for reasons doctors would like to understand, are on record to support hope, and sustain quackery. Beware of both scientific and medical claims that depend on sensory perceptions; the senses can be fooled, as any magician can testify. Insist on seeing test data gathered in an organized, neutral fashion. Check out the sources of such data.

Writers can be lulled into accepting and publishing unethical material through the endorsement of a seemingly legitimate professional or business association. Check out the membership of such associations. Nothing is easier to form than a self-protective association. Check out credentials; in the medical and health care field, there is no such thing as a reliable, unaccredited school.

The National Association of Science Writers holds that you should take all necessary measures to ensure that all information you purvey will be accurate, truthful and impartial. The association also frowns on taking remuneration to permit your name to be used to "promote" a commercial service, product, or organization.

Chapter 11
Broadcasting science news

SCIENCE NEWS REPORTING ON RADIO and TV comes in highly variable package sizes and qualities. The packages range from twenty- to ninety-second "news" spots, sandwiched between local and world events on the evening newscasts, to the elaborate, hour-long *National Geographic* documentaries and the educational "Cosmos" series that made astrophysicist Carl Sagan of Cornell University an international celebrity. Each documentary and each program in a series can take weeks to produce and sometimes months or years. Achieving network technical standards requires elaborate production and film/taping equipment. This makes documentaries very expensive propositions. Furthermore, science and medical shows are perceived as playing to a limited audience.

There have been some exceptions. The University of Texas Health Science Center in Houston produced, for educational and public relations purposes, a series of medical advice program that won nearly two minutes of precious air time on news shows in dozens of cities in Texas and other parts of the country. The success of this series lay partly in its moderator, Dr. Red Duke, an engaging, drawling, bushy-moustached physician whose steel-rimmed granny glasses could not hide his projection of intense concern for patients. He looked and sounded much different from your average family doctor.

This success illustrates two problems electronic journalists face in reporting sci-

ence news over radio and television. In television especially, you need a combination of voice and personality that mesh with the subject matter to hold an audience long enough to win the time necessary to tell most science stories. Personality on radio comes about just as strongly through voice timbre and pace of delivery, combined with the voices of other actors in the drama. Otherwise the tendency of an audience to switch to something more dramatic or magnetic produces low viewership and listenership that a network or local station cannot endure. Low ratings essentially killed a weekly television science show hosted by Walter Cronkite, who had the image and reputation of being the most trusted anchorman in network news. Honesty and trust were not enough to hold audiences once he was away from exciting and often stressful, to viewers, events of daily news.

National Public Radio, a few local stations, and the Public Broadcasting Service maintain commitments to science and nature programs because policy dictates they should. The also deal with a faithful audience of educated and affluent people, ideal science news buffs. The "Undersea World of Jacques Costeau" has been a staple on public television. Cable News Network also used regular medical programs, sponsored by a drug company. The American Association for the Advancement of Science experimented with ninety-second radio spots distributed to commercial stations for free use, and the

American Institute of Physics has tried to interest local TV stations in using two-minute science strips during news shows. Occasional commercial radio statons commit time to science and medicine, and talk show hosts will scatter a scientist among their guests now and then. Often the specialists deal in applied sciences, such as the horticulturist who answers questions about planting methods and tree pruning. There are exceptions. FM Station KGO in San Francisco in 1983 devoted two hours weekly to a science program touching all areas except the social sciences and medicine. Suspicions exchanged among broadcasters indicate that they think conventional science programs attract an audience, estimated at from 10 percent to 20 percent of the total viewers, of hard-core science fans who will watch anything of this genre. Often science-nature programs are scheduled into time slots where viewing is low anyway. One advantage of the short segments devoted to science programming is that they can be slipped into news programs or unsold commercial spots without much disturbance of regular programming. The lack of sure-fire commercial appeal for science contributes to a nagging media frustration among science writers and scientists who see television as an especially effective way of teaching people about science.

Although all three national networks have one or more science news specialists, the on-camera appearances of ABC's Jules Bergman, who is the dean of television science journalists after nearly thirty years with the network, or of Robert Bazell of NBC are limited mainly to short news stories except when "big events" occur in science or medicine. Bergman, for example, gets his greatest camera exposure during space flights or when some other technological event, such as the implantation of the first artificial heart, makes news for reasons other than the science involved. The science specialist supports the news coverage of the event with explanations or interviews interpreting the technical processes surrounding the event itself. Bergman and Phil Lewis, his producer, won the Science in Society award of the National Association of Science Writers for "Asbestos: The Way to Dusty Death." This documentary sprang out of the news event of a public controversy that erupted when lawsuits claiming asbestos-related ailments threatened the financial stability of companies in the asbestos industry. The documentary challenged Bergman to explain the medical, economic, and legal aspects of the story.

Writing for electronic media

The appeal of electronic media, especially television and its variants, attract science writers in spite of the fierce competition for jobs and air time. George Alexander, science writer for the *Los Angeles Times,* left his newspaper after 25 years in print journalism for a year-long Macy Foundation fellowship intended to get more science journalists in broadcasting. His biggest surprise was the adjustment necessary to minimize his own contributions and let his subjects tell the story in their own words. Broadcast journalists may work a day or two on a two-minute story or a week on one running six minutes (Alexander 1985). Many journalists will find they need voice training and a certain level of mechanical aptitude to cope with recording equipment and the complexities of cutting and splicing the magnetic recording tapes.

For most science journalists, the best opportunity for science writing on radio and television will come as a producer. There is little specialization for on-camera personalities with local television news and features staffs because they are expected to cover several news events each day. Many must write their own scripts also. The high salaries of network news correspondents make it uneconomical, in the view of TV management, to have "personalities" involved too long in the logistics of researching a story, setting up film-taping appointments and moving camera crews around the landscape. This work falls to someone known as a producer.

The producer is responsible for researching and presenting story ideas, steering them through the selection process, doing or guiding field research, picking locations, managing the camera crews, organizing. the production sequences, and often writing the first draft (or the final draft) of the script. After all this is in place, the "anchors" come in to review the script and tape the sequences where they appear. Television is a group effort. Although the introduction of new, miniaturized, and lightweight camera and sound recording gear no longer makes TV the two thousand-pound pencil of journalism, it is more cumbersome than print journalism for the journalist. Some TV shows are done as studio productions; "Cosmos," for example, used elaborate, dramatic stage settings to enhance the feeling of accompanying moderator Sagan on a tour of the universe.

Radio reporters need a broadcast-quality tape cassette recorder, one that reproduces conversations and interviews with a fidelity better than the cassette recorders available at the low end of the price scale. A print reporter can make out with sufficient clarity of sound to transcribe key quotes. The radio reporter can bring people into the studio for live interviews on the air, but risks loss of audience if the chemistry produces a dull exchange. Radio reporters can splice together their own commentary with that of people they interview. This technique strips out dull and badly spoken segments from the tape, but it can be abused by distorting the interviewee's words and context. Many public relations people will supply "actualities" for use by radio, prerecorded statements that offer explanation and commentary on subjects in the science or science-public affairs fields. You can even get prerecorded answers, with a set of questions to be asked by the announcer. These come from companies and institutions aiming for free publicity using the name of the scientist to promote the ends of his or her school, company, or viewpoint. Mainly it's free advertising. Public relations offices also produce short video segments for use on in-house communications networks for employee training and information. Such products seldom discuss the less appealing sides of an issue or fully explore depths of controversy.

Wire service reporters also are expected to write for radio and for print. To serve customers of the radio wire, news service writers will also file a short story written for radio stations subscribing to the news services. Often the wire service reporters will read their copy in feeds to stations. Public relations offices also send out tapes and news releases slanted for radio. Radio has the ability to use sound effects and music to evoke pictures and emotional responses in the minds of the listeners. Overuse of these and other techniques in both TV and radio can carry you into that grey, shifting border between information and contrived entertainment. Skillful use of "natural" sound can evoke powerful responses. In 1984 Walter Cronkite made effective use of the soft, clicking sounds of robots at work in an unpeopled, darkened factory for "High Tech: Dream or Nightmare?" The scenes established a tone for the show, which raised questions about the future use of humans in factories and the kinds of jobs, if any, available for most workers. Television is also subject to making writers search for the sharp turn of phrase; Cronkite's term "steel collar workers" describing the robots is an example. These phrases register upon the ear and stick in the brain.

One of the complaints of scientists, some of whom delight in the chance to appear on TV or radio, is that the broadcast journalist is particularly vulnerable to the scientist-operator who can condense or oversimplify a complex situation into a catchy phrase. On television, this is coupled with the dangers of image-thinking in which reasoned and rational arguments supporting a scientific position can be replaced by a series of images and buzzwords that carry viewers to a conclusion faster than the mind—and reason—can follow. The short times allotted any story on a newscast compound the problems and make the medium vulnerable to distortion and misrepresentation.

Writing for radio and television comes more naturally for some science writers than for others. The key to effective radio-TV writing is remembering that you are transferring information through the ear rather than through the eye. The ear accepts information at a much slower rate and requires conditioning the mind to receive through the ear. However as you develop skill at writing for the ear, you can appreciate the beauty of how precisely you can control that marvelous instrument, the human voice, through your scripts.

This control is accomplished through knowing that the normal speaking voice delivers about 150 to 180 words per minute. This allows you or the persons for whom you write to estimate the time on a story in terms of seconds. When you get better acquainted with your own speaking rate or that of someone for whom you write regularly, you can hit the requested time precisely. You and your announcer should read the script through aloud to locate rough and uncertain writing in the spoken version and to get an actual time. (For the same reasons, many print writers will find their stories benefit from being read aloud to reveal similar problems in stories for print media.) Some writers have the knack of hearing a story as they read it silently.)

Because you are writing for voice and ear, which process information much more slowly than the eye, your sentences should be much shorter, more declarative. This requires clear, sharp thoughts. Shorter sentences also give your announcer a chance to breathe. Use an active style wherever you can. Unlike the printed word, conventions of radio and television favor the use of present-tense writing. You can mix present and past tenses, discouraged in most printed works. Although

people usuallly read a story in newspapers and magazines silently and alone, radio and television appear to members of the audience as much more personal than print does. Therefore you can adopt a somewhat more casual, personal writing approach than you might use for a story going into print. Beware guidance that tells you to write like you speak, unless you speak very well indeed. Broadcast writing is writing as you wish you spoke. Only a few specialty stations tolerate slangy, ultracasual expression. Direct address is more acceptable to radio-TV news editors than it is to editors in the print media.

There are some things to avoid in writing for the ear. Do not string "s" and "cee" words or sibilants together. The same goes for percussives, such as "Peter Piper picked a peck . . ." Sibilants and percussives can have your announcer sounding like a short-circuited electric appliance. You will be hissing at the listener. Avoid packing too many facts and numbers together in a single sentence. While print media editors like such tight and compact writing, throwing too much at a listener overloads the ear and brain. Spoken writing is much looser and contains words thrown in to separate the hard chunks of fact that float through a sentence.

Spoken communication is more effective when the ear and brain are conditioned to receive your information. Therefore few radio writers will start a story or a sentence with a name, unless the basis for identification has already been laid in the story. "A physicist said today that . . ." will precede the sentence containing the scientist's name unless he or she is well known. Some routine facts may be omitted entirely. Ages, precise titles, addresses, and sometimes town names lack the pertinence to command time in a short radio or television report. You save every word you can because you will not have enough of them to tell all the relevant facts. Background information also gets little space in electronic news stories.

Radio reporters have an advantage over

their TV counterparts. They can patch or connect a telephone conversation into the broadcast or into their tape recorders without elaborate prior arrangements. You should, however, tell your interviewee you are recording the talk for broadcast use. When editing snippets of conversation out for broadcasting, you need to be careful to keep these fragments in the context of the entire conversation. This is ethical journalism.

Words with pictures

Two things electronic media cannot tolerate are dead air and dead screens. Do you remember driving and listening to your radio? Suddenly there's no sound. Did it startle you? You may have wondered if your radio had broken. Did a power failure knock the station off the air? The announcer may have only stepped out of the booth longer than intended, allowing a tape or record to play out. Whatever happened, it certainly was not planned. As you have seen from timing scripts for 150 to 180 words per minute, you can estimate time down to a split second. The process works in reverse—or simultaneously—for television. Pictures and words are coordinated the same way, against the frames or inches of pictures to be used in the story. This allows you to work pictures into a TV broadcast by coordinating them with the announcer's voice. You must fill the airtime allotted for the story. And the segments of sound must match the segments of film or tape in each scene of the story. Film and tape are timed by the playing speed, as in frames per second for film and inches per second for tape. Seldom are the stories on TV the complete, unedited "raw" tape shot by the camera crew. They are edited down, which you as producer may do also, to preserve only the best pictures and quotations.

You can use "outside" film or tape from a scientist or a public information office in the story by "dubbing" or copying segments and splicing them into your story. Many researchers film experiments or tape examples to illustrate their discussions. In teaching hospitals they may have the assistance of very expert photographers, artists and writers to help them. You need only know the length of time required to show an adequate amount of the scientific action, the fertilizaton of an egg by a sperm, for example. Then you can write the amount of copy needed to cover and explain the picture for the time the film or tape is to be on the tube or movie screen. When you have the accompaniment of pictures, you do not need to put the whole story into words. Let the pictures tell as much and possible, explaining as little as you can. When working with pictures, do not explain what is obvious to the viewer. Use your precious words for background, point out the significance, and explain what your audience does not see but needs to know to understand the picture. Television and film writers and editors follow the rule that "Less is more."

If the tape or film has its own sound, such as an interviewee answering a question or a sound inherent to the action being observed, you will need a pair of transitions. These are words known as a "lead in" and "lead out" designed to condition your viewers to the coming change of scene. If the tape or film has no sound of its own, you must supply a "voice over" to explain what is happening. Again, avoid explaining the obvious.

Scripts may be written in all capital letters or in capitals and lower case. One of the conventions of broadcasting is the "all kaps" script. However a combination of big and little letters is easier to read. Likely your copy will be put into a character generator that will project the script onto an off-camera reading device that allows announcers to follow copy without seeming to read from a script. Often the reading device is a television screen concealed in the anchorpersons's desk. The character generators, much like word processors, can also put additional information and graphic devices directly on the screen. For example you may augment voice information with a "crawler" of words along the bottom of the picture or at key points in illustration. You are not limited, either, to moving pictures or film or tape. A still picture may be "frozen" on the screen to give viewers a close look at some key part of the action. Most stations will have graphic artists who will prepare maps, charts and sketches as still pictures to illustrate your point. These can be fed into the electronic picture from projectors for still photographs and slides. Part of the art of successful and interesting television lies in choosing the mixture of such materials to produce the right effect on your audience as well as illustrating your point.

Seeking the action

Still pictures are considered of low-level interest in television programming, even though they may be the best way of illustrating your story's point. Accept, however, that TV is the medium of motion. Thus a story with lots of action will knock off a story without action. One of the unfortunate visual handicaps of science and medical stories is that many of the most dramatic moments cannot be seen or cannot be photographed—or there is no action. You can achieve simulated animation through various techniques. One technique is time-lapse photography, those pictures where you see a flower unfolding, for example. As with the unfolding flower, time-lapse photography has lost its novelty and become a visual bromide. Sometimes shifting the focus of the camera across various parts of an especially dramatic still photograph of an experiment works to achieve simulated motion in the eyes of the viewer. True animation, the process by which cartoon characters appear to move, is expensive and time consuming, hardly suited for spot news. Faster graphics, including animated graphics, may come from new software programs being developed for microcomputers. For now, these emerging graphics possibilities function best in the hands of expert programmers.

On the other hand, "graphics packages" are becoming more a part of scien-

tific documentation, and many of your news sources may produce them as part of their investigations. Your camera people can photograph these illustrations off the screen of the computer tube or perhaps have them duplicated onto a video cassette tape. Ask about these electronic possibilities. In some universities, government labs, hospitals, and industries, there are graphic artists, photographers, or computer-aided design (CAD) technicians who may be able to produce simulations for you. The investigators themselves or the public relations office can make the arrangements. Computer-generated illustrations that include simulated motion have reached a very realistic level in some laboratories. The programming process is tedious and therefore expensive. As more is learned about programming for such illustrations, this process may offer both scientists and science journalists a more accurate way of portraying for the general audience how the experts think the physical world operates. This will add new dimensions to understanding through seeing the unseeable.

Similarly, motion pictures may document parts of the actual investigation. Copies may be made available if you ask. Many high speed processes, such as wind tunnel and temperature testing, use high-speed photography called Schlieren (shadow) photography, which registers changes in the density of the air around a test object. Some laboratories will have the electronic equipment needed to add false color to black and white photography. This is the way color is added to satellite photographs of the earth, available through government offices. The technique may be applied to other computerized pictures to make the invisible into a picture.

At many news events, such as space shots, the scientists and the public relations office may make available models, called mock-ups, and training aids as backdrops and props to add visual interest to your stories. Doctors often do simulated operations on animals, dummies and corpses as part of their preparation for experimental procedures. This may be strong stuff to put on television. Most experimental surgery is documented routinely, step by step, with commentary by the chief experimenter. The problem of taste may force you to edit out some of the more gory segments or have the nerve and support of management to broadcast material that may shock a large number of viewers. A tiny but growing branch of law deals with media legal responsibility for disseminating material that may have adverse effects on unwarned viewers. Animal experiments may yield protests from animal rights groups as well as illustration for your stories. The writer may want to consider a warning to viewers that such material is coming in a production.

Most illustrations, particularly for news stories, will be taken on the scene by your camera crews. The best of the scientific meetings will provide you with a secluded place for interviewing scientists. If this is not part of the press arrangements, you will have to find your own quiet spot. The lighter, more portable ENG (electronic news gathering) equipment makes this easier, but you must provide the questions. This gets very difficult when you know you will have only a few seconds for the story on the air. Most TV reporters will do a dry run on the interview in advance of taping, helping the subject move toward short, direct answers where possible. But have you ever thought of the problems of explaining DNA in thirty seconds?

Such time restrictions make television interviews seem oversimplified. Another handicap is that TV interviewers seldom are science specialists. They are generalists or have a better acquaintance with the stuff of politics and public affairs. Thus, the ability of a reporter to understand the heart of a story or to compress the questions and answers into a few seconds may guide story choices more than significance of the scientific and technological content. The closer the discovery or application comes to general human experience, the more likely that television, the truly mass medium, will use the story. "As a result this system requires journalists with strong stomachs able to ask embarrassing questions they know to be silly," says Ira Flatow (1979, 10) of National Public Radio. Broadcasters get only one chance at the story.

Because the illustrations on television flow past the viewer, stripping the artwork and the focus of photography down to the most simple elements is more important than for print journalists. A complex illustration in a newspaper or magazine can be studied and restudied by the reader, but it lies beyond the recall of television viewers. Material recorded on video casettes can be an exception if the equipment has a "stop-action" function that will freeze and hold a frame on the TV tube for extended viewing. Some educational material makes use of this capability to allow viewers to study a scene until they understand what they see.

Assembling the sequence of illustrations and accompanying descriptions calls for much the same logic and art used to organize a science feature story for print. The story moves from the opening, through key points and to its climax. The short news story can cover, at best, only one aspect of the story. Avoid bogging the story down in details that eat into time. If you have a longer story, you may want to preview the organization with "storyboards." These are rough sketches, drawn in a screenlike format, of key illustrations in the story, the milestones that help you visualize the organization and progress of a story. Obviously television production involves more than the general steps outlined here. Several books detailing the process of scripting for TV are available, but these basic steps will get you started. Many colleges and high schools offer television production courses, and in many communities the local cable company offers free or cheap access to TV production training as part of its local contract.

Accuracy vs. stereotype

Not all science journalists accept the standards of commercial television, even when financial success comes with the formula. Former NASW president Edward Edelson of the New York *Daily News* called the formula for "That's Incredible" the "worst possible news for journalists who are trying to write seriously about science and medicine in the U.S." The proposed mix of stories that offended him leaned heavily on items about extrasensory perception, "astonishing" scientific achievements, frog and animal research, voodoo, and "great natural mysteries." These are elements of schlock science, pseudoscience that focuses on the bizarre (1980, 2).

One scientist has warned televison interviewers they may be on the wrong track in pursuing the appeal of fear in science. The pessimistic questions of TV interviewers are in sharp contrast with the optimistic questions the scientist says he gets from audiences who see promise in science and technology. It is a mind set that a journalist, print or electronic, can slip into easily (Rosen 1977).

Part of this trap is formed through television entertainment programs. Much of the learning that takes place about science and scientists comes indirectly through entertainment shows. With some exceptions, these programs have stereotyped science as threatening and scientists as cold, calculating, and often reprehensible. Or scientists have been portrayed as superbrains, capable of producing miracles, which may flatter scientists but misses the mark. Another stereotype is the scientist who is brilliant in the lab but bumbling outside it. With the resurgence of interest in science, such attitudes may lead to wrong expectations due to a contrived image or a surrendering of citizen participation in issues and reliance upon the expert.

Physicist Jeremy Bernstein, a science writer for *The New Yorker,* finds objections to using elaborate stage and production techniques to report science: (1) scientific points can get lost in the cuteness of staging; (2) you can make events too visual, beyond reality; and (3) predicted results may not come. Instead of contriv-

ing dramatic effect through sets, it may be enough simply to show your audience the places, the buildings where major science events took place, the laboratories where science is made today. He also advises recreating the famous lectures where scientists unveiled their discoveries (1981).

The effect of television on viewers is powerful and can have unexpected results. The Royal Medical Society entered a serious public fight with the British Broadcasting Corporation (BBC) following a documentary alleging inadequacy in British tests for death before the removal of organs for transplantation. Donations of kidneys dropped 50 percent (UPI 1980). On the other hand, deliberate use of the medium's powerful effect for political purpose was Dr. Bernard Nathanson's intent when he made a videotape of sonograph pictures of a fetus being aborted.

Science journalists also have the opportunity to correct misimpressions of science and medicine as they appear on entertainment shows. Mike Oppenheim, M.D., argued in *TV Guide* that the violence on entertainment shows should be even more violent—showing what really happens as a consequence of gunshot wounds, for example. Although a hero taking a shoulder wound appears fit again after a week with the arm in a sling, the truth is far more painful, and it's long-lasting pain and disablement. Knife slayings are not quick and easy, said Dr. Oppenheim. "Furthermore, anyone who has watched an inexperienced farmhand slaughter a pig knows that the resulting mess must be seen to be believed." Human death is similar. Showing violence as it really is would do much to discourage any fascination with it, he argues. Already beset for showing too much violence, TV producers can barely imagine taking more realism to advertisers for approval (Oppenheim 1984, 20).

"People would watch more science on television and learn more from it if producers could produce a good play instead of a good wildlife lesson. There are some prime time shows that successfully mix medical content with drama," says Barbara Culliton, a former NASW president and news editor for *Science* magazine. There is no evidence that the public is sated with science news, she says. "Rather there is a demand that it be interesting" (1982-83, 4).

Don Herbert, who appeared on NBC for fifteen years as "Mr. Wizard," offers this four-step guide to writing for broadcast that is familiar to anyone who writes feature stories.

1. Catch viewers' attention.
2. Arouse curiosity with promise of interesting things ahead.
3. Develop a "plot": What happens next?
4. Resolve the "plot," fulfill the promise, satisfy the viewer.

Herbert packed this into a ninety-second format to demonstrate scientific phenomena, a magic show. The problem is the same one faced by people who write advertising commercials as minidramas. They achieve these often in less than ninety seconds for a commercial. It takes care and thought, but it could break science reporting out of the stereotyped molds of TV interviews and long documentaries in news broadcasts. Some organizations are trying this now with educational clips on science, medicine and health care (Herbert 1982-83, 9).

CONTROVERSY.   Some of the other problems of television coverage of science and medical events include getting news ahead of knowledge, raising unnecessary alarm in viewers, and frightening people away from treatment. They were illustrated by "AIDS: Profile of an Epidemic." This 1984 documentary about the newly identified disease known as "acquired immune deficiency syndrome" (AIDS) was prepared by the Public Broadcasting System. Recognition of AIDS as an identifiable condition occurred in 1979 and became known outside medical circles in 1981. The federal Centers for Disease Control in Atlanta first warned of its

prevalence among promiscuous homosexual men and regular drug users. The pattern of a breakdown in the victims' ability to resist what are called "opportunistic" infections and a rare cancer was found also among a set of Haitian immigrants to the United States and some victims of blood diseases, such as hemophilia, that require treatment with a series of blood transfusions. Much later it was recognized officially in babies born to some drug users and some possibly bisexual men. Some doctors at Albert Einstein Hospital attempted earlier to get material on babies into the medical literature but were rebuffed (Rubin 1985). At first the disease appeared limited to the United States. As awareness of the disease spread, it was reported by doctors in other countries and, finally, identified as being widespread in Africa. Total cases by mid-1984 were reported as under 4000. Late in 1985, the number of people identified in the United States with AIDS topped 14,000-plus, with more than 1,000 others in Europe. The number of victims appeared to nearly double each year, and the fatality rate seemed near 80 percent. Its victims included several otherwise healthy persons who had contracted the disease through blood transfusions, including one nun. A primitive test for antibodies to the disease, to estimate exposure, was developed after only four years, primarily to screen blood donations. Congress and the federal administration provided emergency funds for research into the causes of AIDS, care, possible cures and potential vaccines against it.

The story of AIDS contained all elements necessary for sensational reporting: sex, threat to health, mystery, and high probability of death. Criticism of all media reporting on AIDS was almost universal. Dr. Virgil A. Hatcher, professor at New York University's medical school and author of a book about AIDS, had both praise and criticism for the PBS documentary. However the PBS story was produced after later knowledge emerged, knowledge unavailable to both doctors and journalists reporting earlier. Dr. Hatcher faulted the program for failing to clearly define the elements that make up the disease. This should have been one of the first tasks of the writers and producers, but it would have been outdated by the time it appeared. Haitians, for example, were later removed as a group at special risk of catching or transmitting AIDS as the general prevalence of the suspected virus became better known. The stigma attached to Haitians by early ignorance of the disease was, in retrospect, unnecessary. However part of the first scares associated with AIDS lay in journalists' ignorance of how the medical community applies the term "epidemic" to any increase beyond the expected "normal" incidence of a disease. Thus an epidemic may involve relatively small numbers for cases of a rare disease. Yet in the unraveling of the AIDS story, the "sensationalist" version may yet be shown more accurate as doctors develop their data. Thus news ran ahead of knowledge. Reporting could not wait for the years needed to develop fuller, and still incomplete, information.

Another criticism involved failure of the media to convey the immense difficulties researchers face in locating the causes of AIDS or any new disease through the slow, painstaking methods of basic research. Epidemiology helps locate, describe, and define many aspects of a new disease, but researchers may postulate several and even conflicting theories or hypotheses that must be tested and verified. During the heat of the AIDS controversy documented by PBS, both French and American scientists identified a virus believed to be the cause of AIDS. By late 1985, the scientific community had not yet reached universal consensus on whether this was the same identical virus or two versions of it, raising the possibility that the AIDS virus, like the influenza virus, just might be able to mutate faster than scientists could develop vaccines.

The AIDS documentary itself seemed contradictory, Dr. Hatcher observed. One of its purposes was to make the point that

AIDS was difficult to transmit from a victim to fellow workers, medical personnel, and to families. This lack of understanding of the disease had caused undertakers, nurses, doctors, employers, blood bank operators, friends and casual acquaintances to ostracize AIDS patients. While generally attempting to bring rationality to this picture, Dr. Hatcher noted, the point regarding the low dangers of casual transmission from one person to another was negated by the show's ending, which warned, "Use extreme precautions when in contact with an AIDS patient." (This was, however, advice that many in the medical community would support from their own knowledge of the uncertainties of science and medicine until all possible evidence on AIDS had been developed, and it was an indication of divergent opinions found in medical disputes.)

Dr. Hatcher praised the PBS producers for giving sufficient and broad description of signs that laymen could use to recognize AIDS in its earliest stages. Yet when one married Texas public official discussed having these symptoms, journalists did not press him for public acknowledgement of the true nature of his condition. Both print and electronic journalists used detailed material from his death certificate, however, to permit their audiences to infer AIDS, although that was never said explicitly. Dr. Hatcher also praised the producers for omitting descriptions and photographs of treatment procedures, which can be gruesome. TV producers, more than print writers, have to be sensitive to the possibility that people needing treatment for AIDS, cancer, or any of a dozen other diseases may avoid treatment after seeing it and its consequences (Hatcher 1984). Doctors frequently turn aside patients' request for such details or gloss over them for the same reason.

In breaking news situations, the powerful effects of television's pictures coupled with crisis situations, such as the 1979 nuclear power plant accident at Three Mile Island or terrorist and aerial hijacking events, has caused TV to become the focus of considerable criticism from others in the media and from outside. One line of criticism holds TV, with help from nonscience writers in the print media, exaggerated the dangers of radiation leaks at Three Mile Island. Critics of nuclear power, on the other hand, accuse the TV networks of underplaying the accident's seriousness. Several studies following that particular incident showed that TV reporters generally acted responsibly but mirrored the confusion among nuclear scientists and engineers at the scene.

After the accident, the one real criticism leveled at TV was the lack of reasoned analysis. Sociologist Dorothy Nelkin (1984a) laid the lack of such analysis in part to the pressures of TV to select visually stimulating material. Talking heads, she says, are not considered stimulating enough to hold an audience. Reality must be transformed into entertainment in the ethos of TV. Because journalists generally, and TV reporters in particular, have limited grasp of technological risks, they tend to rely on government officials as authoritative, responsible, neutral information sources. When government is confused or insensitive to emerging risks, journalists likely will fall back on their preconditioning from entertainment shows. The easiest questions for them to ask are the "What if . . .?" questions that evoke speculative answers drawn from worst-case possibilities.

Whether the medium is print or electronic, there is a primitivism in us all. When the scientists are baffled, as Prof. David M. Rubin (1980) has described at the Three Mile Island accident, an ancient awe leads writers to use all resources for information while conditioned to look for the worst. Dr. Edward Burger, director of the Institute of Health Policy Analysis at Georgetown University Medical Center, told Daniel Machalaba of *The Wall Street Journal,* "The public deserves to be educated about science, but the press emphasizes the simplistic and the scary" (Machalaba 1984). But when the shamans reach the edge of their knowledge, what is out there may well be scary. Most of the

Three Mile Island story has been written (Sills 1982), but the dramas inherent in the search for cure or prevention of AIDS have yet to be played out, along with who knows how many other dramas waiting to be discovered. For example, one of the new puzzles of AIDS emerged in the discovery of a concentration of victims in a small, poverty stricken Florida town. Why? Stay tuned.

Unraveling such mysteries posed by the natural world is what science is about. Putting the erratic progress of science into perspective is what science writing is about, whether you do it by words alone or with sound, motion and pictures. All science writers should be versatile and willing to operate in the medium that conveys the best understanding. Whatever your choice, it will be an exciting intellectual and physical journey, in good company, into the unknown. It should be a satisfying adventure.

Experiments

1. From the science stories you have read, pick one or two subjects that you think fit the requirements for a television program, and explain why in a one-page memorandum designed to convince a TV news director that they can be produced.

2. From *Science* magazine, *New England Journal of Medicine,* or another journal, write two news stories for radio. If you have a tape recorder, record them for playback and class critique.

3. Choose a story from your reading of journals or from experience and prepare a two-minute TV script and storyboards from it. Perhaps your class can tape the best of the stories into a science program.

4. Interview the university's public information person for a radio or video program on the problems of dealing with scientists and science subjects at your school.

5. Arrange to visit the newsroom of a local or university television station during preparations for a daily newscast; observe the selection and editing of stories.

REFERENCES

Alexander, George. l985. Goodbye pad and pencil, hello mike and camera. *ScienceWriters* 33(2):11, 12.

Altman, Lawrence K. 1984. Fewer AIDS cases filed at end of '83. *The New York Times,* Jan.6, 6.

———. 1985. Doctor seeks to limit news on artificial heart program. *The New York Times,* Feb. 2, 6.

Altschull, J. Herbert. 1983. *Agents of Power: The Role of Media in Public Affairs.* New York: Longman.

Ashby, Eric. 1960. Dons or crooners. *Science* April 8, 1165-70.

Associated Press. 1983. Leprosy increases in U.S. *The Houston Post,* Nov.30, 32D

———. 1984a. Judge castigates company chiefs in suit over intrauterine device. *The New York Times,* March 2, 9.

———. 1984b. Radiation risks at 3 Mile Island are found higher than expected. *The New York Times,* Jan. 6, 6.

———. 1984c Shockley wins $1 in libel suit. *The New York Times,* Sept. 15, 6.

Barbanel, Josh. 1984. Report finds psychiatric services in chronic crisis in New York City. *The New York Times,* Jan. 7, 1.

Bernstein, Jeremy. 1981. TV Science: D for Sagan, A for Miller for obeying Bernstein's second law. *NASW Newsletter* 29(3):6-10.

———. 1982. Accepting scientific ideas. *St. Petersburg Times,* April 30, 21A.

Bishop, Jerry E. 1980. The Dunwoody report: She nailed us to the wall. *NASW Newsletter* 28(1):8.

———. 1981a. The editor's letter. *NASW Newsletter* 29(3):20.

———. 1981b. Wall Street insiders cash in while writers observe NEJM release time. *NASW Newsletter* 29(2):4.

———. 1982. Do scientists have a right to publish when they please? *NASW Newsletter* 30(2):2.

———. 1984. Report validating lump removal in breast cancer awaits publication. *The Wall Street Journal,* Dec. 4, 33.

Bishop, Jerry E., and Michael Waldholz. 1983 New genetically engineered vaccines aim at blocking infectious diseases in millions. *The Wall Street Journal,* Oct. 23, 31.

Blakeslee, Sandra. 1983. Fossil may be clue to ancient diet. *The New York Times,* Dec. 26, 13.

Bloom, Mark. 1979. AP syndicates Blakeslee cancer series, but is mum on his cancer society affiliation. *NASW Newsletter* 28(3):1.

Bloom vs. Relman: Panel at Columbia P&S debates NEJM's "Ingelfinger Rule." 1982. *NASW Newsletter* 30(1):6.

Blumberg, Baruch S. 1983. The life of service and the life of science. *The Magazine* 7(2):12.

Boorstein, Daniel J. 1983. *The Discoverers.* New York: Random House.

Bostian, Lloyd R. 1983. How active, passive and nominal styles affect readability of science writing. *Journalism Quarterly* 60(4):635.

Broad, William J. 1985. Reagan's "Star Wars" bid: Many ideas converging. *The New York Times,* Mar. 4, 1.

Broad, William J., and Nicholas Wade. 1983. *Betrayers of the Truth.* New York: Simon & Schuster.

Buchanan, Rex. 1979. Use of researcher feedback in a science writing seminar. Paper presented at AEJMC annual meeting, Houston, Texas.

Burd, Gene. 1981. Press responsibility for health news: Beyond precision and toward prevention. Paper presented at the AEJMC convention, East Lansing, Mich., Aug.

Calder, Richie. 1963. Introduction. In *The Evolution of Science,* ed. Guy S. Metraus and Francois Crouzet. New York: New American Library.

Cardon, Raul Luis. 1962 Needs and difficulties for the scientific and technological development in Latin America: Journalism's contributions to this development. *Report on the first inter-American seminar on science journalism.* Santiago, Chile. Oct. 16-18.

Monograph 341, 1-E669. Organization of American States.

Carson, Gerald. 1981. The Yankee Tarzan. *American Heritage,* May, 60-64.

Chalk, Rosemary. 1983. CSFR begins project on secrecy and openness in technical communication. *Science* 4 (Nov.):497.

Charrow, Robert P. 1983. Advertising prescription drugs. *Science,* June 10, 1106.

Ciba-Geigy v. Mathews, 428 F. Suppl. 523 (S.D.N.Y. 1977).

Communication and medical research. 1964. Proceedings of a national symposium, University of Pennsylvania in Philadelphia, Oct. 17.

Cornell, James. 1977. Ibero-American science writers meeting. *NASW Newsletter* 25(1,2,3 comb.):22.

Cotiaux, Neil E., and Lynn Darling. 1976. Allied Chemical considers plans to help Va. firms hurt by Kepone. *The Washington Post,* Dec. 3, 1C.

Courtright, John A., and Stanley J. Baran. 1980. The acquisition of sexual information by young people. *Journalism Quarterly* 57(1):107-14.

Cowen, Robert C. 1984. Avant-garde science journalism. *Technology Review,* Jan., 6.

Cromie, William J. 1981. Splitting water with light. *Mosaic,* Sept./Oct., 7.

Culbertson, Hugh M., and Guido H. Stempel III. 1984. Possible barriers to agenda setting in medical news. *Newspaper Research Journal* 5(3):53-60.

Culliton, Barbara J. 1981. The president's letter. *NASW Newsletter* 29(3):19.

_____. 1982-1983. Science in the media. *SIPIscope* 10(6):4.

Davis, Alan C., Jerry Bishop, and Pat McGrady, Sr. 1978. The American Cancer Society Seminars, chapter two: Rebuttals and agreement. *NASW Newsletter* 26(3):9-13.

Dickson, David. 1984. *The New Politics of Science.* New York: Pantheon.

Dietz, David. 1977. Giants of science were my friends. *NASW Newsletter* 25(1,2,3 comb.):25,26.

Duncan, Ronald, and Miranda Weston-Smith. 1978. *Encyclopedia of Ignorance.* Elmsford, N.Y.: Pergamon Press.

Dunwoody, Sharon. 1978. Science writers at work. Research Report No. 7, Indiana University School of Journalism.

_____. 1979a. News-gathering behaviors of specialty reporters: Making two-level comparison of mass media decision-making. *Newspaper Research Journal* 1(1):29-41.

_____. 1979b. Science writing study finds: AAAS is master of what makes news at its sessions. *NASW Newsletter* 29(4):1.

Dunwoody, Sharon, and Byron T. Scott. 1982. Scientists as mass media sources. *Journalism Quarterly* 59(1):52-59.

Dunwoody, Sharon, and Michael Ryan. 1983. Public information persons as mediators between scientists and journalists. *Journalism Quarterly.* 60(4):647.

_____. Unpublished manuscript. *Journalism Quarterly.* Forthcoming.

Edelson, Edward. 1980. The president's letter. *NASW Newsletter* 28(2):2.

_____. 1983. McClintock brings flair to science. *Austin American-Statesman,* Nov. 3, J1.

Edwards v. National Audubon Society 423 F. Suppl. 516 (D.C.N.Y. 1976) 556 F. 2d 113 (CA2 1977) cert. denied, 3 Med. Law Reptr. 1560 (US Sup. Ct. 1977).

Elliot, John. 1979. Relman of NEJM accused of restricting free flow of news. *NASW Newsletter* 28(3):5.

Fitzgerald, Mark. 1984. Pleasing the advertiser? *Editor and Publisher,* March 24, 18.

Flatow, Ira. 1979. Radio science reporting is an honorable estate. *NASW Newsletter* 27(2):10.

Forsham v. Califano, 587, F. 2d 1128 (D.C. Cir. 1978).

Forsham v. Califano, 100 S.Ct. 978 (1980).

Frenkel, Karen A. 1981. NYT may use FOI against NEJM rule. *NASW Newsletter* 29(3):15.

Friendly, Jonathan. 1985. Bureau ordered not to speak to a *Times* Reporter. *The New York Times,* Feb. 28, 6.

Gans, Herbert J. 1980. *Deciding What's News.* New York: Random House.

Gastel, Barbara. 1983. *Presenting Science to the Public.* Philadelphia: ISI Press.

Glynn, Carroll J. 1985. Science reporters and their editors judge sensationalism. *Newspaper Research Journal* 6(3):69-74.

Goodell, Rae. 1977. *The Visible Scientists.* Boston: Little, Brown.

_____. 1981. Scientists, not reporters, determined what the press covered in DNA debate. *NASW Newsletter* 29(1):1.

Goodfield, June. 1981. *Reflections on Science and the Media.* Washington, D.C.: American Association for the Advancement of Science.

Gratzer, W.B. 1984. Science has lost its virtue, not its value. *Science 84,* Jan./Feb., 17.

Greenberg, D.S. 1967 *The Politics of Pure Sci-*

ence. New York: The New American Library.

Greenberg, Daniel S. 1978. A court deciding science issues: Will it go to trial? *The (Louisville) Courier-Journal,* Jan. 25, A7.

Greenberg, Joel. 1982. Cocktail party tip leads to major beat by weekly. *NASW Newsletter* 30(3):13.

Greene, Bob. 1982. American beat: By any other name. *Esquire* Sept., 23.

Hatcher, Virgil A. 1984. Documentary. *Video Review,* Sept., 92.

Henahan, John F. 1981. Notes from an expatriate: An interview in a brothel and a few other such tales. *NASW Newsletter* 29(3):9.

Herbert, Don. 1982-1983. Science in the media. *SIPIscope* 10(6):9.

Hildebrand, Joel. 1957. *Science in the Making.* New York: Columbia University Press.

Hines, William. 1984. Ban of EDB use on citrus set for Sept. 1. *The Dallas Morning News,* March 3, 3A.

Hohenberg, John. 1961. Interview with author. New York, fall.

Holder, Dennis. 1983. Forget the old rules: Objectivity, caution. *Washington Journalism Review,* June, 36.

Holub, Miroslav. 1982-1983. Growing Up: Comments from a poet-scientist. *SIPIscope* 10(6):21.

Hrdy, Sarah Blaffer. 1983. Heat loss. *Science 83,* Oct., 73.

Hulting, John L., ed. 1983. *Playing It Straight.* Chester, Conn.: The Globe-Pequot Press.

Hutchinson v. Proxmire, 443 U.S. 111 99 S.Ct. 2675 (1979).

Interdisciplinary Panel on Carcinogenicity. *Science* 17 (Aug.):682-87.

Jeans, James. 1958. *The Growth of Physical Science.* New York: Fawcett.

Johnson, Earl J. 1965. The realities of world news editing. Sixteenth William Allen White Memorial Lecture, Lawrence, Kans., Feb. 10.

Johnson, Kenneth G. 1963. Dimensions of judgment of science news stories. *Journalism Quarterly* 40(Summer):315-22.

Kamin, Leon J. 1974. *The Science and Politics of IQ.* Hillsdale. N.J.: Lawrence Erlbaum.

Kevles, Daniel J., Jeffrey L. Sturchio, and P.T.Carroll. 1980. The sciences in America, circa 1880. *Science* 209(4452):27-32.

Kidder, Tracy. 1983. Science as a contact sport. *Science 83,* Sept., 59.

Knoll, Erwin. 1984. Censors at work. *The Progressive,* April, 4.

Kohlstedt, Sally Gregory. 1980. Science: The

struggle for survival, 1880-1894. *Science* 209(4452):33-41.

Kolata, Gina. 1982. Food affects human behavior. *Science,* Dec. 17, 1209.

Kreighbaum, Hillier. 1959. Public interest in science news. *Science,* April 24, 1092-95.

————. 1978. Perspectives on science writing. Paper distributed at Symposium on Teaching Science and Environmental Writing: The Journalism of Uncertainty, Seattle, Wash., Aug. 12.

Kusch, Polykarp. 1961. Science doesn't have all the answers. *The New York Herald Tribune,* April 12, sec.2, 3.

Kwolek, William F. 1973. A readability survey of technical and popular literature. *Journalism Quarterly* 50(Spring):225.

Laing, Mark. 1978. Asian science writers association reborn. *NASW Newsletter* 26(1):16.

Lear, John. 1962. When is a new idea fit to print? *Saturday Review,* April 7, 41.

Leary, Warren E. 1983. Study says trees may use chemicals to communicate. *Kansas City Times,* June 6, A-2.

————. 1979, Sperm count of U.S. men appears to be dropping, scientist reports. *Louisville Courier Journal,* Sept. 12, A4.

Levine, Steven T. 1981. Readability of genetic engineering articles in newspapers and magazines. Dept. of Journalism, University of Texas at Austin. Unpublished study.

Lewin, Roger. 1983. How did vertebrates take to the air? *Science,* July 1, 38.

Lewis, Howard J. 1985. Jon Franklin wins second Pulitzer—by doing it his way. *ScienceWriters* 33(2):1-4.

Lyons, Richard D. 1983. Science promises revolution in farming and its products. *The New York Times,* Dec. 26, 1.

McDonald, Kim. 1981. A "superstrain" of cockroaches hoodwinks news organizations. *The Chronicle of Higher Education,* Oct. 21, 9.

————. 1983. Limits on early release of medical news are called harmful. *The Chronicle of Higher Education,* Feb. 3, 6.

McLeod, Jack M., and James W. Swinehart. 1959. *Satellites, Science and the Public.* Ann Arbor: University of Michigan Survey Research Center.

Malachalaba, Daniel. 1984. Nuclear fallout: Age of high technology increases problem of press in covering complex controversies. *NASW Newsletter* 32(1):5.

Marcus, Steven J. 1984. "Bugs" that make chemicals. *The New York Times,* March 2, 31.

Marshall, Eliot. 1983. The murky world of toxicity testing. *Science,* June 10, 1130.

———. 1984a. Legal threat halts CDC meeting on lead. *Science,* Feb. 17, 672.

———. 1984b. Newman's impossible motor. *Science,* Feb. 10, 571.

Mehlberg, Henryk. 1958. *The Reach of Science.* Toronto: The University of Toronto Press.

Mobil will pay $100,000 to settle charges by EPA. 1983. *The Wall Street Journal,* July 7, 44.

Moore, Wayne S., David R. Bowers, and Theodore A. Granovsky. 1982. What magazines are telling us about insects. *Journalism Quarterly* 59(3):464-467.

NASW Roster of members, with supplements. July 1983.

National News Council. 1984. Council says *Times* distorted facts of dioxin story. *The Quill,* Jan., 37.

Nelkin, Dorothy. 1984a. Background paper. *Science in the Streets: A Twentieth Century Fund Report.* New York: Priority Press.

———. 1984b. Why is science writing so uncritical of science? *SIPIscope* 12(1):1-4.

Nelson, Harry. 1978. Laetrile. *NASW Newsletter* 26(1):12.

———. 1984. Man's grasp of bionics growing by careful leaps. *Houston Chronicle,* Feb. 26, sec. 5, 90.

Oppenheim, Mike. 1984. TV isn't violent enough. *TV Guide,* Feb. 11, 20.

Osio, Osvaldo. 1983. Celestial swastika story disputed by professors. *The Daily Texan,* July 14, 3.

Pasztor, Andy. 1983. Acid rain could be cured by cutbacks in Midwest sulfur pollution, panel says. *The Wall Street Journal,* June 30, 18.

Perlman, David. 1984. Chinese science writers curious about ET and SF, mystified by PR practice. *NASW Newsletter* 32(2):2.

Peterson, Osler L., and H. Jack Geiger. 1962. Auditing cancer research. *Saturday Review,* April 7, 45.

Phillips, David R. 1978. Newspaper stories about murder suicide. *Science* Aug. 25, 748.

Pitts, Melissa Lynn. 1980. Science news coverage in ten major dailies. M.A. thesis, University of Texas at Austin.

Randal, Judith. 1982. Gene screen: Firms to make tests part of personnel policies. *Dallas Times Herald,* July 11, 8A.

Reinhold, Robert. 1984. Restaurant has recipe for multimillion-dollar computer. *The New York Times,* Jan. 7, 7.

Relman, Arnold S. 1979. Medical meetings should be backgrounders, not news. *NASW Newsletter* 28(4):9.

———. 1984. "Ingelfinger rule" clarified by NEJM editor Relman. *ScienceWriters* 32(3):11. (Reprinted from *Clinical Research* 32(2):21.)

Rensberger, Boyce. 1977. Aztec experts deny as ridiculous professor's charge that they witheld data on extent of cannibalism. *The New York Times,* March 3, sec. 2, 23.

Reuters. 1981. Barber beetle's bite can be brutal. *The Dallas Morning News,* Jan. 18, 42A.

Rosen, S. 1977. A scientist in televisionland. *Television Quarterly* 14(spring):81.

Rubin, David. 1980. Science writers never had a chance in the Three Mile Island nuclear debacle. *NASW Newsletter* 28(1):1,2, 10-13.

Rubin, Rita. 1985. Doctors seeing increase in AIDS among children. *The Dallas Morning News,* July 21, 1.

Ryan, Michael. 1979. Attitudes of scientists and journalists toward media coverage of science news. *Journalism Quarterly* 56(1):18-26.

———. 1982. Impact of personal contact on sources' views of the press. *Newspaper Research Journal* 3(3):22-29.

Schmitt, Harrison E. 1984. Dissent. In *Science in the Streets: Twentieth Century Fund Report.* New York: Priority Press.

Schramm, Wilbur. 1962. *Science and the Public Mind.* Washington, D.C.: American Association for the Advancement of Science.

Schroeer, Dietrich. 1972. *Physics and Its Fifth Dimension: Society.* Reading, Mass.: Addison-Wesley.

Shaw, David. 1977. Science news: Experts see distortions. *The Los Angeles Times,* Jan. 13, 47.

Shepherd, R. Gordon. 1979. Science news of controversy: The case of marijuana. *Journalism Monographs* 62(Aug.):1-35.

Sibbison, Jim. 1985. Pushing new drugs—can the press kick the habit? *Columbia Journalism Review,* July/Aug., 52-54.

Silberner, Joanne. 1981. Bone of contention: Few science reporters bothered to check Harvard's claim of "new." *NASW Newsletter* 29(3), 13.

Sills, David, et al., eds. 1982 *The Accident at Three Mile Island: The Human Dimension.*

Boulder, Colo.: Westview.

Singh, Man Mohan, and Stanley R. Kay. 1976. Wheat gluten as a pathogenic factor in schizophrenia. *Science* 30(Jan):401.

Smith, R. Jeffrey. 1982. Scientists implicated in atom test deception. *Science*, Nov. 5, 545-547.

――――. 1984. Nuclear winter attracts additional scrutiny. *Science*, July 6, 30-32.

Smith, Richard D. 1984. The AIDS elephant. *The Sciences*, March/April, 8

The smooth selling of a wrinkle remover. 1984. *Business Week*, March 5, 66.

Snow, C.P. 1961. *The Two Cultures and The Scientific Revolution.* New York: Cambridge University Press.

Sokal, Michael M. 1980. Science and James McKeen Cattell, 1894-1945. *Science* 209(4452):43-51.

Stephens, Mitchell, and Nadyne G. Edison. 1982. News media coverage of issues during the accident at Three Mile Island. *Journalism Quarterly* 59(2):199.

Storad, Conrad J. 1984. Science writers evaluate their field. *Quill*, June, 29.

Strassman, Erwin O. 1964a. Letter to Bureau of Fair Play. *Houston Chronicle*, Sept. 10.

――――. 1964b. Physique, temperament and intelligence in infertile women. *International Journal of Fertility* 9(2):297-301.

Sullivan, Walter. 1984. Possible signs of proton decay cited. *The New York Times*, Jan. 6, 6.

Sun, Marjorie. 1984. EDB contamination kindles federal action. *Science*, Feb. 13, 464.

Swain, Bruce M. 1982. *The Progressive*, the bomb and the papers. *Journalism Monographs* 76(May):1-45.

Swanson, Charles E. 1955. What they read in 130 daily newspapers. *Journalism Quarterly* 32(fall):411.

――――. 1958. *Science, the News and the Public.* New York: New York University Press.

Tankard, James. 1976. Reporting and scientific method. In *Handbook of Reporting Methods*, ed. Maxwell McCombs, D.C. Shaw, and David Gray. Boston: Houghton Mifflin.

Tankard, James W., and Rachel Adelson. 1982. Mental health and marital information in three advice columns. *Journalism Quarterly* 59(4):592-97.

Tannenbaum, Percy H. 1963. Communication of science information. *Science* 140: 579-583.

Tannenbaum, Percy H. and Mervin D. Lynch. 1962. Sensationalism: some objective message correlates. *Journalism Quarterly* 39(Winter):317-323.

Tichenor, Phillip J., Clarice N. Olien, Anette Harrison and George A. Donohue. 1970. Mass communications systems and communication accuracy in science news reporting. *Journalism Quarterly* 47(Winter):673-83.

Tower, Donald B. 1979. Freedom of information act has potential for abuse. *NASW Newsletter* 28(3):9.

Twentieth Century Fund. 1984. *Science in the Streets.* New York: Priority Press.

Ubell, Earl. 1961. Proton and neutron cores photographed. *The New York Herald Tribune*, Feb. 2, 3.

U.S. Congress, House. Subcommittee on Investigations and Oversight, Committee on Science and Technology. 1981. *Fraud in Biomedical Research.* 97th Congress. Washington, D.C.: GPO.

UPI. 1980. Doctors battle stigma. *The Dallas Morning News*, Dec. 21, 38A

Van Nevel, Paul. 1979. NCI survey shows cancer coverage "fragmented." *NASW Newsletter* 28(3):7.

Ward, Richie. 1978. How to write the science story. *Writer's Digest*, Feb., 19.

Warming up new weapons in the war against frost. *Business Week*, Nov. 28, 138.

Washington Research Project v. Department of Health, Education and Welfare, 504 F. 2d 238 (D.C. Cir. 1974).

Watson, James D., and Francis Crick. 1968. *The Double Helix.* New York: Atheneum.

Westin, A.F., and Michael Baker. 1972. *Data banks in a free society.* New York: Atheneum. Whelan, Elizabeth M. 1984. When Newsweek and Time filtered cigarette copy. *The Wall Street Journal*, Nov. 1, 28.

Wingerson, Lois. 1979. Science writing in Britain: Aggressive reporting of research just isn't done. *NASW Newsletter* 28(4):9.

Wolfle, Dael. 1980. Science: A memoir of the 1960's and 1970's. *Science* 209(4452):57-62.

Yankelovich, Daniel. 1984. Science and the public process: Why the gap must close. *ISSUES in Science and Technology* 1(1):12.

Young, Patrick. 1981. Eye institute puts on blinders as reporter looks for story. *NASW Newsletter* 29(2):12.

――――. 1983. Baltimore researchers provide new insight on aging process. *Houston Chronicle*, Oct. 16, sec. 1, 30.

Ziman, John. 1968. *Public Knowledge.* Cambridge, England: Cambridge University Press.

Zimmerman, David R. 1979. How consumer education, public relations style still translates as press agentry. *NASW Newsletter* 27(2):1-3.

Zukhav, Gary. 1979. *The dancing Wu Li Masters.* New York: Bantam New Age Books.

INDEX

Transplants, 144
Trans-science, 38, 86-91, 100, 119
  references for, 99
Trespass, 119
Troan, John, 30
Truman, Harry S, 125
TTAPS Group, on nuclear winter, xi, 5
TV Guide, 144
Twentieth Century Fund, 11

Ubell, Earl, 25, 27, 81, 132
UCLA, 59
Union Carbide, 44
United Features Syndicate, 30
United Press International (UPI), 28, 42, 116, 144
University of Cincinnati, 103
University of Texas, 137
USA Today, 36, 79
U.S. Congress, report on fraud, 41
U.S. News and World Report (U.S. News), 30

Vaccination, 109, 110
Van Buren, Abigail, 72
Van Nevel, Paul, 63

Wade, Nicholas, 68, 69
Waldholz, Michael, 77
Wall Street Journal, The, xi, 12, 23, 36, 42, 77, 91, 115, 126, 128, 130-132, 147
Washington Post, x, 12, 15, 32, 42, 91
Watson, James D., 6, 34
Westin, Alan F., 107
Weston-Smith, Miranda, 51
Whelan, Elizabeth M., 128
Who's Who, 51, 65
Wilford, John N., 23
Wingerson, Lois, 14
Wolfle, Dael, 20
Wolinsky, Howard, 85
World Wide Medical Press, 129
Wyckoff, William C., 19

Yankelovich, Daniel, 135
Young, Patrick, 77, 117

Ziman, John, 9
Zimmerman, David R., **133**
Zukhav, Gary, 79